KODAK PXP 6057
43

KODAK PXP 6057
44
45

KODAK PXP 6057
46

KODAK PXP 6057
47
KODAK

LEANNE BENJAMIN
BUILT FOR BALLET

LEANNE

BUILT

BENJAMIN

OR BALLET

An Autobiography

LEANNE BENJAMIN
WITH SARAH CROMPTON

M
MELBOURNE BOOKS

Published by Melbourne Books
Level 9, 100 Collins Street,
Melbourne, VIC 3000
Australia
www.melbournebooks.com.au
info@melbournebooks.com.au

Title: Leanne Benjamin: Built for Ballet
Authors: Leanne Benjamin with Sarah Crompton
ISBN: 9781925556575

NATIONAL LIBRARY OF AUSTRALIA
A catalogue record for this book is available from the National Library of Australia

Publisher: David Tenenbaum
Designer: Ellen Cheng
Editor: Charlotte Gurtler

Front cover photo: Johan Persson / ArenaPAL
Back cover photo: Jason Bell
Endpaper photos: Roy Round

To my parents, Jill and Bernie,
who opened every door and allowed me to fly.

To Tobias, my anchor,
who always encourages me to be exactly who I am;
and darling son, Thomas, who keeps me on my toes.

CONTENTS

FOREWORD

WHAT MAKES LEANNE BENJAMIN SPECIAL? It's a question I've thought about a lot as we've worked together on this book. She was undoubtedly a prodigy, a winner of prizes, marked out from the first as a dancer of exceptional talent. But that's not what makes her interesting to me.

Her greatest moments came at the end of her career, in her forties, when she returned after giving birth to her son. She'd always been the most dramatic dancer, voluptuous as well as steely, capable of bringing any role to life, whether it was a fairy-tale bird or a real-life victim. Yet at that moment she seemed to acquire an aura, a sudden confidence in her own ability that made her performances transfixing.

There are a lot of good dancers about. But there aren't that many who leave you unable to tear your eyes away. She had that rare quality of being real on a stage, her thoughts communicated through movements that were at once expansive and precise. She was wonderful in the work of Kenneth MacMillan, particularly as Mary in *Mayerling*, because she so carefully conveyed the character's journey from heady romanticism to a fatalistic acceptance of death. In works such as *Gloria* and *Song of the Earth* she revealed her artistry, her understanding of the music she was moving to, the eloquence of the silent steps she was performing.

She made sense of roles as different as Marie in *A Different Drummer* and Giselle in *Giselle* by not playing up any single aspect of personality, but by seeming to live the narrative minute to minute, describing the nuance of a story in the infinite complexities of classical dance. I'll never forget her in Kim Brandstrup's fragmentary *Invitas, Invitam* where she made your heart ache for lost and unfulfilled love, or in Wayne McGregor's *Infra* where she appeared late and electrified the stage with her presence. In Christopher Wheeldon's *Commedia* she used all her knowledge to weave dances full of delicate phrasing and glorious notes of grace, an intricate, intimate performance that seemed to reflect the history of dance itself.

Benjamin was steeped in that history. She began her career at the moment when the origins of the British ballet tradition were still touchable and was taught by people whose knowledge reached long back into the nineteenth century. She left the stage having worked with a new generation of creators, who will shape the trajectory of dance into the twenty-first century and beyond.

But what's really fascinating to me about Leanne Benjamin is that none of this came easy. She had to struggle repeatedly to get where she wanted to be. From quite early she had the sense that she had special qualities as an artist that needed cultivation and nurturing and she held to her belief that she could be something, even when it would have been quite easy to give up and settle for being less than her potential. It took enormous discipline and courage to keep going when stopping would have been an easier and perhaps happier option.

In this sense, her life is a reflection of an experience that goes far beyond ballet. If you peep behind the curtain of many careers, there's a sense of disappointment, of talent that hasn't quite been realised, of frustration with structures and the accidents of existence that can constrict achievement. Finding the resilience and the determination to carry on when events seem to be going against you is never easy. That Leanne managed to do so, to overcome obstacles so that she finally realised her own dreams is part of what makes her story so inspiring.

We didn't know each other when we began to collaborate, at more or less the same time as a global pandemic began to sweep through the world. When we first embarked on her story, we could meet, sitting in each other's kitchens, sifting through cuttings and letters, sharing memories. As we progressed, normal life closed down, shutting us in our separate homes. Like so many people around the world, we found ourselves looking back and reflecting on the values and people that mattered in both our lives, on what our families taught us, on what art had meant to us.

What binds the characters in Leanne's story together is their passionate commitment to ballet as a living, breathing art form that can motivate and inspire. It is an art that can convey emotions and feelings in ways that everyone can understand, to tell stories that offer insight and consolation.

One of Leanne's most famous roles was in *Requiem*, a ballet made by Kenneth MacMillan as a tribute to his friend John Cranko, who died entirely unexpectedly and far too young. You can watch her performance in the Pie Jesu on YouTube. I'd been lucky enough to see it in a theatre, and I watched it a lot as we worked on this book, marvelling at the way she strips away all false feeling, becoming the essence of both grief and hope.

It's performances such as this that have made me want to watch dance ever since I was a child. Dance matters because it can communicate so directly. What makes Leanne Benjamin interesting is that she has devoted her life to that belief. This book is part of that.

Sarah Crompton

INTRODUCTION

I OPEN THE DOOR FROM the narrow street and walk into another world. It isn't particularly smart or especially glamorous. There's a glass-fronted reception desk to one side, and a security door ahead of me. Both are battered by constant use. Only the bouquets of flowers building up in one corner are a clue to the fact that this is the Royal Opera House, home to Britain's Royal Ballet, a place where every night ambition and imagination come together to make dreams come true. A place of entertainment and fantasy and grinding hard work. A building that has been my second home.

I first performed professionally on this stage when I was seventeen and an anxious student at the Royal Ballet School, which I'd joined from my home in Australia. I was playing the tiny walk-on role of the Bride in *Romeo and Juliet* and I was nervous. I described the experience in a letter to my Aunty Pat, my father's sister, who waited back in Rockhampton for news of my progress, complaining that my costume was at least six inches too long. 'I thought I was going to ruin the whole ballet by tripping onto the stage instead of walking!'

I am still here in my fifties, still metaphorically hitching my dress up and getting down to work, teaching what I know to a new generation of dancers who are learning the same roles that I once performed. As a principal ballerina, I danced all the famous women of classical ballet: the doomed Odette in *Swan Lake*, the tragic peasant girl Giselle, the sparkling Sugar Plum Fairy, a bright Aurora in *The Sleeping Beauty*. But the characters I loved best in that thirty-year career were the ones who didn't need you to put on a tutu and pink tights, the heroines of ballets by choreographers such as Kenneth MacMillan, women with real emotions and passions, flawed and fabulous, with a bit of personality and a lot of spirit. Or abstract roles, where you are asked to twist your body into the most outlandish shapes or communicate feeling by a stretch of the neck or the shape of your arm.

From the age of seventeen until forty-nine when I retired, I wasn't happy when costumes made me uncomfortable. I never liked pulling on a frilly skirt or wearing a wig. I wanted to strip down to basics, to wear a body stocking, or a simple costume, and revel in the pure joy of free movement, expressing my feelings with every inch of my body.

Maybe that springs from one of the most important things about me: I never wanted to be a ballerina. It just happened. It was my sister Madonna who pored over photographs of Margot Fonteyn when we were growing up in the small city of Rockhampton in the middle of Queensland, Australia. It was Madonna who had the perfect bun and the graceful deportment. I was the kid with my hair falling down my back, bouncing around on my pogo stick, screeching with laughter and playing tricks on my neighbours. You can tell the kind of girl I was by the fact that one morning I turned up for dance class—where everyone was very serious in black leotards and pink shoes—dressed as the Easter Bunny, trotting round the studio complete with ears, handing out eggs, and then joining in the lesson as if nothing had happened.

But somehow ballet wormed its way into my life. Getting up for a 6.30am class every day was as much a part of my teenage years as barbecues and swimming in shark-infested seas. I was built for ballet. I was tiny and strong, with long legs and arms and unquenchable energy—and I loved getting into the studio to practise and to improve, to see where my body would take me. I just wanted to be the best that I could be. That feeling pushed me a long, long way. I knew that if I wanted to achieve true excellence, I had to leave Rockhampton and travel halfway across the world to study at the Royal Ballet School. Leaving my home and my country at sixteen years old was one of the hardest things I've ever done—I didn't have the right clothes to get me through a bitter British winter and the only food I knew how to prepare was chocolate cake. But it wasn't just this cold, grey country that felt alien to me. It was the whole world I had chosen to enter. I was a guileless, passionate girl who had barely seen a ballet performance. Suddenly I was trying to navigate a career that asks for obedience and conformity—not qualities I am known for. Perfectionism, yes. Hard work, definitely. But silent yes-saying, not so much. I like to have a laugh, to ask questions, to push the envelope. Those weren't necessarily the qualities that people were looking for.

That temperament has made my life infinitely more interesting, but I've also had some missteps along the way. My career didn't unfold like a beautifully curved satin ribbon, flying through the air in perfect waves as it does in Frederick Ashton's *La Fille mal gardée*. It was definitely full of flight and excitement. By the time I was twenty-eight, I had been principal in four internationally renowned companies, and I then enjoyed twenty-one years as a star of the Royal Ballet. In that time I worked with so many fascinating people, from historical figures who built the foundations of British ballet, such as Ninette de Valois, Frederick Ashton and Kenneth MacMillan, to the dancers, directors and choreographers who are shaping the world of dance that we see today: people such as Wayne McGregor, Christopher Wheeldon, Alexei Ratmansky and Carlos Acosta. The legendary Alicia Markova prepared me for my first role; the equally legendary Lynn Seymour passed on her wisdom to me about my final characterisation on the Royal Opera House stage.

But I've had some ghastly times too, when I felt everything I had worked for was turning to dust around me, when I was in pain, or so miserable that I just wanted to give up and try my hand at something else. With support and belief, I managed to drive through the bad spells and keep going, working as hard as I could. I've always understood that you are the only person responsible for your talent. You have to nurture it and believe in it. Every person is different, but that instinct for survival and improvement is true of us all; as the saying goes, when life throws you lemons, you need to learn to make lemonade and make the absolute best of yourself if you want to succeed.

I did succeed, building a career that has been notable for its longevity and its variety. Though I thought I could walk away, I came to love the world of ballet so much that it has held me in its arms and pulled me back, to pass on all I have learnt to the next generation of dancers. A ballet company really does become your family, one where new babies are arriving all the time and old timers are taking on different roles. When I arrive at the stage door nowadays, it's as if my life is passing in front of my eyes. Now, like everybody, I have to negotiate complicated security measures and use my electronic pass to be admitted. Once upon a time, I'd breeze in and out, and when my mum would ring me from Rockhampton, I'd be called to a draughty stage door to take the call. I feel one hundred years old just for remembering those days. But some things never change. The downstairs coffee bar, plonked in a draughty corridor with wonky tables and black plastic seats, is still a place to meet and chat. You never know who you might encounter in the queue: the world-famous baritone Bryn Terfel might be there, or the Royal Opera House's music director Antonio Pappano. Perhaps I will meet an old friend such as Darcey Bussell, back like me to do a spot of teaching. Sometimes it's quite empty or quiet; when the opera chorus pour out from a general rehearsal it's like a rugby scrum, so noisy you can't hear yourself speak. The corps de ballet in contrast are so much more petite and delicate.

Here, they know that when I order a hot chocolate to take away, that I like it very chocolatey. I've been drinking it all my career. Odd as it sounds, it was always the drink that calmed my nerves before a performance and now it sets me up before leading a rehearsal, so I sip it as I walk. My favourite route to the floors above, where I will be coaching, is around the stage level because it gives me a chance to take a peek at whatever set is piled up behind the stage, with the crew getting it ready for the night's performance, shifting scenery around on huge trollies, driving little cars that look like golf carts. The height of the fly tower is thirty-seven meters, the same as three to four houses piled one on top of each other, so the changes of scene can be flown in and out. Even if I were a bit taller than my five feet, two inches, I'd still feel like a dwarf, overwhelmed not only by the size of everything but the sheer magic of what goes on here.

There are names scrawled on the wings at the side of the stage; I always say good morning to Rudolf Nureyev, whose picture hangs to the right, an inspiration still. When the curtains to the auditorium are open, the red of the seats and the gold and white of the horseshoe-shaped tiers glint in the house lights. This is just about my favourite view in the world, so full of memories, good and bad, of nights when I didn't want the curtain to come down and those—much more rare—when I couldn't wait for a performance to end. At the rear of the stage, there's a door that leads you to the changing rooms, working rooms and studios. Backstage the world over, it's always the case that unless you know where you're going, you get lost. Any stranger visiting the Royal Opera House could vanish into its colour-coded areas and find themselves in a warren of rooms and corridors that only make sense to people who know exactly where they are going.

Fortunately, I do: when I walk into work, I'm heading for the Blue Core where the ballet rehearsal rooms are. It still seems strange to me, as I make my way to the guest dressing room on the first floor, not to be heading for the principal changing room on the stage level that I shared with Tamara Rojo for many years, her side of the room immaculate, mine a chaotic mess. Before we moved in, Darcey Bussell and Miyako Yoshida used it as their dressing room. Now it's occupied by Natalia Osipova and Lauren Cuthbertson, taking their part in that changing fabric of history that seeps into the walls of a big lyric theatre like this. I love the feeling of being part of a bigger parade.

The top floor of the Opera House is the place with the best views across the hustle and bustle of the old Covent Garden market, across the slanted grey rooftops, down to the bright lights of the London Eye, turning so slowly and imperceptibly on the south bank of the River Thames. This is also the heart of the ballet company, with a canteen, and three good-sized studios all named after significant figures in the company's history—the Ashton, the MacMillan and the Fonteyn. There's also the Clore (named after the Clore Duffield charitable foundation that did so much towards the rebuilding of the opera house). This is a studio theatre, often used for public events like talks and demonstrations, and that's where I am heading on a typical day when I bump into Philip Mosley, senior character artist and artistic scheduling manager. I've known Phil forever—we were dancers together at Sadler's Wells Royal Ballet, my first company—and I adore him. He's a roguish Yorkshireman, with a strong accent and a wicked grin. He's also apparently the boy who inspired the story of *Billy Elliot*, having made his way from a working-class family to the Royal Ballet School. If you want to know anything about anything, or anyone, Phil is the man to ask. He's one of the pivotal figures in the Royal Ballet because he controls the weekly rehearsal schedule for ninety-odd dancers, a job that is like constantly working on a room-sized jigsaw puzzle or playing three-dimensional chess against unseen opponents.

His quirky manner conceals an iron grip of scheduling and a remarkable gift for people management. As a dancer, I drove Phil crazy, trying to squeeze in as many rehearsals as possible. He used to call it 'Being Benj'd'—and it was a phrase that stuck. Now I am a coach, I discuss the dancers I am working with instead, being just as pushy on their behalf. If you're going to be great onstage, you need time in a rehearsal room, and you don't always get it. My own insistence on that led to me getting a reputation as being difficult and I probably was sometimes, if I'm honest, but I needed it to be able to give the kind of performances I wanted, for the audience's sake as well as my own.

So many memories of those days come flooding back as I push open the heavy door and walk into the Clore. This was the studio where I struggled to get my head around the fierce geometries of Wayne McGregor's choreography, when he created a role for me in *Qualia* just three months after I'd given birth to my son Thomas. I remember the difficulty of trying to remind my body how to dance again, cramming my feet back into pointe shoes after months of freedom, but I also recall the sheer physical excitement of wrapping my limbs around movement that was quite unlike anything I had ever experienced.

My first rehearsals for *Polyphonia* by Christopher Wheeldon were also in this room. There was one moment when we were rehearsing this complicated piece to the music of Ligeti when the cameras came to film us for World Ballet Day. They arrived just as we were working on a section of duets in unison, and we couldn't get it right, stopping and starting over and over again while the pianist Rob sat patiently repeating the same few phrases. I wonder what on earth people felt as they watched, but at least it gave them an insight into all the discipline and struggle that lies behind a dancer's apparently glamorous existence.

That is what I want this book to do as well. I've had such an amazing life, travelling from the outback to Buckingham Palace, from obscurity to the top of my chosen profession. In that world, I've seen so many changes, watched ballet shift from being a profession that would have been recognisable to its nineteenth-century practitioners, where dancers had to be seen but definitely not heard, to one that is looking proudly forward in the twenty-first century by giving the performers of today much more autonomy in how their careers unfold.

I've been part of that change, absorbing advice from the great dancers and teachers of the past but also fighting for self-determination in my own career. I've learnt how to make things happen, how to take a risk, how to cope when things go wrong. I was a prodigy, yet the very best period of my career came in my forties, after giving birth, when I was juggling being a wife and a mother as well as a ballerina. I know the mental strength you need to succeed, to make your dreams come true even in the face of huge obstacles. I pass those lessons on to the dancers I teach and coach today, but as I look back on my life, I also feel that all the knowledge I've gathered on my journey from little Rockhampton to the biggest stages in the world has some lessons for all of us. This is a ballet book, but one with a difference.

CHAPTER 1

THE TINIEST COMPETITOR

THE GROUND BENEATH MY FEET was as red as my costume, rough, stony and hard on my toes. As I jumped over and over again, soaring through the air like a firebird, legs extended in a perfect line, head and arms thrown back, I experienced a sense of exhilaration overriding the tiredness. The photograph I was posing for felt very special, capturing the essence of who I am—a ballerina who travelled halfway across the world to find her fame, coming home to Australia, dancing on its ancient stones. After all these years living away, I still love my country more than anywhere in the world. I am Australian. I feel Australian. My upbringing shaped me as a person, even though I found my destiny with the Royal Ballet in England.

The photograph, on the back cover of this book, was taken by Jason Bell at the end of 2006 as part of an advertising campaign called *A World Stage*, which emphasised the international character of the Royal Ballet, and the Opera House where it has its home. Other posters in the series, stuck around the London underground and plastered across the front of Covent Garden itself, showed Darcey Bussell posing elegantly in front of the white cliffs of Dover and Sergei

Polunin looking wild by a castle on the Black Sea. That's why I found myself in the outback outside Alice Springs, waiting for my cue in the middle of a great, big, dusty nowhere.

We'd planned the photograph and my costume meticulously back in London. The brilliant costume makers at the Royal Opera House helped me create a Chanel lipstick-red dress with a skirt that would flash out behind me as I moved, and catch the breeze if we were lucky enough to get one in forty-degree heat. Jason's idea was to go for the centre of the continent, where even the colour of the earth tells you that you are in Australia. We'd hoped to shoot in front of Uluru, the country's most famous landmark, but we couldn't get permission to film there. The previous day, the team had been to the iconic domed rocks of Kata Tjuta and I'd had a terrific time, going through my paces on a flat floor, surrounded by looming boulders. It was as if someone had built a perfect set for a shoot.

The next day—the day we actually got the photograph Jason had been dreaming of—the terrain was much rougher, and the weather more overcast. To my surprise, the team had organised for a local 'truckie' to drive an authentic Australian road train slowly back and forth behind the shoot for a few hours. I warmed up clinging to the large grille on the front of the minibus in which we were travelling, before moving into the space, trying various steps and different positions. Nothing quite worked, until I took off into a huge jump. There was no trampoline, and no special effects. There wasn't even a proper dance floor. This was not a stunt photograph, it was me, launching myself into the sky, in touch with the red, red earth of my beloved country.

I adored every moment of that trip, even though at the age of forty-two, flinging myself over and over again into a flick jeté, where you basically get enough momentum to do the splits in the air, was possibly what triggered problems with my left hip that have dogged me for years. It was worth it, though. The photograph is my love letter to Australia, and it took me straight back to my childhood in

Rockhampton, Queensland, where I grew up when its population was just 40,000 (it's now more than 80,000) and which provided the secure nest from which I flew at the age of sixteen.

What can I tell you about Rockhampton? It will explain some of its character if I say that when I finally retired from the stage, the local newspaper, the *Morning Bulletin*, featured a cartoon of me being showered with flowers, doing an arabesque on the back of a bull, on top of a plinth saying, 'Welcome to the beef capital of Australia.' That's the town slogan, but in my honour the word 'beef' was crossed out and replaced with 'ballet'. That's the kind of place it was: proud of its inhabitants, a real community, where people looked out for each other and cared about each other's futures. It was a quiet place to grow up. If you were interested in the arts and culture there was little to see, but it was a paradise for outdoor activities, sports and horse racing. A visit from the circus was a great excitement, the fair was a great excuse for dressing up. It was a safe place and when I look back to my childhood, my memories are happy ones.

My parents, Bernie and Jill, met at the Friday night youth dance at Our Lady's Parish Hall. He was nineteen, she was just shy of fifteen, and there was no way she should have been there because the dance was for Catholics only and she was Anglican. But this pretty girl, with short pixie hair like Twiggy, caught my dad's eye when everyone lined up to choose their partners for the dance. He walked her home that night and then kept taking her out to the cinema and for walks. On Saturdays, they'd go to the Wintergarden and sit in the posh seats upstairs, watching a film and then moving on to the Golden Gate Cafe for ice-cream sundaes afterwards. On Sundays, they'd go with friends to the beach, twenty minutes away, eating home-made cake and drinking soft drinks. Dad was playing trombone in the Rockhampton City Band at the time and would call in at my mum's house when he was supposedly on his way to practice. Not much practising ever happened and as a result he never finished learning to play the trombone.

It was all very innocent and sheltered; whenever they tried to sit in the car together outside Mum's house, they'd hear a cough from her mother on the porch, warning her to come inside. Nice girls didn't sit in cars. Pictures of them taken at the time show a handsome couple: their arms wrapped around one another, ready to face the world. My mum looks a bit like me, all teeth and a smile as broad as the day is long, but I inherited my father's lean muscular frame and long legs.

They knew they loved each other right from the start, I think, but religious affiliations did separate people in Rockhampton at that time, and it took my dad a while to convince his family that Mum was the right girl for him. After finishing his mechanic's apprenticeship, he went to Brisbane for a year to work, but distance didn't stop the relationship. In the end my mother solved any difficulties Dad's family might have had by converting to Catholicism to marry him. They walked down the aisle in 1960 and are still blissfully happy together. Growing up, I could see the difference between their two families. Dad's was conservative and a bit staid: there were a lot of rules, and not much fun. Mum's background was more carefree and less formal. She always talks about wearing shorts to go to see him and the disapproving looks she used to get from his mother. She just did it to push her buttons, I suspect—I take after her, always testing the boundaries, seeing how far I can go. We've got the same giddy sense of fun too.

Dad was the baby of four: his oldest brother, Keith, was thirteen years older; Ray, who went on to become a Catholic bishop, was eleven years his senior; and Pat, his spinster sister who plays a big part in my story, was eight years ahead. Perhaps because he was the baby, Bernie (named after his sister Bernadette who had been stillborn) was always regarded as the lucky one: on the day of his birth, his father, Evan, bought a lottery ticket, and won a share of the first prize. It was enough money to build a new gable-style home in Davis Street, Rockhampton, and transform the family fortunes. All his life, Evan drove around town in a polished white Zephyr, his pride and joy. With a shock of neatly parted hair which had turned white in his twenties, he cut a distinguished figure in an immaculate suit and leather lace-up boots. It was probably from him that my family, who all played the piano and sang, inherited our musical tendencies. He was the organist at the local Catholic church, conducted the choir, and also played the piano that accompanied silent films at the local cinema, improvising his piano playing to fit with the on-screen action. For his own pleasure, he played ragtime, and I used to love sitting next to him on a stool as he played all those great Scott Joplin tunes.

Mum's family lived in Derby Street, not far away from Dad's house. She was also one of four, with two sisters and a brother: Fay, Dell and John. They were also musically talented; after singing in a local Eisteddfod, Dell won a music scholarship to Sydney, but they didn't have enough money to let her go. It was a house full of warmth and affection. Mum's father, my grandad Denis Mulhern, was famous for his vegetable patch and as a child I used to love going to their house because they had chickens—chooks as we called them—that I could endlessly chase round their garden and overfeed. The Mulhern grandparents were the ones who christened me 'Mischief' soon after I arrived in the world on 13 July 1964. I was six weeks premature, which was quite a shock for my parents, but they seem to have taken it in their stride. I was only five pounds and seven ounces but was strong enough to be sent straight home.

As I grew, my mum's father often used to pop round, just to catch a glimpse of me, though sadly he wasn't in my life for long. He died, entirely out of the blue, when I was four and my mum was heavily pregnant with my younger sister Fiona. Having never been ill in his life, he got a blood clot in his leg which travelled to his heart. He'd booked an appointment to see a doctor but collapsed and died that day on the floor of Rocky's famous department store Tucker & Tucker, where he was the manager. After his death, his wife Kathleen sat down with my mum and dad and said she didn't want to live any more without him. Two hours later she died—of a broken heart, according to my mum—and it was hard not to feel that was true. I used her name as my confirmation name: Leanne Faye Kathleen Benjamin.

Although our childhood was incredibly happy, both Mum and Dad were quite driven, a quality I see in myself and my siblings. They had nothing when they met, and in the early days, when Dad was a mechanic and Mum, who had been working in an accountant's office, had given up her job because that was what women did when they got married in Rockhampton in the sixties. She was bored and missed her job. One day, someone gave her an old chair which she renovated and sold. It was the seed of her future business, but at that time, money was very tight. Things were tough, especially once my sister Madonna, who is two years older than me, arrived. But they always had the knack of making the best of what they had. Their first house was on Considine Street, which runs across the area known as The Range on the southside of the city. There were a lot of beautiful colonial houses on the hill up there, each on a separate lot, with tin roofs, and white balconies. Ours was one that Dad had built, quite modest, on the side of a hill with a brick base to level the house and provide room for a garage and laundry room.

It was a lovely place to grow up, but my parents had to put in a lot of hard graft when they first moved in. For the first two years, there was no sewage system and they only had an outside 'dunny', which Australians called a thunderbox. In the middle of the night, they had to take a torch out into the garden to make sure there were no redback spiders or frogs on the toilet seat, or snakes on the ceiling for that matter. It was all just part of life in Rockhampton, a city of extremes, of floods and bushfires, of elegant suburban houses and abattoirs and the heavy cattle trains, taking beef all over Australia. Only when I came to London, and my new friends reacted with horror to my tall tales, did I realise that I'd been dicing with death on a daily basis, avoiding the snakes in the long grass, and the crocodiles in the creeks that I'd swim in. Yet I don't remember growing up with any fear, except a healthy fear of God, instilled in me at church where I spent most of my time when I wasn't dancing.

We lived in Considine Street until I was nine. My earliest memory—around the age of three—is sitting on the kerb outside, waiting for the cream bun van to arrive to give me a treat for tea. Three of us grew up in that house—Madonna, me, and Fiona, who is five years younger than me. It had a grassy backyard, where our clever handyman father built Madonna and me a lovely cubbyhouse—a scene of endless mud pie teas. The yard was also home to our pet kangaroo, a little joey that Dad brought home one day after its mother had been killed on the roads, an accident that was unfortunately all too common in Queensland at the time. Dad was running the local service station and garage by then, and one of his clients brought the baby in, wrapped in hessian. He gave it to Madonna and me and we were thrilled. It stayed with us safely in the backyard for a long time, until one terrible day we came home from shopping to discover that our pet had been attacked and killed, probably by some local dogs. It was traumatic; after that we stuck to dogs, a long succession of sleek alsatians, who lived outside but always became part of the family. When I arrived in London, I missed them so much that sometimes I addressed my letters home to the dog as well as my parents.

Our second, much grander, house was around the corner, at 62 Agnes Street, where we moved in 1973. It was an old-fashioned Queenslander double-storey home—almost unique at the time, because most Australian houses were single-level and built on stilts. My mum and dad walked past it most days, often discussing its potential. They knew the owner, a man called Mr Evans, who had built it himself in 1918 and raised his family there. After his wife died, he moved out to live with his son and put the old house on the market, but because it was so dilapidated and needed so much work, no one wanted to buy it; apart from my dad, that is. By then there were three of us, and Mum was pregnant with my brother Tony. When Dad asked Mr Evans how much it would be, the old man said he would sell it to him for what he could afford, even though that was about $10,000 less than he'd hoped for. It was a lot of money then, but that was that, a done deal, full of great kindness.

The story has an odd coda, because after we'd moved into the house, Mum and Dad were woken at 3am one night by the heavy, slow thud of someone walking up the stairs, and were convinced that there was an intruder. Dad armed himself with a chair and went downstairs to have a look around. There was no one there, and all the doors and windows were locked, so he went back to bed. The next morning Mr Evans' son Clive, who was then our neighbour, called to my father over the fence to tell him that his father had died at 3am the previous night. It was as if he had come to say goodbye. Perhaps he understood he had placed his much-loved home in good hands. Everyone thought my dad had taken leave of his senses, wanting to buy a run-down, old-fashioned house and it took him and Mum years of backbreaking work to do it up and get it how they wanted, but 62 Agnes Street was a wonderful place to live, with a great mango tree out in the garden that plopped mouth-wateringly ripe fruit on our heads. I never ate mangoes much as a child—the parrots who were always getting drunk on them, ate more than we did. Now I love them and regret the waste.

In 1972, the year before we moved into Agnes Street, Dad had made another of his brilliant decisions and bought a piece of land by the beach at Lammermoor, about forty kilometres from Rockhampton. He had just enough money either to put a swimming pool in our back garden, or to buy this little beach-front plot. He chose the beach, levelled the earth, and put up the simplest of rock block houses, which he adapted and developed over the years, building an extension and a proper deck. When we were kids, it was just a couple of rooms with concrete floors and white walls, full of junk shop furniture, on a long, straight stretch of water, with a view across the Pacific Ocean to Great Keppel Island, in the southern portion of the Great Barrier Reef.

On trips across the bay, we used to hang off the side of the boat on ropes, watching the water race past. Sometimes we'd make fires on the beach and cook damper, which is traditional bush bread, without yeast. It was that kind of paradise, a place of total freedom. As I got older, more and more houses sprang up along the shore, but at first there were no other buildings to obscure the view. We'd go there for weekends, and always at Christmas when Dad would give us pieces of cardboard to slide on down the dunes, or a tyre tube to swim in. There were no shark nets, but that didn't stop us, we just plunged straight in. As a child, I'd fall asleep in the tyre on the rough-hewn deck, listening to the sound of the waves; as an adult Lammermoor remained my haven, the place I most wanted to be. When I was injured or unhappy or just trying to make sense of the world, I'd go back there and walk on the beach, and think, and my cares would slip away on the yellow sand. Even now, if I am booking a holiday, I don't want to be in the countryside or the mountains, I need to be looking at the sea. Lammermoor was my happy place in my youth, and it has stayed with me.

All the outdoor activities meant that I grew into a sleek, muscular kid, tiny, with big teeth and my hair in bunches. But I was something else as well: I was a performer who loved being centre stage. It all began, as it does for so many people, because Mum thought that Madonna and I would walk better if we took dance lessons. There was perhaps a bit more going on in her mind than that, because she'd always loved dancing and performing as a child—she and her sisters took music, singing and dancing lessons. When there wasn't enough money to cover the cost of all three, it was dancing they dropped, and she'd always regretted it. In her heart she was a frustrated performer and so she was happy to see if her daughters would like dancing too.

When she saw an advertisement in the *Bulletin* for a Saturday dance class for youngsters at Jan Moore's Dancing Academy, run by Jan Moore herself, she signed us up. I was three and Madonna was five when we started. The school consisted of one room underneath a house, and I remember doing a little concert there for our parents. I was so small compared with the other girls that Miss Moore dressed me as the only boy and the other girls danced around me. When the school expanded, it moved to a bigger space at St John's Church Hall in Parnell Street, just round the corner from my Aunty Pat's house. As in so many of the buildings in Rockhampton, the floor was raised above ground level which provided the perfect opportunity for a naughty boy who was always chasing me around the playground at school trying to kiss me, to wiggle into the under-space and poke dirt up through the floor and onto my feet.

Jan Moore was a beautiful woman with heavy dark hair, like a queen from a Disney cartoon. She must have been quite young, because she was still teaching in 2021, and she ran a good school, a tight ship, but she was very strict. In an interview after I'd become famous, she said she remembered me as a natural performer with a happy smile and a willingness to do anything that was asked of me.[1] That's what I remember too. I just loved dancing and I was always happy to cavort in front of an audience.

My first real moment in the spotlight came in 1968 when, as a four-year-old, I took to the huge stage at the city's Municipal Theatre at the local Eisteddfod. Wearing pink ballet shoes, white socks and an elaborately puffed and primped pink checked cotton dress, with little white nylon sleeves and pictures of animals painted around the skirt, I gave the assembled audience my all-singing, all-dancing version of Shirley Temple's 'Animal Crackers in My Soup'. The result made the local paper. 'The Tiniest Competitor,'[2] read the headline, accompanied by a photograph of me with Jill Cadden, one of the adjudicators, who had come down from her little judging platform in the centre of the stalls to talk to me at the front of the stage. I got highly commended for that performance, while my sister Madonna took second prize for her performance as Thumbelina.

The photograph took pride of place on the first page of the scrapbook that Aunty Pat started making for me that day, and continued to compile all through my career, until she died in 2007 at the age of eighty. Aunty Pat was very much part of our family life. Because she was unmarried and childless, she treated us like her own children, taking enormous pride in our success. After Grandad

Benjamin died in 1973, Pat stayed in the family home, looking after her mother, my grandmother. In her working years, she'd been cashier for the farming and horse supply store Williams, sitting at the heart of the store and managing all the payments.

She absolutely loved horse racing and knew all the owners, trainers and jockeys. Every Saturday was local race day, and if I wasn't at ballet, she'd take me along. We'd head straight for the horses, and she'd get the gossip and inside gen on any possible winners. She was good at picking them too. I'd quite often return from the course with more money than I set off with.

Every Friday after our dance lesson, Madonna and I would walk round to her house and she would cook my favourite meal: home-made fishcakes with tinned mackerel. I don't think Grandma Benjamin approved of our dancing, worrying that it wasn't quite proper or absolutely the thing for a nice Catholic girl to do. But Aunty Pat, though just as devout, relished our achievements; she'd pray for good outcomes for our exams and performances, write encouraging letters and cards. On our teatime excursions, Madonna was always the perfect guest and I was permanently in trouble—probably because I talked too much or answered back—but she never swerved in her encouragement and support of us both.

The Benjamin Sisters, as the local papers were fond of calling us, were more and more successful, so Aunty Pat's scrapbooks filled up. Our weeks were full of lessons and there were concerts and competitions some weekends, where we'd perform in an array of elaborate costumes that my mum enlisted the help of a local dressmaker to provide. We danced everything: tap, Irish, Scottish, a bit of ballet. There are photographs of me in an outsized hat for a 'Beside the Seaside' number, and a little green leotard with a polka dot skirt when the school was competing in another Eisteddfod—and the Benjamin Sisters were singled out for special praise. In 1970, with a spotty red mob cap on my head and a collar to match, I was photographed in my 'Maid in the Garden' costume which I wore for a demi-character dance. I am always the smallest person in any picture and some of my costumes make me smile. I still have the canary-yellow feathered pantsuit with a hood that I wore when I played Tweety Bird.

My passion for my new hobby was driven both by enjoyment and by a certain amount of financial acumen. I realised quite early that if I won first place in a competition, I would earn myself a little brown envelope containing the prize money of $2.50, and if I entered myself for fifteen different categories and won them all, my piggy bank would fill in a very satisfactory way. At a young age I understood that I could make money by doing something that I was good at, which has been an important motivator for life. But I was also a competitive child. Mum and Dad had brought us up to be the best version of ourselves we could be, and to strive to improve ourselves at all times. I practised and practised in the front room, constantly trying out my routines. The only second places I was ever awarded were in tap, but I wasn't that bad a tapper either. Years later when I was learning Kenneth MacMillan's *La Fin du jour* at the Royal Ballet, I had the secret satisfaction of being able to pull off the soft shoe shuffle the piece requires, when other classically trained dancers really struggled. It all went back to those days at the dancing academy.

The dance competitions and concerts mainly took place on the handkerchief-sized stage at St Andrew's Church Hall, which my family remember for its extraordinarily hard benches, where they sat and suffered while offering their daughters endless applause. Backstage, it was equally primitive. We changed our costumes underneath the stage, and as you took your clothes off the rail that ran down one side of the stuffy, cramped room, you could hear all the tapping, bouncing and noise on the boards above. Mum would be there, getting Madonna and me ready. She'd help us into our costumes, pinch our cheeks to give them a bit of colour and send us on. I adored it.

Even Dad got in on the act. He was often so busy working at the garage that Mum and I would drive down to see him, taking his dinner on a plate. But in his tiny patches of free time, he'd make props for us to use. One particularly fine construction was for a Christmas fancy dress competition for which Madonna and I dressed up as Fred Flintstone and Barney Rubble in homage to *The Flintstones*, our favourite TV cartoon. After watching the show on TV and studying the design, Dad built us a car with bits and bobs from his workshop. It was made of cardboard and quite light, so we could put our arms through the sides and parade around holding it, Madonna in front and me directly behind. We won first prize thanks to his efforts. We were always performing somewhere. Every year there was a revue at Our Lady's Catholic church, which had a tiny, constricted stage. It was the scene of my first—and last—piece of choreographic invention, when I performed a solo to Tchaikovsky's 'Waltz of the Flowers' from *The Nutcracker*, with butterfly wings attached to my back. On St Patrick's Day, Mum used to come to collect me from school, and I'd go to dance at an Irish celebration. If I were lucky, she'd take me for a cold milkshake after my performance, instead of putting me back into the last lesson at school. We danced a lot to help people by raising money for charity or performing for people who were disadvantaged in some way. It was all part of my parents' belief in giving back to the community.

People always said the second that I walked on a stage, you could see how much I felt at home, and that I could always tell a story that would hold an audience entranced. I don't think I was even nervous—that came later. I was very lucky to have such support from the community of Rockhampton. We were always in and out of one another's houses, having tea, at 'smoko'—the Australian equivalent of an English tea break, I guess—where people would pause in their morning routine to have cake and tea, to chat and gossip. There was a real sense of togetherness and care, which did a lot for my confidence. In those early dancing days, I wasn't just clocking up a lot of experience of knowing how to perform to different audiences and get them on my side, I also felt wrapped in their concern for, and pride in me. When I retired, my postbag was full of cards and letters from those same friends and neighbours who had followed my progress faithfully down the years. Aunty Fay, my mother's middle sister, who lived with her husband Arthur in the middle of rural Queensland, raising horses, wrote me a letter that summed up the sentiments of many I received, and that touched me deeply. 'I think one of my very best memories of you was "Animal Crackers". You held the stage then and from then on it was yours.'

Dance was slowly gaining its hold on me. But the way I was taught was about to alter radically, and oddly the choice that changed my life was made while we were on holiday. From the time I was six, we used to go on an annual vacation to the Gold Coast, which was, to our eyes, very glitzy and colourful, with gold-bikini-clad Meter Maids walking the streets, boosting business by offering to put a five-cent coin in the parking meters for incoming tourists. These girls were funded by local businessmen because by being there and making life easy for shoppers, they kept people buying in the stores. It all seems very alien now, but at the time, they just added an exotic sense of difference to our holidays from real life.

The holiday always started in the same way, in the middle of the night, with Mum and Dad carrying me and Madonna, fast asleep, out into the already-packed station wagon, and driving south from Rockhampton for about eight hours. As they drove towards sunrise, we'd wake up and start clamouring for breakfast and driving them mad by asking whether we were there yet. Our destination was always the same too: Tom Tait's apartment block on Mermaid Beach, a few kilometres down from the stretch of the coast known as Surfer's Paradise. It was a two-block concrete motel, but it seemed very sophisticated to us, with its apartments shaped in an L around a swimming pool. We'd swim in inflatable arm bands, sunbathe, and eat ice-cream, and then I'd go on the dodgems with my dad, or race cars with him on a huge Scalextric track. It was there, in 1975, that we made a big decision.

Madonna and I hadn't been enjoying dancing lessons. We were both clearly talented dancers and had become more and more serious about wanting to study ballet, rather than the mix of dancing styles that we were learning at Jan Moore's. The school operated on an almost Victorian system, with stars awarded for success. If we failed, Miss Moore would cross out the stars very purposefully. Madonna and I were beginning to struggle with the whole atmosphere, though I was louder in voicing it. I'd had the same issue at school. If a nun asked me to pick something up which someone else had dropped, I'd ask, 'Why?' I wasn't trying to be contrary or rude, but I had a strong sense of justice. My parents took a fairly dim view of my attitude. They were fair but strict at home, expecting us to do what we were asked without arguing and my mother, in particular, tended to take the view that if we were in trouble out of the house, it was probably our fault. They felt that we should solve our own problems, particularly if they were of our own making.

I wonder now if my inclination to challenge things might be why I seemed to get into trouble so much at dance school. I distinctly remember being sent to face the corner in a lot of lessons, gazing at the spider webs that gathered there. They were different times. Miss Moore would discipline her pupils if they made a mistake, sometimes pulling us by the arm to get us into position. In many ways, she was a terrific teacher—she certainly taught me how to perform. But because I was so keen to succeed, I became overwhelmed by the humiliation of being punished. It's an experience that has stayed with me long into my adult life and to this day affects my view of teaching. Having an objective view of excellence and pushing a pupil towards that goal is one thing, but praise and reward are a much better way of enforcing good practice than criticism and the undermining of confidence.

All of these issues came to a head while on holiday at Mermaid Beach and the result was that my father broke off our holiday and flew back to Rockhampton to give our notice to Miss Moore before the start of the new school year. One chapter in my dance training was over—and a whole new one was about to begin.

CHAPTER 2

DONNARANLEANNE

WHEN I WAS THIRTEEN, I nearly died. I ran out of school, straight across the road to meet my mother waiting in the car, and wham! A car coming slowly up the hill hit me full on, catapulting me in the air. I don't remember the impact, but I do remember waking up on the ground, unable to talk, trying to fight my way back to consciousness, with everyone around panicking and trying to resuscitate me. The driver, Mr Limkin, an incredibly nice man, was virtually in tears. Everyone said it was a miracle I'd survived, and I was probably saved by the fact that he was so careful behind the wheel because I'd just shot into the road, not looking left or right. One of the nuns rang my father, telling him to come quickly because there'd been 'a terrible accident'. By the time he had driven through every red light in his panic to get to me, I was sitting in the back of an ambulance looking quite perky. The ambulance whisked me to the doctor's, but because this was the seventies, no one actually did any X-rays. If I could move, I must be okay. I think I broke my collarbone, because years later, someone noticed a crack on the left side and one arm has always been slightly out of alignment, but no one checked anything at the time.

I know exactly why I was moving so fast. I was running away from my piano teacher who I hated because she used to hit me across the knuckles with a long stick if I made a mistake. Since I made a lot of mistakes, I had very sore fingers, and goodness only knows how I stuck it out until I finally got to grade five, when I gratefully gave up. But the accident was typical of my hectic life. I was always racing somewhere, trying to catch up with myself. By that time of my life, my path was beginning to be clear: ballet was where I felt at home, where I progressed, where I felt most confident. School was something I did. My reports weren't bad, but they were pretty average, and I have always felt under-educated. Things weren't helped by the fact that I was sharing my bedroom with Fiona, who was five years younger, and needed the light turned out early, which cut out the possibility of study or bedtime reading. It's astonishing I know anything, and an even greater miracle that I managed to pass all my exams.

What education I had began at Our Lady's, a Catholic school run by some wonderful nuns where my uncle Ray was then priest. It was profoundly traditional. We lined up in the playground every morning, wearing little white hats and navy-blue pinafores and then marched into our classrooms to the sound of martial music playing from a gramophone in one of the upstairs rooms. If you were in particular favour, which I rarely was, you might be allowed to put the LP on the turntable.

The strictly Catholic teachers regarded my dancing as something to be tolerated rather than celebrated. I was let off early one day a week for ballet lessons, but if the principal, the tiny Sister Clotilde, ever saw me pass her room, she'd swish at me with a cane, so I got into the habit of ducking every time I had to pass her window. I wonder now at the way that my family, strongly Catholic in so many ways, and committed to the charitable values of the church, were so encouraging of my talent for dance. I think letting us perform sprang from their deep-seated belief in allowing all four of their children find our own way in life, allowing us to make our own decisions about what we wanted to do. Mum and Dad were both self-made and entrepreneurial and they didn't want to force us into a particular path too young, so the dance lessons continued to run parallel with my formal education, as I moved up to the Range Convent, where I stayed until I was fifteen and a half.

Ironically it was my big sister Madonna who first dreamt of being a ballerina. Her bedroom was dedicated to photographs of the famous ballerinas of the past and her plan was to follow in their delicate footsteps. Her role model was Margot Fonteyn, a beautiful dancer with impeccable manners and grace in all she did. She studied the Princess Tina ballet annuals, and even carried round a little black book in which she wrote poems about the ballerinas. She had reason to think she could succeed: she was really talented and completely dedicated.

At that stage, I didn't take ballet seriously as a career, however much I loved it as a practice. Even then, I was clear in my own mind that I was too open and outspoken to be a ballerina. I didn't fit the grain of ballet like Madonna did—I was the mischievous little sister to her good, serious personality. I was the one who asked questions, not the one who unquestioningly followed discipline. Although I was happy to dance the little solos she choreographed for me to pieces of Chopin, I wasn't that interested in dance as an art. The first ballet I ever saw was in 1971, when the Royal Ballet's film version of *The Tales of Beatrix Potter* came to the Wintergarden. Later, when I arrived in London to study at the Royal Ballet School, I was excited to discover that the stars of that film, Michael Coleman, Wayne Sleep, and Lesley Collier were not only still dancing, but were also rehearsing in the rooms next door to the students, it was something I could never have imagined as a child. The first live ballet I saw was when I was actually chosen, at the age of eleven or twelve, to perform a Scottish reel in the Queensland Ballet's version of *La Sylphide*, which is an indication of how back to front my experience was. I was performing before I could appreciate ballet's essence or understand how it acted on you if you were a member of the audience.

I saw professional dance from an auditorium in around 1978, when we went to Brisbane to see Margot Fonteyn, who was touring Australia in a programme called Stars of World Ballet. She was almost sixty, and a year off retirement, so although I was conscious of watching a legend, I was also disappointed that she was so clearly past her prime. She danced a little solo from *Raymonda*, and as a critical teenager, I could see that she was struggling. It put a note in the back of my mind about the right moment to stop when I was getting to the end of my dancing career.

There was another reason why the idea of making dance a profession seemed unlikely. Around my early teens, I began to have problems with a very stiff joint in my big toe on my right foot. I don't know what caused it—perhaps it was when I caught it in the pedal of the bright red second-hand bike that dad gave me for my birthday—but Dr Forbes's words stuck with me: 'You've got osteoarthritis. You'll never be a professional dancer with that toe.' It was a shock, but fortunately I just ignored him, although in a way he was right. I really shouldn't have ever been a dancer with that toe, and I've had to work around it my entire career. I've got no flexibility in it at all, and it has meant that in later life, I couldn't dance in soft ballet shoes. I missed out on parts like Mats Ek's *Carmen*, which I would have loved to perform, because it's choreographed for a dancer with her feet in flat shoes. On the plus side, this meant that as soon as I went up on pointe, I was comfortable and at ease. I was always praised for my tremendous high runs and my bourrées when I was performing, but little did the critics know that I was forced to go right up on the top of my metatarsals because I couldn't go down! If I pushed into the toe too much, it would begin to throb. In the early years, I used to try to cure it with heat lamps but latterly, I just used to take an ibuprofen and carry on.

At no point, however, did I think about giving up, whatever the doctor said. Without my knowing or encouraging it, there was something in dance that was beginning to hold me. I enjoyed going into class, for one thing. I liked the work, the sweat, the challenge of challenging myself. What's more, I had the right body for ballet. I was naturally skinny, with long limbs. Madonna, though incredibly talented and a beautiful dancer, had to work harder. She had the kind of physique that meant she had to diet to stay as slim as she needed to be, worrying about her line and her appearance on a dance stage. I could eat whatever I wanted and was very strong. We were entirely different in our aspirations and our view of ballet yet we both had an incredible stroke of luck. Quite by chance in Rockhampton there was a ballet school that was already producing world-class dancers, who were finding success in Australia and in Europe. When my parents decided we had reached the end of the road with our first school, they enrolled us with Valeria Hansen, and it was thanks to her inspiration and training that both Madonna and I became professional dancers.

Valeria Hansen began her career in Brisbane in pantomime and variety shows, taking her Royal Academy of Dance qualifications as she performed. She founded her school in Rockhampton in 1937, teaching 'Operatic Dancing and Acrobatics', and from the very first day she turned out young dancers who stood out. The *Bulletin* reported on her success in an early recital, saying she 'deserves credit for the way in which she has trained these juveniles'.[1] By the time I pitched up on her doorstep, she had sent a succession of girls to dance schools and companies around the world, including Mary McKendry, who went to the Royal Ballet School, London Festival Ballet (later English National Ballet) and Houston Ballet before finally returning to Queensland Ballet to work alongside her husband Li Cunxin.

Madonna and I already knew how good a teacher Miss Hansen was. We'd seen her in action at the Eisteddfods, where the teachers would sit down one side of the room, watching their charges perform. Miss Hansen stood out. In a town where everyone looked natural and a little weather-beaten, she had an immaculately powdered face, so white it looked as if she never saw the sun. Her hair was a perfectly coiffed halo of black, and she wore neat little Dior-style suits, with high collars, low black Cuban heels, and stockings.

Her school was in Buffalo Hall on Denison Street, about a ten-minute drive away from our home, and a few blocks back from the river. The building doubled as the Masonic Hall, so it often stank of beer when we arrived after the weekend and made our way to the upstairs room where Miss Hansen had her studio. It was a nice, airy space with a wooden floor and big windows down both sides—you had to jump on the double barre that ran along the walls to open them in order to get a draught running through. The main railway through Rockhampton was a stone's throw away, and lessons were punctuated by the sound of the heavy transport trains rattling past the windows.

Once we started going there, our days took on a new shape. There were no sleep-ins at Agnes Street. At six in the morning, my mum would call up the stairs 'DonnaranLeanne', running our names together like a song, and down we'd rush, in time to pile into the car to head off for our 6.30am ballet class. Actually, that's not quite true. Madonna would make a calm and measured progress down the stairs, with her hair done neatly in a bun and all her ballet gear packed carefully in a bag. About ten minutes after, as late as I could possibly leave it, I'd follow her, harum-scarum, everything flying, hair tumbling down, grab a cup of Milo—which was my favourite chocolatey drink, reputedly full of vitamins, though it was the chocolate crust I really liked—and fall into the waiting car. Quite often, I'd be so late I wouldn't have managed to get out of my pyjamas and would have to change in the car, while Madonna sat looking smart and collected.

It's the story of my life: I've always been late for everything and it started with those early mornings in Agnes Street. The reason for the unearthly starts was practical. In central Queensland, it can hit forty degrees in summer, and we were on our way to rigorous exercise in a hall without air conditioning. Even beginning early, I remember the air as sticky and heavy, like a blanket lying over the day. It was also the only way we could find the time to train properly; if we were serious about learning to dance, we had to squeeze class around school, with early morning and early evening lessons.

Before our lessons, a couple of the older, more responsible girls would open up the hall, and then we'd wait, with two sentries peering out of the window on lookout duty, so we could stop messing around and get into some semblance of order by the time Miss Hansen was getting out of her car. She drove a sporty little blue Mazda that she bought from my father, who by then ran the dealership in the town. By the time she arrived in the studio, where we were pretending that we had warmed up, it was like a parting of the waves as she walked down the room to her desk, placed dead centre. She put a briefcase and a cassette recorder on the table, sat down, and we began. On the wall behind her, there was a portrait of the Queen and she was like a queen in her own kingdom as she sat there, framed between two doors that led off to a little kitchen area at the back.

Her method of teaching was unique: she'd rarely move from her chair and barely demonstrated a step. I remember just the occasional illustration of a rond de jambe, where she would lift her skirt a millimetre and flash a rather elderly leg. But her instructions were clear, and she'd correct us verbally in a quiet, calm manner. Everything was about following her voice, learning to work for ourselves, and feeling the movement in our bodies.

There wasn't a mirror in the room—or at least there was, but it was closed in a cupboard, so we hardly used it, and it felt like a big deal when she produced a key so we could open the cupboard and see a particular position. Because I wasn't looking at myself, I never thought of myself as being fat, thin, tall, or short. I was just there to learn to dance and to perfect what I was doing. As I took the Royal Academy of Dance examinations, I was told in the reports that I had good proportions, an expressive face, and nice, high extensions, but I didn't develop those by looking at myself, just by following

Miss Hansen's instructions. This saved me, I think, from one of the most difficult things for young girls about learning to dance—it can encourage body dysmorphia.

Teenage girls in society at large are obsessed with their image, with the way they look. Dance is an extreme example of that. It's a very visual profession, based on a particular aesthetic. You're barely clothed. You have to deal with seeing yourself in a mirror on a daily basis, and it's amazing how the mind can play tricks on you. Depending on your mood, you can have a different opinion of your body. Because one day you'll feel fantastic, you'll think you look fantastic—and then the next day, you think your legs look terrible, or your bum is sticking out. It's a difficult profession because of that, and you can't really get away from it.

One of the many benefits of Miss Hansen's teaching was that she never mentioned weight; she just taught the girls in front of her to dance as well as they were able, teasing out their talent with her gentle guidance. I wasn't super-thin in my early days, and I had a bit of a tummy, but what Miss Hansen taught me was not to obsess about my appearance; to obsess instead about dancing, communicating and loving what I was doing. Now when I am teaching, I really don't like it when people are constantly looking through me to the mirror. I ask dancers not to do it. I am in front of them, and it's my eye and my judgement they need to trust. If dancers spend too much time examining their reflections, they distort their positions and are not fully engaged in the movement itself. As a professional, sometimes you need to see what you are doing in order to embed it in your muscles and bones, but I never grew up with that. It wasn't a fixed way of behaving for me, and I believe that was of an immense benefit. I learnt from Valeria Hansen how to share a love of dancing and to encourage someone to be the best they could be, without ever compromising her standards. Although I am not the same kind of teacher at all—I am always moving energetically around a studio, in trainers and casual clothes, and I am considerably louder—I have tried to absorb her philosophy. She was strong and strict, but I don't remember her raising her voice in anger or being condescending. You always felt the respect flowing from her to her pupils. I never talked to her in the way that some dancers today would chat easily to their teachers; I was too much in awe of her, but I think she had a soft spot for me. There is one photograph of me sitting on her knee, and we're both smiling. You can see the warmth between us.

My weeks began to fall into a regular pattern. Class in the morning and in the evening, and then on Saturdays, lessons all day, with Scottish and Irish dancing in the afternoon. For some years, the morning lessons were shared with older girls, but as they gradually left to take up their careers elsewhere, or as they stopped doing ballet entirely, I had Miss Hansen to myself in the mornings, and for eight months before I left for London, I had private coaching because everyone else in my year had gone. Under her gently critical eye, I steadily worked my way through the Royal Academy of Dance Examinations, treating them as another form of competition, determined to do as well as I possibly could. I always passed with honours, and was rarely nervous, though Miss Hansen used to watch my progress anxiously through a little hatch built in the wall at the top of the stairs.

My report for my intermediate exam contained only two negative comments, that I should 'avoid tendency to pitch the weight back' and 'at times adjustment of weight should be more forward' in pointe work. Those were two corrections I was given my entire career, and this backs my theory that although you can improve as a dancer, your weaknesses will likely remain the ones you began with. Miss Hansen quite often unorthodoxly opened class with allégro training, so I had no worries as a dancer about jumping or speed. But grand pirouettes, or turns in attitude, made me anxious, because I'd never really been taught to turn. I always marvelled at dancers such as Carlos Acosta or Marianela Nuñez who are brilliant at turning on the spot, because they were trained as young dancers in ways that gave them the feeling of the turn. Dancing is often about confidence; perfection follows once you have the sense of the movement.

Miss Hansen's school was surrounded and nurtured by a network of supportive mothers, who provided moral, financial and practical support as she taught their daughters to dance. On Saturdays they were much in evidence. One mother, Mrs Graff, would stand in the kitchen dispensing home-made cakes and snacks—I remember Jatz biscuits were a particular hit at twenty cents for four. I also remember sneaking out to buy chocolate, which would instantly melt in the heat. I was in England before I realised chocolate could be eaten in any state other than molten. Another mum, Mrs Veretennikova, whose daughters Anna and Nina both went on to have great ballet careers, accompanied us on the piano that sat on a raised platform at the end of the hall. Mrs V, as we called her, also ran the local ballet shop, Centre De Danse, on Musgrave Street on the northside of town, a treasure trove of costumes, shoes and everything else an aspiring dancer could want.

I tried on my first pair of pointe shoes there when I was thirteen (I started dancing on pointe relatively late) and felt a wave of excitement as I felt the hard tip close around my toes for the first time. Mrs V and Mrs Graff were also on the yearly Eisteddfod committee, for which Dad was the treasurer. Mum stayed clear of committees; her support came in the form of endlessly chauffeuring us to all our lessons, sitting in the car outside, waiting for class to finish. Sometimes it would run over by an hour, and the supper she had painstakingly prepared earlier would be dried up, but she didn't moan and nor did we. Or at least not often.

Being so busy with dance didn't stop me having friends, but it did alter the way I interacted with the other girls at school. I wasn't popular and I wasn't unpopular, but I was certainly never interested in being part of any clique or group. I just got on with everybody. My social life, such as it was, was built around Agnes Street and the families who lived nearby. On Saturdays, after dance class was over, our family would sit around with other families in the garden and there were beers for the grown-ups and pies for us all. I'd be there in my pink tights and flip-flops, peeling the lid off the pie with great deliberation, and to everyone's amusement.

My best friend Terri Williams lived round the corner and all the Benjamin siblings spent a lot of time at her house, where there were seven children. Terri and I went to Our Lady's and the Range Convent together and on occasion we ran the tuck shop, although we weren't very reliable salesgirls. Bored with my daily regime of a vegemite sandwich and a piece of fruit, we used to peel off the underneath of the sausage rolls and eat them before we sold them on. Terri was my great confidante, and we did all the girly teenage things together: hanging around, lying on the bed giggling, looking through magazines. She saved me from being that stage-struck kid who loses track of the real world around her. With Terri, my friend to this day, I could always be a normal teenager; I had other friends at ballet school, but she grounded me.

So did events like the sheer embarrassment of the school prom, when I was about to leave school for good. At fifteen, I had finally got rid of the great orthodontic apparatus of braces, rail tracks, neck brace, head brace, the lot, that I wore without any inhibition for most of my teenage years, but I still wasn't the type that any teenage boy was likely to look at. I was thin and flat-chested and not interested in boys at all. I didn't want to go to the prom, but my mum insisted I should attempt to find a partner and in desperation, we looked to Mum's best friend, Coralie McKendry, who had eight children. Mary McKendry was dancing in London by this point, but I was friendly with her sister Josephine, who was also studying ballet, and one of the boys, Patrick, was the same age as me. He didn't want to take me to the dance, but his mother shamelessly bribed him with the idea that one day I would be such a famous dancer that I would be in the pages of the *Australian Women's Weekly* magazine, and he would be able to say he had been my date. Years later, I actually did make its pages so at least we both fulfilled our sides of the bargain.

By my early teens, my mother had taken on a new project. She'd always been interested in antiques and Dad built a small cottage in the back garden where she could sell her increasing stock. There was a little display area for jewellery at the front, and then a larger space in which she displayed furniture at the back. As her reputation grew, more and more people came for a chat and to see what she had for sale. This was in the days when no one locked the doors, so people started to come to the house, walking through the front door, thinking our house was the shop. We would be watching TV or eating dinner and find people in the living room, asking how much we'd charge for the table, or picking up lamps to examine them. That was the point Dad decided he'd had enough and found a piece of land where he lovingly designed and built a double storey, colonial-style building that Mum could use as her new business base. She turned it into a thriving concern, where characters came and went, and I'm sure it's where I inherit my own love of interior design and antiques. Her business has always been a labour of love and she taught me a lot about buying, whether it was property, paintings or antiques: you should never buy solely to make a profit but because you love something. If it makes money, great, but you will always have the satisfaction of enjoying it, which is the most important thing.

The greatest change in my growing up, though, came when Madonna decided that she wanted to follow her dream by going to the Royal Ballet School in London. I think Miss Hansen must have told my parents that the best dancers went to study there, and my father doesn't recall having much choice in the matter. Of course, Madonna was in seventh heaven: she had longed to go to London to follow in the footsteps of all those beautiful ballerinas she so idolised. Her departure was a big deal. The furthest anyone in our family had travelled was Japan, where Dad had been on business, and the idea of settling somewhere with a cold climate threw everyone into a panic. Madonna remembers us all heading to Brisbane to buy her a wardrobe which included a fur coat and snow boots—completely over the top for an English winter. There was a big send off at Miss Hansen's studio for both Madonna and Karen Donovan, who went to the RBS at the same time, and subsequently made a career with Sadler's Wells Royal

Ballet. They were presented with a scholarship cheque raised by the ballet committee and the entire town seemed to turn out to wave them off at the airport. Mum and Dad went too, accompanying Madonna to London, via an extremely scary emergency landing in Bahrain when their plane lost an engine. They were so distraught when it came to leaving their sixteen-year-old daughter alone in England that they cancelled the holiday of a lifetime they had planned on the way home. All this goes some way to explaining why my own decision to follow in Madonna's footsteps and apply for the RBS just seemed to progress as a matter of course. It wasn't a big deal because Madonna had paved the way. She'd made all the decisions and I seemed to ride along in her wake.

These days to be considered for the Royal Ballet School from Australia you have to send a twenty-minute video and be prepared to travel to London for two days of intensive auditions, interviews and a medical test. In my day, the process of application was considerably more primitive. I had to send photographs of myself in three positions, which were taken by a local photographer who stuck me on top of a table, next to the barre, presumably because it looked better to have the high windows behind me. He clearly didn't know anything about dance, because that meant the whole angle of the shoot was dreadful and, I am amused to notice, draws attention to the fact that I have a ladder in my tights, which is just so typical of me.

Studying the photos now, with my teacher's eye, I think they're pretty terrible, but I'd want to see that girl. I've got a nice physique, good proportions and good muscles, and though my right finger is sticking out when my arms are meant to be gracefully curled above my head—a ballet fault I've worked on my whole life—I'm holding the pose quite well. But I do look young. I was fifteen, but I still look like a child: flat chested, with those coltish arms and legs. Apparently, the school nearly didn't take me, because I was so thin and they got in touch with Miss Hansen to say I looked great, but was I eating properly? She assured them I was, and I got my place in October 1979, which I'd take up in September the following year. When the letter arrived, I was jumping around the house. It was one of the great moments of my life. There's a horribly posed newspaper photograph of me, holding that acceptance letter, surrounded by my classmates, all with our feet slightly awkwardly folded, one behind the other. With all the success I had, I never felt the slightest sense of jealousy towards me from my classmates. I really liked everyone and never got involved in the gossip that can go on in dance schools. It just didn't interest me.

I made the papers again when, competing against fourteen other girls from across Australia, I won a $1000 bursary from the Royal Academy of Dance, the first time I had ever had any money towards my training. I danced to Beethoven's 'Piano Sonata No. 8', the Pathétique, music that I have decided I want played at my funeral, and did have played at my wedding, I love it so much. The same newspaper reported that I was going to London with my father for Christmas to see Madonna, who was dancing in the corps de ballet of *Swan Lake*. By then, Madonna had left the school and been taken into the Royal Ballet, and obviously part of the reason for our visit was to go to see her. We all missed her terribly.

The other motive was to try to dissuade me from becoming their second daughter to leave the nest and settle in London. Mum and Dad didn't want to lose another child to the UK; I had a place at The Australian Ballet School as well, and I know they hoped that I might change my mind and go there. Throughout my childhood, I'd always loved spending time with my dad. He took me to stock car races, and we once saw the daredevil antics of the stuntman Evel Knievel. A treat, on the days he was free from work, was simply to get into the car together and just drive, listening to music and chatting. There was never a particular destination. We'd cruise around Rockhampton, or travel to places not too far away, like Mount Morgan, an old gold, silver and copper mining town. Going to London was the same kind of adventure but on a bigger scale, and he made it into a wonderful trip. We went to Stratford-upon-Avon, visited Shakespeare's house, took rides on London buses, went on walks in Hyde Park, and took in a couple of shows.

London was extraordinarily cold, grey, and full of terraced houses crammed together, with no space between. For a girl from sunny Queensland, it seemed unbearably dirty and oppressive. To my fifteen-year-old eyes, Sydney with its Opera House and its harbour seemed a far more beautiful and impressive city than London. I hated it. But then I walked into the foyer of the Royal Opera House, with its deep red carpet, cream and gold walls and its atmosphere of artistic endeavour, and I was blown away. I sat in the stalls, clutching my programme, watching Madonna perform in a dreamy version of *Swan Lake*, and I knew I wanted the same experience. My path was set, and I was determined to follow it.

I came back to Rockhampton, and waited, filling in time. If I'd chosen to go to The Australian Ballet school in Melbourne, I'd have started in January. For the Royal, I had to wait until September. I carried on studying with Miss Hansen, enjoying our long mornings together; I passed my Advanced RAD exam, and I represented Queensland in my last Australian competition, in the Commonwealth Society of Teachers of Dancing Sun Cup. For a final time, in January 1980, I went to Sydney for the dancing summer school run by Martin Rubinstein, a legendary teacher who, over the three previous summers, had expanded my horizons beyond Rockhampton. He'd been an important player in the development of ballet in Australia: one of the stars in the 1940s of The Australian Ballet, founded as the Borovansky Ballet by Edouard Borovansky, who had once toured with Pavlova. As a dancer, Rubinstein was famous for his high-flying elevation and his theatricality, shining in roles once made famous by Nijinsky; but when a double bout of tuberculosis forced him to retire from dancing, he refashioned himself as a teacher. By the time I met him he was a stout, characterful man, with a twinkle in his eye and a cheeky sense of humour. Because I was still ignorant about ballet history, I didn't register how important he had once been as a dancer, but I knew he was a terrific teacher.

I loved those summers in Sydney, confiding in a letter home that: 'Mr Rubinstein is lovely, but can be very sarcastic at times. Mrs Graff, our chaperone, is a big grump.' Poor Mrs Graff. She was charged with looking after us, when all we wanted to do was explore a big city. She was appalled when I nearly managed to start a fire in my room at our hostel with the sunlamp that I carried everywhere in order to treat my arthritic toe. Fortunately, the damage was just a hole in the carpet, but quite rightly I got the most enormous telling-off. What I most remember is going to Luna Park, the huge amusement park, and screaming with delight as I rode every ride. I also took a trip to Government House, over-awed by its sense of history, and never imagining that one day I would be part of its story.

There was a sense of filling in time that year. I wasn't looking back or feeling nervous about leaving home. I couldn't wait to be gone. I was like a horse at the gate before the race, desperate to begin my dancing career. Finally, September came, and my parents threw a big barbecue for me to say goodbye to all my friends before we all set off for London. Just before I left, Aunty Pat gave me a card of encouragement, with the poem 'Thinking' inside.

If you think you are beaten, you are
If you think you dare not, you don't,
If you'd like to win, but you think you can't
It's almost a cinch you won't.
If you think you'll lose, you've lost
For out in the world you find,
Success begins with a fellow's will
It's all in the state of mind.

CHAPTER 3

'I'M NOT HOMESICK, JUST A BIT LONELY'

IF AUSTRALIA WAS SUN, BLUE skies, warm earth and bright green tropical trees, then London was brown, grey and dingy. Even the clothes I wore were in shades of maroon and beige, and usually a few degrees too light for the weather. In Queensland, I'd either been at the beach, or in ballet class; I'd no idea how to dress in winter and all I had with me was a lot of badly fitting corduroy and the inappropriate fur coat that my family felt was perfect for the English weather. I arrived at Heathrow early one morning in September 1980, carrying a huge black suitcase containing an assortment of possessions, including a small teddy bear that someone had given me as I left Rockhampton. Mum and Dad flew over with me, turning my move into a three-week long trip to see Madonna. I think that's why my arrival didn't seem as momentous as it was. It was like hand-me-down clothes syndrome: I was leaving home at sixteen, settling in a city I didn't know, living alone and unfriended. But Madonna had done all that two years before me and was now a member of the Royal Ballet company. Big balletic adventures had become a pattern in the

Benjamin family, and though I was excited about it, I didn't stop to think just how different it would be.

Nevertheless, it's hard to describe the shock. My new home was a three-storey boarding house on Glazbury Road in West London, its forbidding brick frontage covered in soot, grime and pollution. This was the kingdom of Stella Wilson and her partner Eileen Ward, who shared the basement and the ground floor with twenty-five cats. The whole place smelt of cat pee, and I am sure it's there that my lifelong aversion to cats began. The accommodation, bedsits for around eight boarders from the Royal Ballet School, rose up from a staircase, with one communal phone halfway up. There was one shared bathroom, with a bath, a plastic hand shower, and a meter for the pilot light for hot water. On the top floor we had a minuscule three foot by three foot kitchen consisting of a couple of rings, a tiny, disgustingly greasy oven, a sink and another hot water boiler. Next door was a small sitting room, with an old-fashioned gas fire that you also had to put fifty pence in a slot to get started, a rug (brown stripes), a table (brown) and a tatty old sofa (also brown). There was one single room, two doubles, and then, on the top floor under the dormers, an attic room which I was to share with two other girls. It was crowded with the kind of furniture that looked as if someone had rescued it before it went to the dump: a couple of chairs, wonky white cupboards and a chest of drawers that had all seen better days. It was also so small that there was barely any space between the beds. My single bed was in one corner, with a rattan table next to it, a couple of anonymous Athena posters on the walls and a (brown) shelf above one end, on which stood a dying spider plant and a radio.

For someone who had just days before been rushing round a large colonial house in Queensland, folding myself into that tiny room felt like torture. Though my roommates were friendly, they seemed as alien as the décor. They were just so English, and so refined, compared with my big, rough Australian ways. One was Mary Goodhew, who went on to run Elmhurst Ballet School, the other was Donna Richardson, who later danced with the Royal Ballet. Both were incredibly kind, but they were so different from me. They ate, breathed and slept ballet; the walls above their narrow beds were plastered with neat rows of photographs of the dancers they admired and wanted to emulate. I have never, in all my life, only wanted to talk about ballet. I learnt to fit in with my ballet-mad fellow pupils, but I never felt the same as them. As my years at the Royal Ballet School continued, I became more expert on the history of ballet, choosing dancers to admire and whose careers I wanted to follow. But even when I understood the significance of Margot Fonteyn, Antoinette Sibley, or Lynn Seymour, I wanted to carve my own path, not follow in their footsteps. I have always been interested in more than ballet and I amuse people even today when I say I'd rather go to the theatre than to a dance performance if I've got a free evening.

For all its inconvenience, boarding at Stella's had two big advantages. The first was that Madonna had stayed there before me, so Mum and Dad felt that Stella would keep an eye on me as I navigated life in London as a teenager, essentially alone. It seems extraordinary in some ways, given how protective they had always been and how strict about the way I had to behave, that they let me go so easily. But in those days, I think we were much more independent. We were fending for ourselves; there were certain rules, but we were left to our own devices. No one was telling us what to do and what not to do. We got into trouble only if we did something that was clearly wrong—as I did the day I managed to leave the bath taps running and flood the entire house, which my dad had to pay to put right.

The main plus of staying at Stella's, however, was that it was only a few minutes' walk away from the Royal Ballet's Upper School at Barons Court, which was the reason for my coming to London in the first place. Nothing else much mattered. Ninette de Valois, founder of the Royal Ballet, opened her first school in 1926; it moved to the Barons Court building in 1947. Down the decades, it was reshaped and extended in various ways, providing a rabbit's warren of studios and classrooms where balletic and academic education were combined.

I loved it. It was all a bit dirty and grimy, but you could taste the history in the air, and since the company also rehearsed there, every day as a student you'd rub shoulders with the dancers who were creating new chapters in the story of ballet. As you walked in, you were faced with a large studio surrounded by internal windows, like a goldfish bowl, where the company often worked. To the left was a corridor leading to the company offices, changing rooms and a studio, and a winding staircase that led to the most beautiful wooden-floored studio, which was where the Royal Ballet mainly rehearsed. If you turned right when you went through the doors, you found yourself in an elegant central lobby with doors and stairs off it. Along on the right and down a little, there were more big studios, one for the company and two for the school, but if you went up to the second floor, you came to a spot where you could see into the Royal Ballet's room. Students used to huddle round that half-glazed door, gazing inside, absorbing and learning. I remember spending long periods peering (illicitly) through the glass, watching stars such as Lynn Seymour and Jennifer Penney at work. Seeing Seymour dance was a revelation; she later became important in my career, but I remember even in those early months watching her in awe. She didn't look like a dancer, with her curling hair pulled back in a wide bandeau, and her heavily kohled eyes. She always struggled with her weight. But the second she started to dance, it was transformative. Watching her taught me that you have to wait to see what is inside someone to know their quality, and what was inside Seymour was passionate and eloquent.

The studios we mainly worked in were at the other end of the building. My favourite was at the furthest point away from the main door; like all the other rooms it had a wooden floor and a barre running around three sides. The windows looked out across the busy Talgarth Road and the District and Piccadilly tube lines ran behind the building, with the trains constantly rattling past, just as the trains did at Miss Hansen's ballet school in Rockhampton—a little reminder of home that always felt like a comfort. In the basement was a canteen, shared between the school and the company, but the company had their own room in which to sit and, in those days, smoke. You might bump into Merle Park, or Antoinette Sibley in the food queue, or see Marguerite Porter buying a toasted teacake, and feel inspired by the simple fact that at some level these dancers, who had made such great names for themselves, still worked and lived in the same way that you did. We didn't presume too much and always tried to keep our distance, particularly after the day one of my friends got into trouble with the Russian ballerina Natalia Makarova when he clattered into her and spilt her cup of coffee over her. But it was somehow important to feel that we were all in this weird world of ballet together.

After a week of acclimatising myself to my new surroundings, taking open classes at the Urdang Academy in Covent Garden to keep in shape, I turned up at the famous door for an audition class. In those days, the Upper School had four first year classes—one for the students who had come up through the Royal Ballet's junior school at White Lodge, which was effectively the top class, two classes that mixed English students and those from overseas, and one that was purely for dancers from abroad. But there was some flexibility in the choices and our level and ability were assessed on that first day by a beady-eyed panel of teachers. Think of the scene in the film *Billy Elliot* when Billy performs at his Royal Ballet audition panel, and you will have some idea of what it was like.

I wasn't nervous, even though I had to dance first when the girl before me didn't turn up. I had confidence in my talent and the class went so well that I got into the White Lodge class, alongside eight dancers from the Royal Ballet's junior school and two American imports—Eva Nissen, a tall blonde Midwesterner and Sarah Green, a beauty from Washington with a wicked sense of humour. I was glad not to be the only outsider in the class, and the three of us formed an instant bond. Such success was thrilling, and like most things in my life from then on, it was posted on a message board, which was on the wall in the central circular hall at Barons Court, just outside the teachers' common room, for the entire world to see. My luck in getting into that top class was greater than I knew, because it meant I studied with Nancy Kilgour, who was an exceptional teacher. Canadian, vibrant and energetic, she had great vivacity and so much to give, particularly to someone like me who was fizzing with energy. She used to dash around the class, handing out corrections, shouting instructions. She was loud, cheerful and endlessly encouraging. From the first day I felt she appreciated the way I wanted to work. From my own teaching experience, I know this is a wonderful bond, especially when the student has talent as well. If a pupil is willing to accept your help, you can push them on. I was very willing, and Miss Kilgour gave me so much help. I always felt she was excited about how I would turn out, which is enormously good for your confidence when you are learning.

Even with this inspirational presence in front of me, class at the Upper School was quite different from anything I'd experienced before. There were strict uniform rules—we wore black leotards, with yellow ribbons around our buns to show we were in Miss Kilgour's class, then maroon leotards in grads, as our second year was known. Lessons were much more communal than I was used to. I'd been taught in one studio, with very few other people around. I'd never learnt a properly choreographed ballet solo in my life, other than solos that Miss Hansen made up on the spot. I didn't know the steps for famous ballets such as *Swan Lake* or *The Nutcracker*. I had never been partnered or danced in a studio alongside so many people who were at my level or above.

It was astonishing to see people who were better dancers than me, but I wasn't intimidated, even though I was working with people who had known each other from childhood. I felt separate and a little shut out, but not over-awed. It was such a huge adventure, and I was hungry for it. I didn't stand at the back: I wanted to make sure

I was seen. I am a fighter, and however hard it was, I was there for a purpose, and I owed a lot to the people who had made their own sacrifices to get me there. I didn't have a scholarship at that point, and there was no government support or a grant to put me through ballet school. Mum and Dad were paying a hefty fee (£1,647 a year, plus accommodation) for the privilege of my learning—I wasn't going to let them down.

You might think all dancers are like this, utterly determined to be the best. But I don't think they are. As a coach, I was once asked by a mother if I'd give her daughter, who was being taught in one of our best schools, some extra tuition and I happily agreed, saying I could fit her in on Sunday mornings. As soon as I said that, her mother jibbed, saying that her daughter needed a lie in, so could it not be too early. I was shocked. At her age, I'd have got up at 4am if that were the only time Lynn Seymour, or someone else I admired and respected, had said she could teach me.

That's one of the qualities I try to instil in the people I teach. It's not all about technique or talent or brilliance. It's not even always the best dancer who gets a role. Sometimes getting to where you want to be as a dancer is about commitment and attitude, with a little bit of luck thrown in. Take Adam Cooper, who became known to so many people when he danced the swan in Matthew Bourne's brilliant version of *Swan Lake*. He wasn't by any means the best technical dancer in the Royal Ballet, but he was pleasant, quick, a good partner, a brilliant actor and he cared about his performance. That's why I loved dancing with him, and I suspect that's why Sylvie Guillem, who was famously (and justifiably) demanding about who she worked with, was happy to be partnered by him in difficult ballets. When I'm teaching, I talk about people like Adam. I think it's important to realise that if you work hard, then someone might see something in you. The young dancers I am drawn to are the ones with a desire to succeed in their eyes. They might not be the best, but I know that person will work to fulfil their ambition; they are the ones practising all the time at the back of the class, they aren't doing the steps once and then sitting on the floor chatting. Character matters, in dance as in life.

In terms of my own career, the other thing I've learnt is that you must adapt and keep going. Disaster lurks around every corner, and it's how you cope with adversity that's going to define you as a dancer and a person. At the end of my first week at the Royal Ballet School, on 24 September 1980, I was about to face one of those moments. My parents had been allowed to come in to watch class and it was all going beautifully. Then we got to the final section of the lesson, where the dancers start to jump across the room. I was always a good confident jumper, so I took off happily into the final grand jeté but managed to land awkwardly on the floor, bashing the side of my foot. The pain was excruciating, and Miss Kilgour immediately whisked me off to Charing Cross Hospital for an X-ray which confirmed the worst. I had a hairline fracture in my fifth metatarsal.

I went to stay for the weekend with Madonna, who pampered me and made me feel better, but she couldn't wipe away my disappointment: after my brilliant start, I was going to be out of action for six to eight weeks and could only sit and watch class. The injury jeopardised all my plans. I had hoped to take my RAD Solo Seal exam that autumn, and also to enter the Adeline Genée competition, which had been held by the Royal Academy of Dance ever since the 1930s and awarded its gold medal to the most promising young dancers. Madonna had won the top prize two years earlier; I knew how important it was as a marker of talent and I was so downcast.

I was also by this stage effectively on my own in London. Shortly after my injury, Mum and Dad had to fly back to Australia to be with my brother and sister. Madonna was mainly busy with the difficult business of making her way in the Royal. She had just been cast as the notoriously challenging role of Fairy Autumn in Frederick Ashton's *Cinderella*. I think Mum and Dad thought she would keep an eye on me, particularly after I was injured, but she simply couldn't cope with that expectation and the stress of building her own career. In any case,

.d her own adult life to lead, her own friends, and I was still .ctively a child, young for my age. We had always been chalk and cheese because she was so organised, and I was so easy-going and chaotic. I think I was like a puppy wanting to play with a cat.

Nowadays when we discuss it, she says she wasn't there for me as much as she should have been, but I understood even at the time how difficult it was for her and accepted that I had to fend for myself. The problem was that I didn't have a clue how to look after myself. I began to buy frozen meals from the local shop and eat them every night; I don't think I ate any fresh food, just pies and burgers that I could heat up in the little oven at my digs. With the enforced lack of exercise and my terrible diet, I began, for the first time in my life, to put on weight. Barbara Fewster, who was principal of the school, called me into her office for a chat and gently pointed this out. I adored Miss Fewster, as I think most people did. She was strict but had a heart of gold, and I suspect that after noticing I was struggling, she kept a careful eye on me. She must at least have been impressed by my determination because having said I couldn't study both for my Solo Seal and the Genée, in the end she let me enter for both.

My next stroke of luck was that as my foot healed, I had private classes with a wonderful character called Joan Lawson. She was another legendary figure, having studied with the notation pioneer Margaret Morris and the Russian dancer Serafina Astafieva, and later in Moscow and Leningrad. She became an expert on Soviet Ballet, but also wrote influential books and manuals which outlined her anatomical approach to the teaching of ballet. She had been a teacher at the RBS, with a particular interest in remedial dance, and developed great skill in getting dancers back after injury—work she continued after her official retirement.

It was my good fortune that she was the teacher chosen to help me bring my foot back to full working order. As a gauche sixteen-year-old, I knew none of this. As far as I was concerned, she was a slightly dotty, grey-haired old lady in ballet shoes and a floaty skirt, who looked as if she had just wandered off the stage, and who called everybody 'Ducky'. But she was, I now realise, an extraordinarily good teacher and she got me into shape with remarkable speed. By the end of October, I was back in class and according to my diaries, Miss Kilgour told me that my dancing hadn't lost anything. If anything, the injury had helped, because it had made me more relaxed.

My diaries of that time, erratically dated and enthusiastically punctuated with multiple exclamation marks, are a vivid record of both how babyish I was and how seriously I took my new world. Some sample entries catch the tone.

'Day went really well. I did a really good big jump and after class Miss Kilgour said she couldn't get over it! So I felt really good. She said I've got everything and only need to keep dancing.'

Later I confide. 'I'm scared for the future and what it will bring ... Ballet really is a world of its own. I must work and keep my muscles toned and become a second Natalia Makarova. Remember—nothing is impossible! I hope I marry.'

Two days later still, I am in a pensive mood. 'Why aren't I ever homesick? I'd love to look into the future. Will I regret my profession? I must reach the top! My height will go against me I presume. Think positive as Dad would say!'

The life I am describing with such stream-of-consciousness breathlessness was a strange cross between a boarding school novel, with a lot of young girls crammed together in an atmosphere that was both frantically competitive and sweetly supportive, and a more expansive picture of life in London during the eighties, where punks strutted down the King's Road, the IRA were beginning to mount a mainland bombing campaign, Mrs Thatcher was taking on the unions and a recession, and I was buying clothes in Mary Quant and Hyper-Hyper on Kensington High Street and listening to the heated discussions at Hyde Park's Speakers Corner.

I was a curious mixture of the naïve and the worldly. I was still going to Mass most Sundays and writing to Aunty Pat to ask for her prayers. 'I'm not homesick, just a bit lonely,' I told her in November. But I was also encountering boys for the first time, recording primly that I didn't like a school party for Halloween where 'everyone was drunk and paired off'. I didn't seem to fit in and disguised my insecurity with over-confident teenage assertions that make my grown-up heart bleed: 'I'm so glad Mum and Dad brought me up to be a lady.'

I seem to swoon whenever a certain boy walks by, without having the first clue how to speak to him. I was lucky, though, in my new friends, particularly Maria Almeida, a calm and restful personality, who had kind parents nearby to look after us, which helped my loneliness. She later became a principal with the Royal, but retired very young, out of love with the art form. She was the most wonderful dancer, with a beautiful lower leg and foot. I adored watching her dance even as a student, because her natural ability, quality and warmth were apparent in every step. In our second year studying together she started to go out with Jonathan Cope, who was in the third year at the time (boys studied for three years, girls for two), and they are still married today. With pals like them at my side, I did all the things young people did in London at the time—dinner at the Hard Rock Cafe was a particular favourite, as were trips to London parks, and constant visits to Harrods where I was beginning to assemble a proper winter wardrobe. I obsessed over knitwear. More seriously, I was also worried by the fact that I had left school at fifteen with the most rudimentary education, which prompted me to sign up for evening classes in the history of art at the institute opposite Barons Court (now the West London College), trying to squeeze some study into the time I had free from dancing. Desperate to expand my brain and my knowledge, I also took myself off to every movie I could manage, and every theatre show I could afford, the more obscure the better.

But what I mainly did was dance, falling into the pattern of each day with something like pleasure. School began with class at 9am and then we'd study particular areas: pointe work, pas de deux classes, repertoire classes and modern. We had special lessons in

Cecchetti technique, a system of training that develops the essential skills of dance—balance, poise, strength, elevation, flexibility and artistry—which had hugely influenced the style of British ballet, and also classes in notation, which I was always trying to skip because I found them boring. The rest I lapped up. Saturdays were a particular joy because you had an open class, with male and female teachers, which was more free than our lessons in the week. It was all new to me and it was wonderful, though I was always anxious when we had to face an assessment. On 2 December that first year, we had to dance an assessment class in front of a truly terrifying set of judges, who included Miss Fewster, ballerinas Pamela May and Merle Park, the then head of the Royal Ballet Norman Morrice, and James Monahan, director of the Royal Ballet School. I did well, but ever the perfectionist, I was disappointed with my marks.

The weeks leading up to the end of the year passed in a whirr of activity. I was so busy that my diary doesn't record whether I was sad that I would be apart from my parents at Christmas for the first time in my life. What it does suggest is that I am excited that I am about to embark on two competitions: the Genée, and then—to my enormous surprise—the world-famous Prix de Lausanne, held annually in Switzerland, which has proved a springboard for many dancers who have become household names. Originally, I had thought I hadn't a chance of being chosen to represent the Royal; a girl called Elizabeth Tullock and Maria had already been picked when I was sitting around injured. But then, at the close of the year, I met another one of the teachers, Kathryn Wade in the street, and she asked me if I wanted to be the cover for Lausanne, because both Liz and Maria had slight injuries.

'Even if they still do it, she might be able to squeeze me in!' The predictable exclamation mark could hardly sum up the extent of my happiness. Being chosen for Lausanne meant I was regarded as being one of the three best dancers in the school. I was on my way.

CHAPTER 4

'REMEMBER THE NAME LEANNE BENJAMIN, WE SHALL UNDOUBTEDLY HEAR MORE OF HER'

The 1980 Adeline Genée competition was held at Sadler's Wells Theatre in North London on 5 January. For the previous week I'd worn myself out, rehearsing and practising. Then, as usual, on the actual day of the event I was late, thanks to my normal lack of organisation, taking twice as long to get my act together because I was conscious someone was waiting for me. I'd planned to catch a tube from West London to Islington, changed my mind and got a taxi, then had to direct the driver because he didn't know where the theatre was. Since I barely did either, by the time I got to the stage door, I was already frayed. The day started with class, and then a stage rehearsal which went disastrously because, for the first time in my life, I was dancing in darkness. From the stage, I could see only blackness, with blinding lights on either side.

I'd never worked like that before and was convinced I'd mess up the performance. Darkness is hard to become acclimatised to, particularly if you are trying to communicate with an audience. I learnt to cope with it later, but at sixteen the sudden strangeness of everything made me nervous in a way I hadn't often been before. I was also, and again for the first time, performing on a raked stage, which slopes upwards, away from the audience. If you've always danced on flat floors, that slight slant is terrifying. It has a tendency to throw everything backwards and push your alignment out. One of the strongest rakes I have ever danced on is at the Paris Opera, which has such a fierce slope that you feel you are falling over; it's agony on the calves if you are only dancing there occasionally. Sadler's Wells isn't as bad, but in the old theatre it was still strange enough to make me feel at sea.

I forced down a cheese roll and an orange juice, then gave myself a talking to. My mum had always suggested that when I felt anxious, I should distract myself by imagining our next-door neighbour, a boy called Graham Baker, in his pyjamas. The thought always made me giggle, and by the time the competition began, I was much more relaxed. It started with an onstage class with ten other girls, taken by a man called Alan Hooper, which we had been rehearsing for two days. Then I performed two solos that had been choreographed for me by Julia Farron, one of the dancers in Ninette de Valois's Vic-Wells Ballet company, who was at that point the grads' year teacher at the Royal Ballet School. I felt, unusually, that my performance went quite well and was pleased to hear loud applause from the auditorium at the end of each solo. Out there in the dark in a full audience was another frighteningly knowledgeable judging panel: Phyllis Bedells, a British ballet pioneer, who went on to become an outstanding teacher and a founding member of the organisation that became the Royal Academy of Dance; the great male dancer David Wall; ballerina Pamela May, and—most famous of all—Margot Fonteyn, headline-making star and the ultimate ideal for every British dancer. She was judging the competition in her role as President of the RAD because it was the fiftieth anniversary of the competition. I felt honoured that Fonteyn was my judge. It didn't increase my anxiety, instead I told myself that her presence would make me dance even better.

Whether this was true or not, after a break all the finalists were asked to line up onstage and Miss Bedells announced the winners. She said that there was too big a gap between the standard of the bronze dancer and the standard of the gold winner, so the judges had decided not to award a silver medal. Instead they had unanimously decided that the gold medal was going to be given to dancer number two. Which was me! I'd like to say I remember every second of what happened next, but the truth is I don't. It's all a bit of a blur.

Fortunately, my teenage-self recorded the moment that Dame Margot handed me my prize. 'Margot,' I wrote casually, 'asked me how old I was and where I trained now and previously and I kissed her when she gave me the medal … I was so glad to be the winner and not the loser. I know what it feels like to lose—your stomach just goes hollow'. I went off into the night on cloud nine, with Madonna, Mary McKendry and some other friends, who gave me chocolates and a teddy bear, and then hit the phone when I got home to share my news. Standing near the scruffy stairs at Stella's I called my parents on the pay phone, and Miss Hansen at her new house in Brisbane where she settled after retirement. I could hear her pride all the way down the line. Although I was relieved it was over, I couldn't sleep much. I felt over the moon and lucky that I had danced so well in front of company directors and other important people. I finally fell asleep wondering what my future would bring.

It was a question on other lips as well. The reviews that greeted my win at the Genée were truly extraordinary and I've cherished them all my life. Ann Nugent in *The Stage* called me an 'outstanding talent': 'Leanne Benjamin showed that she had overcome all the main technical hurdles, her legs extended high and strongly, her jump was easy, and her turns were neat,' she wrote. 'She danced as if she really loved it, even managing to project a delicious moment of humour into one of the solos … she subconsciously found the inner grace of each moment. Remember the name Leanne Benjamin, we shall undoubtedly hear more of her.'[1]

In the *Daily Telegraph*, Fernau Hall's piece was published under the headline 'A Star is Born': 'Very rarely does a young dancer become established as an artist of star quality at a single performance, but that is what happened yesterday … this extraordinary artist seems bound to make a considerable impact on the ballet world.'[2]

These reviews, and others like them, had a huge impact as they circulated to Australia and back again. Miss Hansen saw them. My bank manager in London sent me a copy and forwarded one to my parents in a letter saying he hoped I'd keep up the hard work. I don't remember anyone being anything but kind to me; other girls at the school may have been disappointed that they hadn't been entered for the competition, but it didn't translate into obvious bitchiness. Jealousy is something I've navigated carefully all my career; I've not been conscious of it from others, and I have tried very hard not to feel it myself. My philosophy is that there are enough places for many people to shine. I was happy to look and learn from other people, and never wanted to put anyone down. My family, keen to keep my feet on the ground, have suggested that I never felt envious because I got what I wanted. But I didn't always. There have been long periods when I have had to struggle, to wait my time. Even at moments of glorious success, such as this one, I was brought up to be aware that it is just a moment, and you must consider the feelings of others as well as your own. It was a good lesson to learn early.

In any case, I didn't have time to get big-headed because I was immediately thrown into getting myself ready for another bigger and more daunting contest. On the Monday after my Genée win, Miss Fewster gave me a kiss of congratulations and asked me if I'd like to go to the Prix de Lausanne. I couldn't have had better news. The Prix de Lausanne is one of the most important ballet competitions in the world. Founded in 1973, by a Swiss industrialist called Philippe Braunschweig and his Russian wife Elvire, who had been a dancer, it's open to all nationalities and to all students of dance who want to pursue a professional career. Its record in picking winners is exceptional—the top prize having been taken by dancers such as Darcey Bussell, Diana Vishneva, Carlos Acosta and Alina Cojocaru. In 1981, because it had been running for less than ten years, it wasn't quite as much of an institution as it is now, but it was still a signpost for future success. Previous winners from the Royal Ballet had included Bryony Brind, Alessandra Ferri and Deborah Bull. That meant that I felt the pressure as I prepared two solos, one classical, one new. For my classical, the school chose the Sugar Plum Fairy solo from *The Nutcracker*, and then Derek Deane, one of the Royal Ballet company principals who was interested in choreography, created a modern solo for me to a sad song from Carl Orff's *Carmina Burana*.

I loved the freedom he found for me in his piece, full of little runs, deep bends and delicate arms, but I struggled to master the classical niceties of the Sugar Plum solo. I wrote in my diary after a long rehearsal, that my performance was 'disgusting'. My flat attracted the same adjective. It was a continual mess, we couldn't use the fire because it was giving off fumes, and the hot water boiler had been waiting weeks for someone to come to fix it, which was quite a contrast with Australia where someone arrived instantly to mend everything. Given my angst, it's no wonder that a friend phoned Madonna and told her that I was down in the dumps. She turned up at the school with the excellent combination of steak and chocolate, which proved very soothing. Miss Hansen also sent a cheering letter from Australia. 'They are not giving you much time to prepare but I know how hard you can work, and I have every confidence that you can do it.'

The party that set off for Switzerland on 28 January consisted of me, Liz Tullock, one of the star pupils in our year, my lovely friend Maria Almeida, and another talented student called David Yow. Miss Wade, one of the teachers, accompanied us, while other members of the Royal Ballet School staff travelled separately. By the time we arrived, I had perked up considerably. Lausanne was heavenly: crisp and bright and beautiful. We were staying at the Hotel Alpha Palmiers, which seemed the height of luxury, especially after the misery of Stella's, and which was just round the corner from the Palais de Beaulieu where, over the next five days, the competition unfolded. Although I felt shaky, everything was exciting, and the days were so packed with practice I didn't have too much time to worry. There was such a lot to take in. I had done competitions all my childhood, but never experienced anything on this level. There were dancers from all around the world who looked amazing, doing triple pirouettes on pointe as if it were the easiest thing in the world.

As the days progressed, I found I had to shut the other dancers out. I also felt alone, especially since quite a lot of the other girls had their mothers fussing over them, whereas there were three of us with just one teacher, and she was someone I didn't know very well. I had to focus and remember why I was there, and I was much helped by Liz and Maria with whom I was sharing a room. We spent some time sizing up our rivals and there was one French girl we were relentlessly giddy about, nicknaming her Makarova. She was really good, but we felt she knew it and we were pretty horrid about her. How salutary it was for me when, ten years later, I found myself dancing alongside her at Festival Ballet. Christine Camillo was one of the nicest, most modest and loveliest dancers I had ever worked with and I blushed for my teenage silliness. I was learning a lot of things.

'I adore Switzerland,' I wrote to Aunty Pat. 'Special to me as they speak French and I'm learning French just being there.' Since French had been my worst subject in my entirely undistinguished career at school, I can't imagine why I thought that, and one night in the hotel restaurant I got in a terrible tangle when I ordered something which I didn't understand from the menu and discovered it looked like raw bacon. I stuffed it in a napkin and gave it to poor Maria who put it in her bag, managing to avoid Miss Wade's attention as she did so. Later, I realised it was steak tartare—I had obviously not understood it was served raw.

Meanwhile the competition was moving forwards, though with predictable lack of organisation I nearly missed my turn. Having practised my Sugar Plum solo the day before, on the morning I was due to dance it I went into a big fluster. I couldn't find my number to pin to the costume and was in the loo when my turn was called. Not surprisingly, I went on quite nervous, but it went fine, though the music was played too slowly. When the results were announced in the evening, I discovered I had got through to the semi-finals; the following night, after performing both solos again, I heard I was in the final. So were Maria and David, but Liz missed out and was distraught.

The next morning, presumably to calm us all down, Miss Wade took us to the lake at Ouchy. It was glorious, covered in sailboats and swans, a tranquil place to be before the high energy of the evening's final. We weren't just competing for the glory of it, either. The prize at stake was a scholarship and I was extra anxious about the results because I felt it would help my parents if I could win a free year of tuition.

As the prizes were announced, I became more and more convinced I hadn't won one of the scholarship places. Then, at 11pm, two final numbers were called. The winners of the Prix de Lausanne were seventeen and five. One was Christine Camillo and the other was me! I recorded my feelings in my diary when I got back to the hotel. 'I didn't know what to do when I went onstage. I just sort of walked around bewildered. After the curtain was down all the judges congratulated me and commented mostly on the lovely quality I had, saying this is what the other dancers lacked. They were technicians not dancers. There was a buffet party afterwards which was huge and elegant. I didn't feel like eating. I only wanted to ring home and tell them the good news! I loved the experience.'

There's a film of my performances at Lausanne, and if I had to put my critical eye on, I'd say I definitely didn't win on my technical ability. My Sugar Plum solo is adequate but not exceptional and you can see I don't feel entirely at home in that tutu and with those steps. I fall off pointe a little on one turn. But Derek had created the loveliest solo for me, which played to my strengths and let me show something of my personality.

What I didn't realise at the time is that I could create atmosphere, bringing the audience into my ambit. I was good at putting steps together, melding the tiny moments between the movements into a sense of pure dancing. Some of the kids I teach today can do a great arabesque, or a pirouette or a split jump, but a great technique also involves taking care of the smaller, in-between steps. How do you take off and land, or how do you prepare and finish a pirouette? Ballet is an art form and requires more than athleticism. Steps should look seamless and effortless to an audience. As a coach, I have to remind myself not to get bogged down with technical corrections; there is so much more to think about, including developing a dancer's individual style.

I often use the Royal Ballet's principal Marianela Nuñez as an example. She is an outstanding technician and was an amazing, prodigious dancer even as a teenager. But what I want people to watch is the way she articulates her feet, or extends her arms, how she makes even the smallest movement beautiful, how she links steps together. People tend to get competitive about executing the biggest jeté or the highest arabesque, but to be an artist it takes more than that. If you don't have control you can't knit everything together into a satisfying and artistic whole. Technique, charisma, dynamics, control, emotion and likeability all go together to make a performance—when you get that, then you have a true artist, like Marianela.

One place that many of the world's great companies go to find such artists are competitions. There are a number of them: they give the dancer a chance to grow in confidence and show their quality on a stage, and company directors the opportunity to find the best and brightest talent. I believe that there is enormous value for a dancer in learning to perform to a wider public in this way. Most of a ballet student's time is spent in the classroom and there's a danger that they lose sight of the fact that the step they are practising so laboriously each day is a means to an end. Working in depth on a particular piece for a competition gives them a chance to develop and to put all they have learnt into practice, to perform rather than simply repeat. School performances tend to highlight the dancers who are already known to be rising stars; others don't always get much of a chance to shine.

It's important, I think, to get out there and compete, learning from what you see in others, and pushing yourself to be better. Ballet is essentially a meritocracy. You need to find your level and one way you can find that is through competitions. I am aware of a number of young dancers who were desperate to get into prestigious schools and had been turned down, only to find that when they'd been seen in a competition, the director had offered them a place. Some people stand out and come alive on a stage in a way that they do not in a classroom.

The Prix de Lausanne was a boost to me and my confidence. It was, and is, exceptional because it concentrates on teaching, rehearsal, and preparation rather than simply being a competitive event, which is probably why it has such a good reputation for spotting talent. While I am broadly of the view that a bit of healthy competition is a good thing, I do have reservations about some aspects of competitions themselves. I don't think students need be in full costume and make-up although I understand that it is an opportunity to have the full experience centre stage. For the Genée, we all wore black leotards and a simple tutu which was democratic, fair and enabled us to concentrate on improving our performances.

It's expensive for parents to buy elaborate tutus and it sometimes discriminates aesthetically; if a youngster is wearing a tutu that doesn't fit, or make-up that doesn't suit, it's far harder to see talent than if everyone was dressed in simple leotards and tutus. You are looking at potential, not at a fully-fledged artist. Entry now is generally via a filmed link and that too can be expensive for families. I am often asked to coach young dancers to prepare them for these videos and I wonder about the expense. It can discriminate against families on lower incomes, and they might be better spending their money on lessons rather than competition entries and fancy costumes. It's a big debate, and there are arguments on all sides.

My parents were certainly thrilled I had won the Prix de Lausanne, and I was so glad that I could give them something back; they never complained about the cost of putting Madonna and me through the Royal Ballet School, but it must have been a strain. In a little box of memorabilia that I have kept down the years, the Prix's flowered embroidered pennant has pride of place, as does the tatty number five I pinned to my costume.

When I got back to London, basking in my success, Miss Fewster warned me not to let it make me big-headed, which was fair but unnecessary. I was also firmly told that my scholarship would be at the Royal Ballet School. In my innocence, because I'd been told I could study anywhere, I'd raised the vague notion of transferring to the School of American Ballet in New York, but that was swiftly dismissed. They'd paid for me to enter the Prix—they were keeping me close. This was also the point at which I left the bath water on and flooded Stella's flat, so I went from star pupil to being in literal hot water overnight. It was also the moment that I remember encountering Ninette de Valois, or 'Madam' as she was known to everyone, for the first time when she came to watch our assessments. Every time she arrived in the building, it was like the coming of a god. She was eighty-two by then and a little uncertain on her feet, but still a formidable presence. The room fell very silent when she appeared. I was dancing Crystal Fountain variation from *The Sleeping Beauty*, and naturally I was the one girl in the room who had the straps of her tutu held together with a safety pin. Likewise, when the school went to Russia that April, I was the one who forgot to pack my air ticket; there was uproar when I arrived without it, and much rushing around to secure me a duplicate ticket. I must have been unbelievably annoying, but I found it impossible to shake the scattiness out of my personality, however hard I tried.

The Russian trip should have been sensational. My class stayed in Moscow and Leningrad (as it then was) for fifteen days, travelling by train in between the two cities. It was such an adventure, a rare chance to see companies who forged the classical style and were regarded as among the best in the world, and an even rarer chance to explore a country that was still a closed book to most people in Western Europe. But I didn't really register any of that at the time. My diary and my letters home reveal me moaning about the smelly Aeroflot plane, the endless trips to museums and churches—'once you've seen a couple, you've seen them all'—the fact that the food gave me an upset stomach and the discovery that, outside the hotel, there was nowhere to eat.

My fur coat finally came in handy in the snow, although I noted that everyone stared at me when I wore it, because 'no one seems to have one, probably because they can't afford it.' I found the Moscow architecture frightening and forbidding, liked Tchaikovsky's house, but was bored by Tolstoy's, and adored the Moscow State Circus. The discovery, after a party at the Moscow Embassy, that our rooms were bugged sent me into a panic. 'Hope I didn't say anything wrong!' Worst of all, I was disappointed in the standard of dancing both at the Bolshoi and at the school. I sent a postcard to my parents from Moscow complaining: 'We were expecting wonders and we were so disappointed.'

I found Leningrad more exciting, because I knew it was the artistic home of Makarova, Nureyev and Baryshnikov, and the streets seemed less dangerous, though I was alarmed when Maria and I met some drunken Russians who approached us and seemed very forward. I was impressed by some of the dancing at the Vaganova School, but was disparaging about a performance of a modern work at what was then the Kirov. 'Technique was non-existent and their expressions false and fake', I wrote with the confidence of my extreme youth. I have no idea if my judgements were correct, but I do regret being so blasé about the opportunity I had been given; I feel I should have made more of it. I should also have eaten the suitcase of caviar that I purchased. It was the only thing in the shops, and I bought loads of it because it was cheap, but you can only eat so much of it at a time, and I eventually forgot it in the fridge back in London until it went off.

I had other concerns on my mind, I suppose. For one thing, I was agonising about men. 'I'm so immature bodily no boy will ever like me', I wrote. I didn't understand about sex. Sex education was frowned on in Catholic schools and although my mum had given me *The Joy of Sex* and some other books, they were too embarrassing to read. Everyone around me seemed much more mature and knowing than I was. I was also working hard to improve myself. School was always busy, and I seemed to rush breathlessly from one thing to the next. The days were full of training, and in the evenings I was racing around London, trying to see things, to educate myself about ballet by watching performances at Covent Garden from the standing room in the gods, high in the amphitheatre at the very top of the theatre. The school was given a limited number of passes for this purpose. In the collection I have kept, I notice that I have cheekily altered the dates in order to use them more than once. I doubt I fooled the ushers, but they never threw me out, and though you couldn't see that much from up there, I caught some great performances, building up a ballet database in my head and absorbing the music, which I always loved.

During this time, the choreography of Kenneth MacMillan began to make a huge impact on me. Madonna was chosen to play one of Isadora Duncan's pupils in *Isadora*, his new ballet, and I went to see the dress rehearsal. Its impact overwhelmed me; I felt it was quite the best thing I had seen. Madonna also hid me into the wings for a gala to celebrate fifty years of the Royal Ballet, where I soaked up the atmosphere and glimpsed the famous stars of the past such as Fonteyn, Robert Helpmann, and Frederick Ashton, all taking their bows on the stage where I made my own debut in the school's performance in July, as one of the chickens in *La Fille mal gardée*. In between rehearsals, I sneaked off to Wimbledon, where I managed to blag a pass towards the end of the day, and found myself on Court One, evading the ushers, and managing to get a seat to watch my hero John McEnroe. There's something about tennis that reminds me of dance; you have to live so much in the moment, reacting to the next point. It requires strength of mind and a strategy to do well, as in ballet really. Oddly, two of the men I have loved, including the one I married, have been really good tennis players. It's the one sport that has a real place in my heart.

There's one mystery about this time in my memory. At some point, according to my letters, Dame Ninette suggested that the Royal Ballet Company should consider taking me on at the end of my first year. The school thought it was inadvisable because I hadn't had enough time to improve, and to master pas de deux in particular. I was obviously disappointed, but I don't at any point seem to have been consulted. My father wrote reassuringly from Australia that he was sure it was all for the best, that I should feel proud of myself, and that he and Mum agreed that it was a bit early for me because I was so young.

The curious thing is I remember barely anything about a conversation that could have altered the trajectory of both my life and career. It's true I was very young and extremely inexperienced. But as a position in the Royal Ballet Company was what I had always dreamed of, it seems odd I should have accepted the idea that it was too soon so readily. My first-year report, in the summer of 1981, reveals the reservations the school had about me as well as the talent they saw. Nancy Kilgour's general report praises all I had accomplished but says I had 'a sure and easy technique which this moment is well beyond her physical maturity. She needs to work slowly and carefully in order to bridge the gap between being a very appealing and promising student and becoming an adult artist.'

Under the heading pas de deux, it notes: 'Leanne's turns are good. However, often tends to do combinations her own way rather than as set. Stubborn.' That adjective was an indication of a theme that would pursue me in future.

CHAPTER 5

'A GISELLE LIKE NO OTHER'

IN MY SECOND YEAR AT the Royal Ballet School, I felt I was progressing every day, growing as both a dancer and a person. I had moved up into Julia Farron's class; she was calmer than the energetic Miss Kilgour, softer-spoken, preparing her students to be professionals as well as dancers. The combination of the two of them as teachers in the RBS at that time was the perfect balance, and every day I tried my hardest to win their approval, which was not always easy. Miss Farron pushed me gently onwards, and I was longing to be told I was something more than good. That desire to succeed meant my technique got much stronger. At the start of the RBS, I'd struggled to do multiple pirouettes on pointe. By the time I left, inspired by both my teachers and other exceptional students, I was throwing them off like a spinning top.

Outside the classroom, things were also improving. After much agonising, I'd moved out of Stella's, which had become oppressive to me. I hated the mess, the shortage of space, and the smell of cats. I also found it difficult sharing digs with a lot of other hormonal teenage girls, who would stay up into the small hours chatting when all I wanted to do was fall into bed, exhausted by my efforts of the day. In October 1981, I took a flat in Comeragh Road, still only five minutes away from Barons Court and just around the corner from Stella, who was still at that point my technical guardian in London. I was sharing with Bruce Sansom, who joined the Royal Ballet in 1982, and an Italian girl from the year above called Simona, who I was thrilled to find was an excellent cook. It was clean, cosy, and I finally had more space.

The other major advantage, as it turned out, was that since I was beginning to get bit parts with the company, I could sometimes travel home from Covent Garden with Bruce, which probably reassured my parents, since I was still only seventeen. In October 1981, I was drafted in as cover, understudying in case any of the cast were injured, for the Royal Ballet's production of *Concerto*—my first major exposure to the choreography of Kenneth MacMillan.

At this time, Madonna was trying to make some big decisions about her future because she wasn't happy in the Royal Ballet. Just as she was beginning to have doubts about staying with the company, in walked her little sister, all bright and eager and being much talked about. I was in her territory and I was being noticed, and people tactlessly compared our talent which, for me, made those rehearsals both sweet and sour at the same time.

I learnt the third movement of *Concerto*, with Maria, Jonathan Cope and Bruce. We never actually performed it, but it was thrilling to me to expand into the glorious shapes and extensions of the abstract choreography; it felt like such a step up from learning the corps de ballet parts in *Swan Lake* and *The Sleeping Beauty*, which was our bread and butter at school at the time. I was also rehearsing for my tiny part as the Bride in *Romeo and Juliet*, the one I wrote to my Aunty Pat about. The entire thing seems to have sent me into a terrible fluster, not least because there is a moment in the scene where the Bride is kissed by Romeo, who is dreaming of his own marriage to

Juliet. In my case, Romeo took the dashing form of principal Wayne Eagling, who was a star I idolised from afar. He sensed how nervous I was, and in a bit of laddish banter, landed a huge sloppy kiss on my lips. It was the first time I had been kissed by anyone.

My first professional dancing performance on the Royal Opera House stage, or at least the one that was significant enough to make the database of performances kept in the archive, was on 25 February 1982. I was a Shade in Rudolf Nureyev's production of *La Bayadère* Act IV, known as *The Kingdom of the Shades*, in which he starred as the dashing warrior Solor, alongside Merle Park as Nikiya, the ethereal bayadère, or temple dancer. It was the only time I appeared onstage with the legendary Nureyev, and quite a way to start. This act, where Solor dreams he goes to visit Nikiya in the land of the dead, is one of the most beautiful sections in any ballet. It opens with a devastatingly simple yet technically demanding sequence for the corps de ballet, featuring thirty-two ghostly dancers in white tutus who appear one by one, in procession down a ramp. It works by repetition, as each dancer arrives onstage, she performs a slow arabesque penché, dipping forward with one arm extended and then pulling back into a tendu, with the other arm unfolding gracefully behind her head, before another dancer appears and repeats the sequence. These two movements performed repetitively over and over again build into one of the great triumphs of Russian ballet, utterly spellbinding.

I was the final Shade to start my descent down that seemingly endless slope and absolutely petrified. It all went well, until the section where the dancers line up across the stage, and then do another controlled step on the spot. On the first night, I started wobbling and grabbed my classmate Tracy Brown, the dancer next to me, gripping her right arm with my left. We clung to the position with great grit and didn't fall and since we were on the back row, hopefully no one noticed and we didn't ruin the otherworldly atmosphere. It taught me how nerves can wreck a performance.

This was also the first and last time I danced at the Opera House with Madonna, who was the third Shade down the ramp. Just as my ballet career was taking off, she had made up her mind to give up hers. At the end of this year, when we were sharing a flat in Beaumont Crescent together for a time, she took the brave decision to leave the company, go back to school to take her A-levels, and then go to Oxford University. This was the only moment, since childhood, that the Benjamin Sisters were back onstage together again.

By then, my own sense that dance was the life for me had been cemented by the most extraordinary piece of good fortune. In January 1982, Maria Almeida and Liz Tullock had left our class to join the company, which meant they were no longer available for the school's performance in the summer. At the end of January, the casting was announced on the board, a very public way to learn about the shape of your future. Traditionally in dance companies, when a new production is announced, everyone's name and role goes down on a piece of paper, which is pinned up for all to see. It still happens, though now it's usually alphabetical to make it a bit less obvious who is getting the opening night.

Throughout my career, the casts were typed in order of role and of performance, with the first cast first, the second second and so on right down to the end of the run, and the smallest role. This meant that every dancer had to cope with their excitement or disappointment in front of everyone else. It's incredibly painful when your name isn't next to a role that you want to dance or learn, but the most uplifting feeling when things go your way. On this occasion, there was thrilling news: I was down to play Giselle. But there was also a doubt: my name was second on the board, and another girl's name was first. Jonathan Cope and Bruce Sansom were chosen to learn Albrecht. But it wasn't clear who would dance with who—and which couple would get the prestigious performance at the Royal Opera House before we danced a week of performances at Sadler's Wells Theatre the following week.

I was so excited I could hardly breathe. It was like being given a gold star, the absolute seal of approval. It also felt so massive I couldn't quite take it in, all the more so because the school's performance was very rarely a full-length classical ballet. But my competitive self was still in play. I very much wanted to dance the role with Jonathan, because he was such a brilliant dancer and a great partner, but he is over six feet and I feared our height difference would rule it out. As we began to learn one of the most significant texts in Romantic classical ballet, we mixed and matched. I knew Jonathan would get the Covent Garden performance, because he was the outstanding dancer of his year; my own fate hung in the balance. I knew I was good, but the question was whether I was good enough.

When my parents had arrived for a surprise Christmas visit, they had met with Miss Farron. She said I was a lovely dancer and was doing well, but 'with faults they are still trying to correct, i.e., head always in inclination and fingers which are either stiff or curled'. Reading my parents' letters from this time, I can see how hard I was working and how sensitive I was to any criticism—I can hear them trying to keep up my flagging spirits.

'You know you will never dance like the English and would you want to?' Mum wrote at one point. 'Miss Farron may be testing you out so see if you can see it out. Take your corrections and just improve. You have a very special talent so keep the chin up and show them what you can do.' She adds a warning: 'Love, you must not be late for class. I know you don't mean to. It's not well mannered to be late.' My father sent me jokes, including a letter written on a loo roll because I had demanded a long letter. I write back apologising for spending too much time on the telephone to them, worrying about the cost of international calls, but adding plaintively: 'I know I am a bit naughty, but most times I can't bear to leave your voices.' Underneath all the correspondence, you can see the lineaments of the girl I was in those days, ambitious about my dancing, but always driven, worrying I needed to be better, and completely at sea in the ways of the world.

Cutting things fine was my most intractable problem. I used to leave everything to the very last minute, as I had throughout my childhood, so I'd burst into class or into a lesson at the last possible second and be reprimanded for my lack of organisation. It was a source of real tension, and I never quite shook it off, even when I was performing at the Royal Ballet. I've had more warnings for lack of punctuality from the Opera House than anyone apart from Rudolf Nureyev. I am not proud of it, I know it is rude and profoundly annoying and if any student of mine turns up tardily, I'm not happy. I think it sprang from nervousness. I wanted everything to be perfect. I got into the habit of changing my shoes just before curtain up, or being late leaving my dressing room because I was changing them again before running to the stage. Pointe shoes have, in fact, been a huge issue for me throughout my career, probably because I was always coping with an arthritic toe, and though as a student and young dancer I wasn't quite as finickity about what I wore on my feet as I later became, they were already becoming a preoccupation. That was one reason I was always rushing at the last minute.

Inside the classroom, however, things were going well. I was coached for *Giselle* by an absolutely astonishing team, led by Lynn Wallis, then deputy principal of the school, who went on to become artistic director of the Royal Academy of Dance and one of the most expert teachers in the ballet sphere. I loved working with her. She could be tough and positive at the same moment, always finding the perfect balance. I know some students found her scary, but after all those years with Miss Hansen I was used to someone strict at the front of the room.

Then in March, Peter Wright, director of Sadler's Wells Royal Ballet, arrived to put the finishing touches to the production—and chose Jonathan and me as the opening cast. It was a dream come true: the partner I wanted in a show I wanted to dance, and an opening performance at Covent Garden, the theatre that was the home of the Royal Ballet. I wrote excitedly to Aunty Pat: 'I'm going to need your prayers to help me through. You'd adore my Albrecht. He's tall, dark and handsome.' I felt it was a game changer, which it was, though not necessarily in the way I had imagined, because it was the start of my working relationship with Peter Wright, who was about to become one of the most significant forces in my career.

Wright had been involved in British ballet almost from the start. In 1949, he was taken into de Valois's Sadler's Wells Theatre Ballet, the company that evolved into the Royal Ballet.[1] He became a reliable leading man in works by Frederick Ashton and his great friend John Cranko, and since his retirement from dancing, had taken up the reins of the Royal Ballet's touring company, then called Sadler's Wells Royal Ballet and now Birmingham Royal Ballet. Since the early sixties, he had also made his name as a producer of classic ballets. His productions are in the repertories of ballet companies around the world.

He was utterly steeped in the significance of *Giselle*, which revolutionised the idea of ballet as a storytelling vehicle when it was first seen in Paris in 1841. In the first act the ballerina plays a poor but happy peasant girl in love with a man who turns out to be an aristocrat called Albrecht in disguise. When Albrecht's true fiancée turns up at the village as part of a hunting party, Giselle's world collapses. She goes mad, and kills herself. The first act, then, is set in a recognisable world. The second act is supernatural. In death, Giselle becomes one of the wilis, the spirits of girls who have died on their wedding night because of the faithlessness of men. When Albrecht, now heartbroken and guilty, comes to put flowers on Giselle's grave, the wilis attempt to dance him to death but he is saved by Giselle's love. All in all, the ballet was a big challenge for a girl who was just about to turn eighteen. Quite apart from mastering the steps, I hadn't even been in love when I began to learn it. I had to imagine all that emotion and passion. But the part suited me, because it gave me an opportunity to act, to trace that arc from happy girl to ghostly sylph in a long white skirt, and to make people believe in it.

I relished working with Peter Wright. 'I just adore him, and I'm told it's vice versa,' I wrote home in March. We'd only had four rehearsals by then, because the performance was being twinned with a new work by Eric Bruhn, to give the boys a chance to show off, since the second act of *Giselle* is almost entirely female. The presence in the building of one of the most significant male dancers of our time—on a level with Nureyev and Baryshnikov—added to the excitement of the process, even though I wasn't involved in his rehearsals and his requirements left less time for Giselle.

By June, I was feeling the pressure, not so much physically but mentally, trying to understand the part. Then something magical happened: Alicia Markova arrived to help us rehearse. I was a bit naïve about a lot of famous dancers, but I quickly learned who she was and was astounded at the honour of being coached by her. She had begun her career at fourteen with the Ballets Russes, where Sergei Diaghilev changed her surname from Marks to Markova to make her sound more ballerina-like and Russian. After Diaghilev's death, she went on to become the hallmark for what a ballerina should be in the early days of British ballet, the fledgling Royal Ballet's first prima ballerina. Giselle was her signature—she titled her autobiography *Giselle and I*. It was a role she was inspired to dance when she saw the Russian ballerina Olga Spessivtseva perform it. That meant when Dame Alicia, who had a phenomenal memory, walked into my rehearsal in Barons Court in 1982 and began to help me with my interpretation, I was reaching back almost to the beginning of a great classical tradition. Ballet has always been taught, as the Russians say, arm to arm and leg to leg. Dancers of one generation pass what they know onto the dancers of the next. I shall always feel privileged that the moment I started to perform coincided with a time when these legendary figures were still alive, with their minds full of so much information about ballet's rich development.

By the time I met her, Alicia Markova was a lively 71-year-old with a full head of hair backcombed out into a kind of halo which surrounded her pretty, mobile face. She was kind to me. She sat very quietly at the front of the class, immaculate in a shirt, slacks and loose cardigan, watching closely, speaking rarely, but occasionally offering careful advice on style and particular aspects of technique. As a dancer she had been famous for her airiness, for appearing never to touch the ground, and her advice was all about the line. She told me not to jump into the air in the pas de deux, but to let my partner lift me. That approach wouldn't necessarily go down well with most male dancers today but with tall, strong Jonathan behind me, it wasn't a problem. It was such a rare and precious experience, full of genuine work.

By learning Giselle in this way, I absorbed more than I could have done in class because I was building the strength, the simple puff that you need to carry you through a ballet that is all jumps and hops and lightness from out front, but incredibly arduous to dance. I learnt precision and a lot about partnering too. The mad scene was my favourite challenge. I was trying to find a way to go deep, to make it entirely real and entirely mine.

I recently found a handwritten record of how I learnt the scene: 'Wedding. Daisy. Sword. Stab. Hilarion. Bathilde. Collapse. House. Mum. Tree. Tree. Music. Dance. Agony. Blood. Dirty hands. Cold. Hysteria. Run round. Curse side to side. Hilarion. Collapse. Run to Mum. Traviata. Die.' It is just a list of words that might not mean much to people, but if I look at it, I can remember every single step and every emotion. I've often learnt scenes in this way: the words provide a trigger for the movements. I can lose myself inside the dance simply by reading them. For the mad scene, they provided the vital impetus for emotion: I don't think I have ever managed to get through the scene either at school or in my days as a professional without actually crying.

By June, we had our first run through of Act II, with the entire school staff and some of the governors watching. We were performing in the big company studio, and I could see some of the professional dancers glancing through the door. I was understandably nervous, and I felt I mucked up some steps, but wrote in my diary that I'd been 'passable'. The day of the school performance at the Opera House was

22 July, and it arrived with terrifying speed. In my mind, it's all a bit of a blur. It was a matinee and I remember walking into the stage door of the Royal Opera House with a huge bag of pointe shoes, and then sitting in a tiny room having my hair and make-up done by Ron Freeman. Ron was part of the fabric of the Opera House, a larger-than-life character who knew all the gossip and who was meticulous about his work. His greatest skill was judging what everyone needed before a performance, whether they wanted distracting with a lot of chat, or to be treated quietly so they could calm down.

Anyone before a big event needs to find out what suits them in terms of mental preparation. I always wanted people to make me laugh before a show, because I needed that to help me relax. Ron was a brilliant man, part of the backstage team who are so vital to every theatre and whose massive contribution is recognised by everyone who works there but rarely by the outside world. His attitude to make-up, however, on that day at least, was as old school as his manner. I emerged with dark painted eyes, pink cheeks and huge false eyelashes. Later in my dancing days, I always went for a much more natural approach, but then I looked like a pretty doll and I had to do class in a studio on the fourth floor, feeling like a lemon, with my hair and make-up all done.

That *Giselle* is the first time I really remember feeling anxious before I went onstage. From the second I had walked through the stage door, I felt the responsibility for my own performance and for the success of the entire ballet. I'd celebrated my eighteenth birthday just ten days before; it was a big weight to carry on such young shoulders. I knew how much was riding on this, my first starring role, and I was conscious that my mum and Miss Hansen, my much-loved teacher, were going to be in the audience. I was sharing a dressing room with Tracy Brown, who was dancing the Queen of the Wilis. It was just next to the stage and we were told it had once been Fonteyn's dressing room, which added to the sense of occasion.

My costume was hanging up all ironed and I started to get ready, putting on my tights and my shoes, while a dresser fussed round tidying my hair. People popped in, wishing us well but by the time of the half-hour call I was just trying to get into the zone. My mouth was dry, my heart racing and my mind darting around, going through the steps in my head, checking and rechecking things constantly. I felt incredibly sick and that was the first time I settled my stomach before a performance with a chocolate drink, something I am not sure any dietician would advise for an athlete, but it worked for me. I don't know if it was psychological, but certainly it took me back to childhood, to those cups of Milo in the car, and it seemed to calm me down.

Before I knew it, I was at the side of that huge stage, putting my belongings on a chair: tissues, hair spray and pins, a mirror, a spare pair of shoes for disasters, a glass of water. Some people like to run through their big moments on the stage before a performance; I was more concerned with going through things in my mind, mapping the steps, checking the distances. There are some pitfalls, like dancing round a bench in a series of light, big jumps and I wanted to be sure I knew the space I had to move in. I also checked the daisy that Giselle picks from the garden to see if Albrecht loves her in a game of 'loves me, loves me not'; the petals are cut halfway through so you can pick them off easily, but you've got to be sure which ones you need to tear, or it can ruin the story. Then I was standing behind the door of the cottage through which Giselle first appears, breathing in the heavy smells of rosin, paint and sweat that filled the air, waiting for my entrance. On my music, I opened the door, bounding out into that incredible space and flinging myself heart and soul into a role that not many ballerinas ever get a chance to dance, let alone a green eighteen-year-old student.

At the end of the performance there must have been curtain calls and applause, but I don't really remember. I do remember waiting around while Miss Fewster, Ninette de Valois and the governors came onstage. Madam congratulated me, though I can't recall exactly what she said. All the critics were in the audience, and the reviews were flatteringly ecstatic. Mary Clarke, writing in the *Guardian*, said I was a lovely dancer who was 'no carbon copy of any Giselle I have seen', although she sounded a note of caution. 'For a debut it was amazing … important however to remember it was only a student performance. She is to be treasured and helped but should be safeguarded from over-praise.'[2] In the *Observer*, Peter Williams said that I 'played and danced the part with a depth of understanding and assurance rare in even experienced ballerinas'.[3]

In many ways, though, it was Clement Crisp in the *Financial Times* who provided the most insight into how I danced that day. He wasn't entirely uncritical—he said I was too uncontrolled in the first act. But he added: 'There is, intriguingly, a suggestion of fantasy, of nervous vitality in her manner which ballerina coaching and experience should shape into something vividly communicative in the theatre.'[4] It was quite a reception.

The odd thing about *Giselle* is that even though I have danced it all over the world with a lot of success, it has never been a ballet I have felt comfortable dancing. I feel I have struggled with it. I don't know if it was because I always felt I had to live up to the reputation of my school performance, or whether it is just something in the ballet itself that I have never got to grips with. I loved the second act, where I could fly across the stage with high, light jumps, floating through the air, a loving ghost, but I didn't ever enjoy the first act, because I couldn't imagine myself into being an innocent peasant girl tricked by a man, and I wonder now whether that is because I find the story too unrealistic, or perhaps because I was taught too precisely. When you see someone like Natalia Osipova perform the role, she has an extraordinary freedom in her interpretation. I never felt I achieved that, except perhaps on that very first day when I ended my mad scene with a high, hysterical jump that I know was totally my own.

I loved working with Peter Wright, and felt I learnt huge amounts of stagecraft from him, but he was very exact about how *Giselle* should be danced and that damped down my own instincts. I wanted to do what he said because he was my director, but it killed the ballet for me for a long time. If I went back and danced it today, I would do it entirely differently, and in fact I did perform it better towards the end of my career, when I was dancing with Edward Watson.

There was a long patch in my mid-career, however, when I was always dancing Giselle, and I was often uncomfortable in the first act, with that dress that's all bunched around the middle, and the small voice in my head saying this is silly, I can't pretend to be a little girl who is picking a flower to find out whether her lover loves her or not. If you're dancing these classical ballets, you have to immerse yourself completely. If you do something half-heartedly it feels dated; it's only if you believe in it that you bring it to life. It is also possible that my complicated feelings about *Giselle* were caused by what happened next.

By that point, I had been told that I wasn't going into the Royal Ballet, which was my dream, but into Sadler's Wells Royal Ballet, the touring company. This was supposedly a cause for celebration. I appeared, again, in the Australian papers,[5] who dug out the photograph of me singing 'Animal Crackers in my Soup' at the age of four and added headlines such as 'From a little jig to Royal status' and 'Little Leanne takes London by storm'. Kevin O'Hare, now director of the Royal Ballet, then a student in the year below me at the school, sent congratulations in a birthday card, showing a hippopotamus balancing on a tightrope and joking, 'Is there no end to your talents?'

I was happy to have a job, by no means a given for an overseas dancer at that time. Yet looking at my letters and my diaries, it's clear that from the first I had doubts about joining the touring company. There's a note from my mother—undated like most of her letters—which she must have written just as I was leaving school, discussing my worries. 'I think you will be fine when you start work Lee and give it a go. I always have the feeling you are not too keen to join Sadler's. If you really feel like this, you must go and have a talk with Miss Fewster. It's your life. On the other hand, you may love it.'

CHAPTER 6

ON THE ROAD

ON 12 SEPTEMBER 1982, THERE was a photograph of me and Jonathan Cope on the cover of the *Observer* magazine, under the headline 'Fame! The kids on the way to the top.'[1] One of Britain's most prestigious newspapers had decreed that we were the stars of tomorrow. The feature inside dwelt on my height. 'Leanne Benjamin is so small that when she sat on a bench on stage at Sadler's Wells, she had to sit on pointes before her feet touched the ground; so delicate that when she moved across the stage, she seemed to float rather than walk.' It also pointed out that while Jonathan had begun his career in the Royal Ballet, I was only going to graduate from school in December and would then join the corps de ballet at Sadler's Wells Royal Ballet. I emphasised that it may be years before I am promoted, and we agreed. 'This is the beginning. From now on, it's the long slog.'

One thing I envy about the dancers of today is their ease, the way they feel they can discuss things with people in authority and have some rights of self-determination in their career. When I was eighteen, I was still treated like a child, and definitely wasn't consulted about what was best for me after my success in *Giselle*. By the time that *Observer* interview took place, my future had been decided, not by me, but by the people around me when I wasn't even in the room.

I was called into an office and told what would happen next; it was assumed that I was going to join Sadler's Wells. In some ways it made perfect sense: I had a rapport with Peter Wright, who ran the company. I think he hoped I would rise through the ranks to become his next starring ballerina, succeeding older dancers such as Marion Tait, Sherilyn Kennedy and Margaret Barbieri, who were already taking the leading roles. On one hand, I felt quite pleased about the idea, because I knew that I would get opportunities, and I'd loved working with Peter on *Giselle*. On the other, I just wish someone had discussed it with me. I don't remember a single conversation about whether it was the right move and whether it would suit me as a dancer and as a person. After that school performance, I could have probably chosen to go to any company in the world, but as far as the Royal Ballet was concerned, two years of training meant I belonged to the institution. Peter Wright wanted me in the touring company and so I went.

I couldn't join immediately. The company was on tour in New Zealand and Australia, but I was judged too young to join them. That upset me too because I wanted to go home, and I didn't want to have to stay at the school for an extra term. I went to see James Monahan, the director of the school, someone I always liked, and explained that I couldn't afford to pay another term of fees. Something must have been worked out, because in the end, I did go back, but I struggled with how odd it all felt. One minute I'd been on the stage at Covent Garden, the next I was at Barons Court with a group of classmates I didn't know, back in lessons, while my friends such as Maria and Jonathan were beginning their careers with the Royal Ballet Company. I was happy for them, but anxious for my own future.

Difficult though that time was, I did have a stroke of luck. In that term, we were taught by Mona Vangsaae, a Danish ballerina and the mother of Peter Schaufuss. At that point Schaufuss was one of the most glamorous stars in the world of dance, performing with companies around the world, famous for his virtuoso qualities. He was short but dashing, with a little scar on his upper lip and golden hair and I was quite impressed when he turned up to watch class. He seemed modern and of the moment, when so many people associated with ballet at that time felt old-fashioned and rooted in the past. When we talked in the corridor afterwards, I noted his air of confidence. He was the kind of person who knew everyone and everything and he was passionate about the art of ballet. That first encounter was fleeting, but he went on to become the second of the two Peters who were hugely significant in shaping my early career.

This was also the time I got to know Monica Mason, who was winding down her career as a dancer with the Royal Ballet and had been appointed répétiteur to Kenneth MacMillan in 1980. She was also moving into teaching, with a specialisation in the rehabilitation of dancers who had suffered an injury. When something happened to my back, she was drafted in to help me. Today, there would be hot and cold running medical experts and physios running around with a proper diagnosis. Then, it was just a bad back, perhaps caused by over-straining, and definitely not helped by the way I used to dance with my weight too far back. I am very long legged with a relatively short body, and I tended to arch my lower back, so Monica, who has an expert eye for line and technique, was asked to assist. It was a privilege to work with her because she was already very busy assisting MacMillan and teaching dancers in the company. You could tell she was busy; she arrived and we worked, then she ran off. There was no idle chatter, but she was kind, firm and energetic, and because she never had a pianist, she would sing as I danced in a tiny little studio the size of a bedroom in Barons Court. It was wonderful and it built a trust between us that has persisted to this day.

I was finally ready to join Sadler's Wells in December, making my debut with them in their Christmas season at Sadler's Wells, the theatre that provided them with their London base. There were a lot of injuries to senior dancers, so I got the chance to dance the little American girl in their production of Leonide Massine's *La Boutique fantasque*—a light-hearted meringue of a ballet that no one dances much anymore. I wore a blonde wig, flat black shoes, and got some more good reviews, with Mary Clarke saying I was the best 'obstreperous American girl' she had ever seen,[2] and John Percival in *The Times* noting my vivacity.[3]

In January 1983, I caught another critic's eye when dancing in Ronald Hynd's *Papillon*, set to the music of Offenbach, which was a tribute to Emma Livry, a ballerina who—horrifically—died in 1863 when her ballet skirts caught fire. Jann Parry said I looked like drawings of her: 'Slight, gawky and oddly appealing.'[4]

For all my outward success, behind the scenes I was starting once again to have terrible problems with my feet. I still had the arthritic right toe, but now I also had an ingrown toenail and a new problem with my left foot. I wrote to Aunty Pat: 'At the moment I'm sitting with my foot in a bucket of hot water because my toe is very sore. I am in a state.' I couldn't put any pressure on it, let alone walk. The company was just about to go off on a long regional tour, taking us to Manchester, Glasgow, Bristol, Leeds, Liverpool and Birmingham, but I had to come home and take time off. I wonder now if I was wearing shoes that were the wrong size. No one had measured my feet since I arrived at the school, and I was wearing a dainty three-and-a-half for the first few years of my professional career when my feet had, as I later discovered, grown to five-and-a-half.

By June, when I'd returned to dancing and been one of the cygnets in his production of *Swan Lake* in its run at Covent Garden and a leading fairy in Ashton's *The Dream*, Peter Wright called me into his office and observed that whatever was going on with my foot was stopping me from dancing correctly. He suggested I should try to sort it out and I was grateful to him for his intervention. He seemed to me such a lovely, patient, optimistic person. 'Such a light relief after seeing the big wigs who treat individuals like a kind of cattle,' I wrote home at the time. But the company physio, a doctor in London, and a doctor that Peter Schaufuss had recommended in Surrey all failed to come up with any solution. I began to feel pressurised to accept that the injury was psychosomatic—a devastating idea given that it had disrupted so many months of dancing—when the ballerina Merle Park recommended a Danish specialist who took one look at it and said I had an inflamed bursar under my toe. In the summer of 1983, I had an operation that successfully sorted it out, though not before I'd taken part in a Royal Gala which celebrated Ninette de Valois's eighty-fifth birthday at our home base at Sadler's Wells.

We were dancing *Checkmate*, the ballet de Valois created in 1937, in a programme of mixed excerpts by different companies. Peter Schaufuss partnered Eva Evdokimova in *La Sylphide*, Antoinette Sibley was Aurora in an excerpt from *The Sleeping Beauty* and I was knocked out by the performance of the Stuttgart Ballet superstars, Marcia Haydée and Richard Cragun. Mary McKendry, who had graduated from Miss Hansen's five years before me, was also performing that night. I was flustered because I was covering for someone else, which meant I was playing a different pawn on the chess board and had only had one rehearsal. In the middle of the performance, I caught my leg with another girl's leg, tripped and fell over. I've never bounced back from a tumble so quickly. I was so embarrassed to fall in a gala, with an audience full of dignitaries. At the end, everyone gathered to make speeches, and all the dancers Madam had ever taught—or so it seemed—paraded across the stage, each trying to outdo the other in graciousness. My youthful self didn't think much of it. 'All we wanted to do by 11.30pm was go home,' I moaned in a letter to my mum. 'We had to wait two hours after our turn to sing Happy Birthday to Madam, still in our costumes, which are so uncomfortable anyway. Typical of Sadler's Wells! We all went next door to the pub for a drink while waiting.'

I loved the camaraderie of company life, hanging out not just with other dancers but with the orchestra and all the crew. Life on the road could be amusing. My letters from a boarding house in Exeter, for example, reveal that I was staying, along with another dancer, with the horn section of the orchestra. We had a jokey argument about whether Australian or English men were better—I argued for the Australians, naturally—and then high jinks broke out. 'We managed to short sheet their beds,' I wrote to Aunty Pat. 'You can imagine the trouble when they found they couldn't get into bed. Then we went to town, playing tit for tat, putting toothpaste on their doorknobs and being foolish for hours.' Later, I went plane gliding with them. 'Which was quite terrifying but enjoyable except for the fact that you have to keep catching turbulence to get to a higher altitude and hence one becomes quite dizzy.' It sounds stupid now and rereading my letters I realised how very young I was, but it was high-spirited and fun.

The flip side of all that was the exhaustion of constantly being on the move, and emerging from the theatre late every night, and trying to find something to eat. England in the eighties was a different country than the one it became by the turn of the twenty-first century. Everything was usually closed except for a local curry house, and so that was what we would eat. When I'd finished the school performance, I'd been at the absolute peak of my physical form. Injury and the relentless lifestyle of being a member of SWRB started to make me feel out of shape.

I was eighteen and in my first job and there was no manual on how to cope with life in a touring company. My fellow members of the corps de ballet were lovely. We had fun and they rallied round each other supportively. But historically it was meant to be a rite of passage that dancers higher in the hierarchy told the younger members of the company, who were low in the pecking order, what to do. Some of the senior dancers were not always kind, telling me off for little things like not washing the ribbons on my shoes, sending me back to the changing room to clean them before curtain up. If I made a mistake—and I made a lot at that time—they were quite quick to point it out, even if it related to my personal behaviour. It was particularly difficult to put up with when we were all at such close quarters all the time. I felt pent in, stopped from being myself. I was exuberant and lively, but the structure of the company was very old-fashioned.

But I also began to wonder whether in a touring set up like Sadler's, I would ever be able to excel. Someone like Marion Tait was the iconic professional dancer, always ready to go on, always immaculate. She was lovely to me and great fun too, quick to write a song and rally everyone in a singsong after a show. She seemed to thrive in the circumstances I found so difficult. I didn't know how to work against the odds of touring and give my best. I was immature and I needed help on how to stay in shape, or how to prepare to perform when you've just arrived in a town and you've had no time to get ready. I recognised I had a lot of natural talent, but I felt frustrated by my inability to reach the peak I knew I could attain. I was like a dog paddling: I would make the shows, but I wouldn't feel I danced very well. Whether that was objectively true, or was a result of how pressured I felt, I don't know. There were good moments and some not so good moments, and life felt very up and down.

Once my toe was sorted out, 1984 became a good year for me, one where the opportunities seemed to open up. In January, I was cast as one of Swanilda's friends in Peter Wright's lovely production of *Coppélia*, getting another favourable review from Mary Clarke in the *Guardian*, who was watching benignly over my development. 'It was a special pleasure to see Leanne Benjamin again—she brings to the smallest supporting role a quality and a presence which were noted when she danced her graduation Giselle and which are blossoming gently.'[5] She clearly wasn't watching on the night when, as one of the villagers celebrating in the third act, thanks to the fact that everyone was crammed into one dressing room, I somehow managed to make an entrance with another girl's bra hooked on the back of my costume. Someone pulled it off and I tried to hide it under my skirt, amidst much hilarity. Fortunately, it was a very short number.

My first stage performance, age four; singing and dancing 'Animal Crackers in my Soup'.
Photo: Personal Archive

Being congratulated by the adjudicator, Jill Cadden, post-performance.
Photo: Personal Archive

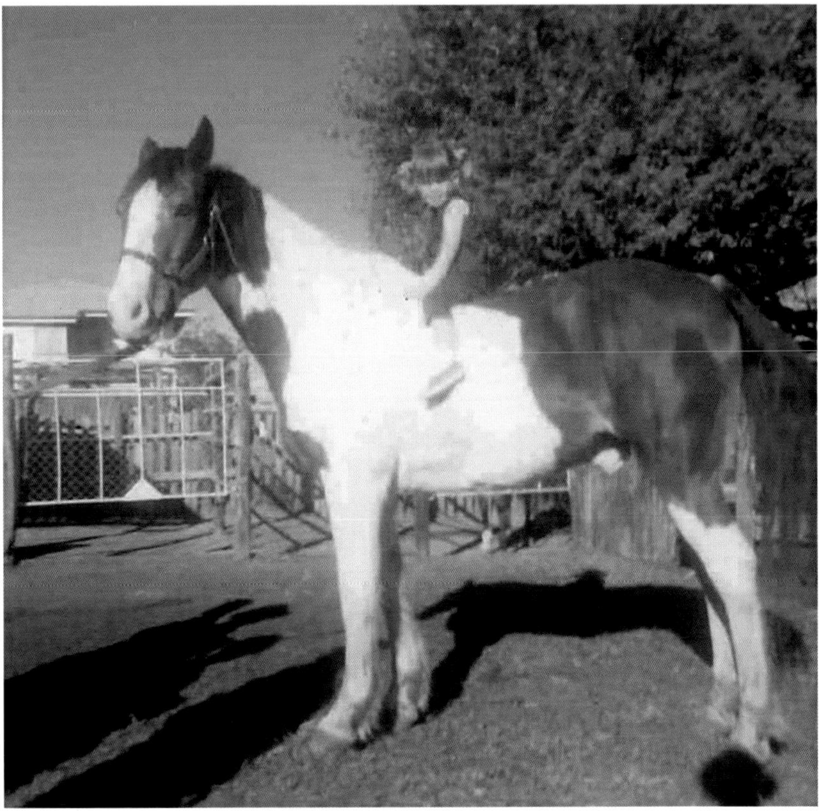

top: Cheeky as ever on holidays at Tom 'Tommy' Tait's Motel near Surfers Paradise.
Photo: Personal Archive

bottom: On my favourite horse, Pie-Pie in Rockhampton.
Photo: Personal Archive

top: Our Lady's Primary School class photo (sitting front left).
Photo: Personal Archive

bottom: Dressed in my favourite outfit for church in Rockhampton.
Photo: Personal Archive

top left: Madonna and I ready for big girl school!
Photo: Personal Archive

top right: All dressed up for a family portrait outside our Agnes Street home. I chose my hand-made green polka dot dress for the occasion.
Photo: Personal Archive

bottom: Proud Aunty Pat standing in front of my first magazine cover shot.
Photo: Personal Archive

top left: The photo that got me a place at the Royal Ballet School; can't believe they took me, even with the ladder in my tights!
Photo: Personal Archive

top right: Practising in Buffalo Hall at Miss Hansen's School of Dancing.
Photo: Rockhampton Bulletin. Photographer Unknown

bottom: Posing in my neighbour's garden after performing an Irish Jig for charity on St. Patrick's Day.
Photo: Personal Archive

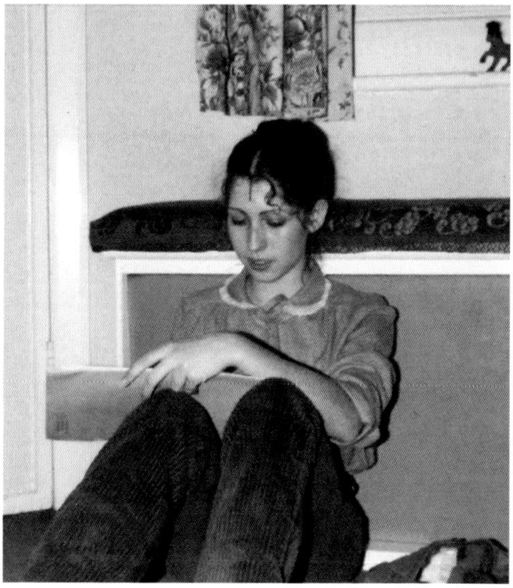

top: Post gold-medal win at the Adeline Genée Awards at Sadler's Wells Theatre. With Judges (from left to right) David Wall, Margot Fonteyn, Pamela May and Phyllis Bedells (seated).
Photo: GBL Wilson / ArenaPAL

bottom left: Writing home during my first year at the Royal Ballet School, 1980.
Photo: Personal Archive

bottom right: My friend Nicola Tranah and me at Stella Wilson's boarding house in my first year in London, 1981.
Photo: Personal Archive

top: Best friend Terri Williams and me at home.
Photo: Personal Archive

bottom: Having fun on holiday at Brampton Island, Queensland.
Photo: Personal Archive

In February, I was struggling with a very cold guest house in Eastbourne with not enough blankets, but I was also feeling that I was beginning to find my feet balletically, dancing the tricky pas de trois in *Raymonda* and, most exciting of all, beginning to build up to my first created role in David Bintley's *Metamorphosis*, a version of Franz Kafka's strange story of a man called Gregor who wakes up one morning to find he has changed into a giant insect. A new ballet always makes for a different atmosphere in the rehearsal room. If you're learning a role that's been created before, you've got to shape yourself to the template that someone else has made. But when you're creating something, you are the pattern, it's your personality and your style that are going to inspire the maker.

David, one of the SWRB's best character dancers, with exceptional comic timing, was in the early stages of his choreographic career, but already much acclaimed. He chose me from the corps de ballet to create the part of Grete, Gregor's sister, telling me he had waited a long time to find a dancer who could embody what he had in mind. His faith in me, the fact that he had given me this opportunity and believed in my ability to create this intriguing role, made me feel wonderful. I soaked everything up, and threw myself into the creative process, absorbing myself in the storytelling and the drama. The piece absolutely suited my instincts: I could wear a checked dress not a tutu, I could get dirty. I didn't have to be pretty with a tiara. My personality meant I always wanted to be real onstage, to communicate, to tell an audience a story with my body and my feelings. *Metamorphosis*, which premiered in April 1984, was the first time I got a chance to do that, and I'll always be grateful to David for giving me such a big break.

Mum, Dad and my brother Tony all made it over for the London premiere, when the critics all arrived to give their verdicts. There was a general sense that the ballet had confirmed David's promise as a choreographer and his importance to the British dance scene and my own reviews were equally complimentary, because he had used my qualities to create such an unforgettable character, full of anguish at what had happened to her brother. Probably the nicest review came from Kathrine Sorley Walker: 'The focal role of the sister gives Leanne Benjamin a generous opportunity to affirm her great talent as a dramatic artist. She dances it with splendidly impassioned fluency but what is even more promising for her future is the force and feeling she is able to express in complete stillness.'[6] There was a lot about my feet. One critic called them flamboyant,[7] which is the first and last time they've been called that; another said they were 'hyper-arched like a scorpion's pincers'.[8] It was all incredibly exciting, especially when the Australian newspapers once again picked up on the story, so my success was reflected back home.

Summer that year brought a blissful holiday in the South of France with some of my fellow dancers, including Russell Maliphant, who later became my first boyfriend, and a very lovely one at that. I'd first spotted him cleaning his car when I was a student because he lived across the road. Once we were in the company together, I used to sit with him, enjoying his conversation. We were complete opposites. I was happy-go-lucky while he was serious and contemplative. I was attracted to his seriousness and his intelligence and we had a very happy few years together before he left SWRB to pursue other interests. Even then he had the authenticity and absolute integrity which he went on to exhibit in his hugely successful career as a choreographer; I love his work partly because it is so much a reflection of the truthfulness he brought to his life. That summer, we travelled together to Rome, where I saw Pope John Paul II, though couldn't hear a word he was saying because all the American tourists in front of us were talking so loudly. Aunty Pat was proud that my Catholic upbringing had sent me to see him, nevertheless.

I took class with the Rosella Hightower School while we were in Cannes, because I was so keen to keep up my training, but on the whole I just relaxed and sunbathed and mucked around on the beach like any twenty-year-old. The break was all the more necessary because the autumn was dominated by a long and gruelling tour of our new production of *The Sleeping Beauty* which Peter Wright had created as a tribute to de Valois. It was fine and handsome, but it put an enormous strain on our dancing resources as we battled round the country, often performing in a Big Top which we erected on the largest bit of open land we could find in a given city. The stage was as wide as Covent Garden's, but the dancing conditions were not quite as settled: in the summer it was as hot as the classroom at Miss Hansen's and considerably more stuffy; in winter or on a cold day it got very damp and chilly. You often found yourself getting changed in tiny Portakabins with uneven temporary floors and then warming up clinging to a prop at the side of the stage. I found this a challenge, but I really loved that Big Top and our audiences, and admired the way that the company was so committed to taking ballet—and big classical ballet at that—to as much of the country as it could reach. In this, Peter Wright was a genius. He was so galvanising and his whole ethos was to get out there and put the show on the road. It didn't make it any easier for me, however, to know that what we were doing was undoubtedly a good thing.

One letter to Aunty Pat, after I got back from Manchester by sleeper, shows the realities of life on the road. 'I am very homesick and in need of a bit of homely love. This profession sure as hell is a tough one and very time consuming indeed. You wouldn't believe how hard they make us work and not only how hard but the length of hours. Eight shows a week, with rehearsals during the day, and usually when we're supposed to have a break there's an urgent rehearsal put in because someone might have got an injury, or someone is suddenly ill … so it's a complete reshuffle of people only minutes before the show when you thought it might have been possible to have a cup of tea! I do enjoy it, but I just get tired of adapting to theatres and hotels weekly'.

The repertory was packed as well. In that autumn, I danced cygnets in *Swan Lake*, the Songbird fairy and a pas de quatre in *Beauty*, and all the usual corps de ballet roles. I wanted to be exceptional not average, but there was no time to be perfect in anything. I did, however, relish the range of parts and was thrilled to be cast as the youngest of the five sisters holed up under their mother's oppressive control in *Las Hermanas*, another ballet by Kenneth MacMillan, based on Lorca's play *The House of Bernarda Alba*. Worming into the character of that frustrated unhappy girl suited me perfectly; in real life, I was always up for a laugh and a joke. Once I got on to a stage, it was the opposite, the darker the character the better. It was like the comedians who can make people laugh but are themselves miserable. I was the reverse. I had come from an uncomplicated, sunny upbringing but there was nothing I liked better to delve into complexity, undertaking my own education in feeling by experiencing emotions in the safety of make-believe. Roles such as this and Grete in *Metamorphosis* were helping me to understand the kind of dramatic dancer I wanted to become.

SWRB's spirit of the hard-working ballet troupe was very much a throwback to Ninette de Valois's own vision of a dance company, forged in the war, where the groundwork for the creation of ballet in Britain was laid by extensive touring, which won her company the abiding loyalty and love of those who saw it. De Valois was not only the guiding spirit of British ballet but of Peter Wright himself, who admired and adored her. He obviously had so much respect for her from the way he spoke about her, and because of that she often popped in to watch our progress at matinees at Sadler's. My first proper encounter with her was when she came in to teach us *Checkmate* and I was one of the red pawns. I could stand up and dance it for you now, even though I haven't danced it since that first year with SWRB, and I can see in my mind's eye her coming into the top-floor studio at Sadler's Wells to teach it to us. She was frail in body then, but her mind was strong, imaginative and fertile, and though she worked mainly with the principals, she had corrections for us all, because she was very specific about what she wanted, about the way we held our hands, or the shape of our bodies.

As pawns, the corps de ballet all started with our bodies pitched forward and our feet in fourth, with the palms of our hands turned down and our heads slightly inclined at the same angle and in the same direction. It's incredibly difficult when you take into account the different shapes and sizes of dancers in the corps to achieve a uniform look, but that was what she wanted, and we were determined to achieve it for her. Madam's instructions were never mean, or personal. It was all about the ballet. The effect of her presence was to make us perform better: suddenly you pull up your posture and straighten your back and become very alert. It was very exciting to be taught by her and impossible not to feel over-awed. She'd often come to socialise with us at end-of-year celebrations, sitting in her wheelchair while we stood around socialising. We'd all go to say hello, but not much more. It's a shame we were all so shy, because it would have been a golden opportunity to hear about history from someone who had made it. I wish I'd had the courage to ask things, but I revered her too much.

Possibly, she wouldn't have had much to say to me anyway because whenever she was watching me from an audience, I seemed to perform terribly. The worst day, arguably the lowest point in my professional career, was when she came to Sadler's Wells in the Christmas season of 1984 to watch a revival of *Les Patineurs*, Frederick Ashton's ballet about skaters. I was cast as one of the girls in brown, and I was having trouble with my shoes, as usual, partly because they'd been painted to match the costume, so I didn't have a choice of which pair to wear. Because they felt uncomfortable, I took them off and started to put them on again, just as the orchestra struck up. Everyone was hissing at me to hurry, but I couldn't get them tied fast enough. There are four couples in that section of the ballet, who all 'skate' on in unison.

On that day, only three pairs appeared. They took up their positions in what should have been four corners of a square; the space where I should have been was on the far side from where I was stranded. My partner, Iain Webb, patiently took me by the hand and waited in the wings until we could find a space in the music to sort of glide across the stage in a sequence of entirely improvised chassés and take up our position. After this chaotic arrival, I launched myself into the next section, a series of jumps crisscrossing the other couples.

I took off into a grand jeté, and promptly fell over, landing on the floor, swearing loudly.

I wanted to crawl into a hole and vanish and felt even worse afterwards when Peter came backstage, utterly furious. 'I've never been so humiliated in my life,' he said. He had been sitting in the audience with Madam and his intention had been to promote me to soloist after the performance, but I had utterly blown it. I was mortified and I had no one to blame but myself.

Ironically, the same day a writer from the magazine *Dance and Dancers* came to interview me and saw the whole thing. Here's the interview: 'Leanne Benjamin went on late in *Les Patineurs* one Saturday afternoon and got into hot water. I know about it because we met just after it had happened, in the gap between matinee and evening, during SWRB's Christmas season at its home theatre. Our dialogue went like this:

"Do you often miss entrances?

LB: No, but I am often late for things. I don't know why. I just am.

But surely you are professional in your approach to your work.

LB: They don't think so. I am a last minute person. I don't know what it is. Take today. I was doing my warm-up before *Patineurs* and working away in the wings, so it's actually not as if I don't care.

Did you feel terrible?

LB: Yes and it was naughty but it's done and you can't do anything about it, except not do it again."'[9]

I did feel terrible and I totally deserved the telling off. Even giving me the benefit of my youth, I certainly hadn't shown the kind of behaviour you'd expect from someone who was about to become a soloist. If I were a director, I wouldn't have promoted me that day either out of respect for the other dancers. But if it wasn't funny at the time, we managed to laugh about it eventually. Years later, Iain Webb, who went on to run Sarasota Ballet, sent me a card of good luck saying, 'Just remember, the show starts at 7.30pm!' I was never late onstage after that, though my tense energy pre-performance meant I often ran it tight. Skating seemed to pose a particular challenge. Putting on roller skates for my first entrance in my debut in the leading role of the full-length version of *Anastasia* at Covent Garden some years on, I nearly repeated my *Patineurs* mistake. My partner was virtually having a heart attack as he waited for me, but I got the skates on just in time.

I didn't have to wait too long for my promotion. It arrived in January just after I'd been involved in another new creation. Jennifer Jackson, a dancer in the company who had started to choreograph, made *Median*, a semi-abstract piece about warring factions. Once again, I loved being part of making something and the neo-classical work asked me to show my speed, requiring sharp shifts of weight, and long supple lines, both of which suited me. Once again, the critics were kind. Peter Wright gave an interview to the *London Evening Standard* in which he said: 'She is a natural with unlimited talent, but she is still young and now she has to be developed very carefully.'[10]

CHAPTER 7

IN THE STUDIO WITH SIR FRED

I HAVE TO GO BACK to explain what happened next. Some months earlier Peter Schaufuss had phoned. He'd just been appointed to the directorship of London Festival Ballet, later known as English National Ballet. My sporadic diary keeping had started again, and an entry in July 1984 tells the story: 'It all began with a phone call from Peter Schaufuss—we went out for a meal and he asked me if I would like to do some work with him and eventually some performances, maybe abroad. God I was so scared on our first meeting but I was able to talk to him and actually enjoyed his company.' He quizzed me about Sadler's Wells—'I hope I didn't say too much'—and later, by phone, asked me if I'd like a contract with Festival.

On 29 July 1984, we went out again. I really enjoyed the evening, which ended with a trip to a club in St James Square after dinner, and then we went back to his flat in Grosvenor Square where we watched part of *Dancer*, a BBC TV programme about male dancers that he was appearing in and narrating. I wrote in my diary: 'God he's such an amazing dancer. I'd feel embarrassed to work with him because he's just so fantastic. I know I'd improve by working with him. I hope he is not assessing me too much because on leaving he said I had a big head. That shocked me and made me concerned. I'd hate to appear like that. He thinks one half of me is insecure, and the other half knows I'm good.'

Over the next few days, I saw a lot of him. He took me to *42nd Street* at the Theatre Royal, Drury Lane and then out to dinner and back to his flat where we talked for hours: 'He shocked me by asking if I wanted to do some practice the following day … He said it was a shame I won't be joining Festival this year because he had planned a few solos for me throughout the year and it's so important to him to do things when you're young.'

The next day we met at three in the afternoon at Festival House, did a barre and then rehearsed the Act II pas de deux from *Giselle*. 'He's such a fantastic teacher. Within an hour he had taught me a lot. At the barre he helped me with positions—really closing into a crossed fifth, using inside thigh to maximum and really stretching my legs and body to the fullest. When doing *Giselle* other faults were that I wasn't lengthening my line at all. I must rotate the top of my back and neck from East to West with the arms and legs. I hadn't felt my back being used like that for ages … It's good to be getting some interest for once. I hope I will improve with Peter. We're planning on working on Sundays when possible.'

Throughout August, these encounters continued, faithfully recorded in the diaries I was keeping regularly at the time. His appeal for me was complicated. He was a glamorous figure, at the height of his fame, and he was also an exceptional teacher and coach. He was brutally honest with me about my dancing, saying I was losing the form that I had exhibited in my final year at school. I relished the sense of getting personal attention, being helped to be better by someone who had the time to do it. I wasn't stupid though. I knew that one reason he was interested in me was that he wasn't that tall; he needed a small, light partner and I would just about fit the bill. I was also wary of his intentions. I didn't want to mix the professional and the personal, and I knew I was treading on dangerous ground.

On 19 August, he took me to see Al Pacino in *American Buffalo* in the West End: 'I decided the best thing was to not get involved and just keep a friendship.'

Two days later, we went out for dinner, and talked both about my dancing—'he's not sure whether all of me wants to be an excellent dancer'—and us. 'He's just been so nice to me … but he hasn't swept me off my feet. I'm still playing the practical woman and I won't be influenced by anyone if I think something is wrong.'

These late evenings at his flat were hard to walk away from, but I was a strong character, and I knew that, however exciting he was, I should not get involved. I also, after slightly longer consideration, turned down his offer of a contract. I was lucky to be at Sadler's Wells and however much I felt stuck and worried, I respected Peter Wright, appreciated that he was looking out for me in a fatherly manner, and felt I should stick with the decision I had made to stay with the company.

After that, Peter Schaufuss mainly vanished from my life and the pages of my diary as I got on with the business of dancing, but in October he reappeared, coming to the first night of *Las Hermanas*. We met after the show. He dangled an enticing prospect in front of me. He was planning to mount a production of Frederick Ashton's *Romeo and Juliet* the following June and he wanted me to dance Juliet. He suggested I should just come along to the studio for a few rehearsals to see how it went. It was an offer I really couldn't refuse.

In September 1984, Frederick Ashton, founding choreographer of the Royal Ballet, had celebrated his eightieth birthday. SWRB threw a late party for him when he came to the Big Top in Cambridge at the start of our autumn season, to see a matinee performance of *La Fille mal gardée*, and I was embarrassed at having to stand around singing 'Happy Birthday' to him. He seemed too big and great a man for such a little tribute, because if it was Ninette de Valois's determination that drove ballet in Britain, it was Ashton's choreographic vision that shaped and sustained it. Without his ballets, the Royal Ballet would have just been a pale imitation of its more historic counterparts in Paris and St Petersburg. But Ashton gave ballet in this country a way of being different: he invented the English style.

Early in his career, in 1955, he made his version of *Romeo and Juliet* to Prokofiev's famous score, not for the Royal Ballet but for the Royal Danish Ballet, where Peter Schaufuss's mum, my old teacher Mona Vangsaae, created the role of Juliet, with her husband Frank Schaufuss as Mercutio and ten-year-old Peter as a page boy. An intimate vision of a big, classic story, it was a success at the time, but was later eclipsed by Kenneth MacMillan's 1965 version, which—in a generous twist of fate—Ashton himself commissioned for the Royal Ballet when he was director.

With his family's involvement in the creation of the piece, it was natural that Peter Schaufuss would want to mount Ashton's ballet as one of the first splashy showcases for London Festival Ballet, since it was a perfect vehicle for him as a dancer and for his ambitions for the company now in his charge. If he wanted me to be his partner, it was like putting a chocoholic next to a bar of chocolate. How could you not eat it? Peter had insisted that I could come in as a guest, dance *Romeo and Juliet*, and then go back to my career in Sadler's Wells. Today, people would probably have walked into their director's office and asked permission before they started. Dancers such as Carlos Acosta and Tamara Rojo were, in my time at the Royal Ballet, allowed to guest all over the place. Then, it felt too daunting to raise the matter with SWRB. I thought it was better to be forgiven after the event than to be prevented beforehand, so I didn't say a word to Peter Wright. I feared he would say no, I suppose. We all do silly things when we don't know how to behave. It caused enormous ripples later, but I have never for a second regretted saying yes, because it gave me the gift of one unique opportunity to see Sir Fred up close in rehearsal.

Peter had wanted to revive the ballet for years. He'd spent a long time persuading Ashton that it was a good idea, rebuilding the choreographic text with the help of Niels Bjorn Larsen who had filmed the original production. Our meetings, as he taught me the ballet, were conducted in secret. I'd gather up my rehearsal clothes at the end of the day and take myself off to London Festival Ballet's headquarters in Jay Mews, round the back of the Albert Hall. I always loved that building, with its slightly down-at-heel atmosphere and its expansive mirrored studio on the first floor.

It made me feel good to work there and never more so than those evenings early in 1985 when I turned up late at night, after everyone had gone home. The building was empty and quiet and working amidst a pool of darkness and silence was magical—so concentrated and intense. On one occasion in February, Ashton himself came along to work with me. I'd seen him at the school when he came in for castings, but had never met him before, although I was beginning to be familiar with his ballets, such as *La Fille mal gardée*, *Les Patineurs,* and *The Dream* from performing them at the school and Sadler's. Other ballets I knew as a spectator included the *Beatrix Potter* adaptation that had first caught my attention in the cinema in Rockhampton, the Russian-flavoured *A Month in the Country*, the abstract *Monotones*, the joyful *Les Rendezvous*, and spiky *Façade*. Ashton's ballets are works of genius, with touches of gentle humour, and steps of eloquent beauty that mould the human body in graceful, constantly inventive ways.

Working with him late into the night, I began to understand in much more depth the very distinctive movements that those ballets require. He was incredibly specific. Some choreographers let you evolve your own way of achieving what they want to see; Ashton wanted you to produce the step in an exact manner. His work looks simple, but if you do it properly, it's extremely difficult because there is a lot of opposition built into it, your arms and your legs are often doing different things in harmony at the same time and there are multiple, fleet-footed changes of direction. It's like a tennis player wrong-footing an opponent. You think the ball is coming one way and you go to hit it, but you have to change direction so quickly in order to meet the ball, that sometimes you miss. The choreography asks you to think ahead all the time. When you're dancing Lise in the second act of *Fille*, you have a jump and as you are in the air, you know that when you land you immediately need to change direction to prepare for the next step which will change direction again. It takes a lot of practice to execute properly because it is so swift and light. You can't possibly dance *Fille* full out if you are even slightly injured. Or take *Rhapsody*, which I danced a lot later in my career. The footwork is intricate and you have to do the most extreme movements to make the choreography look as Ashton intended, accentuating each curve and bend. Above all, you have to concentrate on feeling that every part of your body is connected into your arms, so that when you make the luscious curves of his port de bras you are moving with your whole being.

In person, he was distinctive, with a great wave of grey hair swept back from his distinguished features and a cigarette permanently glued between his fingers, the ash dropping all over the floor as he moved and corrected our poses. He was an elegant figure, too, dressed in a suit and a white shirt, scarf draped around his neck, smelling of soap and tobacco. There were only a few people in the room—Alexander Grant, who'd brought Ashton to the rehearsal, the stage manager Johanna Adams, and her husband Richard Farley, who took photographs. It was such an amazing atmosphere, working through the ballet in such a short space of time. I arrived ready to dance and I was too busy to be in awe of meeting the great man. Given that we were trying to learn so much of the ballet in such a short span, there wasn't much time to ask questions. We just had to push on.

What I noticed was the way he wanted to create stage pictures that made the ballerina look as beautiful as she could be. He seemed to put women on a pedestal and to want to make glamorous, magical creatures out of us. He'd insist that even when you were in repose, your feet were turned out in a very classical position; standing still you were in what we call the B+ position, as if you were about to curtsey. This runs entirely counter to Kenneth MacMillan's version of *Romeo*, where he was aiming for a naturalism in the dancers' presence, actively encouraging feet flat on the ground and normal walking and runs when possible.

For Ashton, everything had to be balletic, lyrical, gorgeous. Even the acting, though dramatic, was classical—it couldn't break the lines. His insistence on a particular épaulement, the graceful placing of the shoulders, neck and head, meant that when we were rehearsing, he would gently move our arms into position so that we would know how something should look. In a way, it was like working backwards. Instead of feeling the action arise from the flow of our bodies, we would know the requisite end shape, and then need to discover how to get ourselves into that pose. If we bent down, he wanted a full bend, not a small dip. If we raised our arms, they had to curve and then curve more. Everything had a meaning, everything was placed. It was stylised, hard to achieve and utterly sumptuous. I went home with my body aching and my head full.

That was the only time I worked with Ashton. He died three years later after a period in which his health had begun to decline and his ties with the Royal Ballet had weakened. I can only compare that evening to opening a jewel box and finding it contained a diamond, so precious and valuable, an incredible encounter. In the end, I didn't dance in the British premiere of *Romeo and Juliet*; that honour went to a young skater called Katherine Healy, who had trained at the School of American Ballet.

As soon as I told Peter Wright that I wanted to be allowed to guest with London Festival Ballet, I was told in no uncertain terms that it was not going to happen. I could leave Sadler's Wells and join Peter Schaufuss's company, or I could stay at SWRB and not dance in *Romeo and Juliet*. It was a moment of decision, and I had to weigh up the options. On the one hand, I was desperate to have that first night at the Coliseum; on the other, I felt that Peter Schaufuss had not been entirely straight with me. I think he suspected that I wouldn't be allowed to guest while staying at Sadler's. I expect he assumed I would leave and come to work with him, and I didn't like the feeling that I was being enticed to do something in a less than straightforward manner.

For Peter Wright there was a double twist: according to the first edition of his autobiography, he thought he had an agreement with Ashton to stage his version of *Romeo* with me in the lead, and then Schaufuss had nipped in and offered an alternative scenario, but still with me.[1] I didn't know anything about the power struggles behind the scenes, but I did know I had to make my own decision. For someone so young, I was pretty decisive, and I always followed my gut instinct. In this instance my gut instinct told me that Peter Schaufuss wasn't necessarily thinking of my long-term interests: he wanted me, that was for sure, but it might be a fast burn rather than a slow development. Peter Wright, on the other hand, was promising to develop and guide me. I was torn between the place I knew and the one I didn't. I chose the security and safety of Sadler's.

For all the fallout, it had been a wonderful experience, one that made me feel I was coming alive, blossoming, learning, getting better at the work. It was also an example of the way that life throws things at you which seem terrible at the time, but sometimes have good consequences. If I'd been allowed to join Sadler's in order to go on their tour of New Zealand and Australia, and not kept behind at the Royal Ballet School for an extra term, then I wouldn't have met Mona and Peter Schaufuss when she brought him to the studio. Without that chance encounter, I would never have had the opportunity to work directly with Ashton, whose influence on the whole world of British ballet has been so strong and important. It was a treasure, and the memory of that evening working with him informed the way I danced his ballets. The strange thing is that although I was known in my later career as a dancer who excelled in the dramatic works of

Kenneth MacMillan, I actually danced just as many of Ashton's ballets and there is so much of his work that I love.

His wonderful humour made *La Fille mal gardée* one of my favourites to dance. One of my strongest memories of SWRB is of dancing Lise in a Big Top in Scarborough, with the rain pouring in so hard it was being caught in buckets placed on the stage, while I balanced on pointe on one leg, holding the ribbons of a maypole, pretending it was a sunny day, and laughing because it was actually raining on my head while I did so. The third act, when Lise and her lover Colas manage to outwit her over-protective mother and end up locked in a bedroom together is particularly yummy to dance, full of little touches of imagination and fun. Ashton's work is perfect when you're a young dancer—exuberant, charming and pretty. I also adored dancing *Cinderella*, and Titania in *The Dream* became one of my signature roles. It has incredibly nimble footwork, and lots of quick turns and little hops on pointe. To make it look clean is really hard and there are very few moments of stillness to let you catch your breath. The big reunion pas de deux with her fairy lover Oberon, lovely, lyrical, full of yearning arabesques, was for me probably the easiest part of the entire ballet to perform.

I was taught *The Dream* by Antoinette Sibley, the dancer on whom it was created, and in my generation probably the perfect Ashton dancer, just as Lynn Seymour was the epitome of a MacMillan dancer. Antoinette was beautiful, speedy, but also elegant with a real air of something special and mysterious about her, the je ne sais quoi, that made her Ashton's muse once Margot Fonteyn, his greatest inspiration, had come to the end of her career.

I learnt *Rhapsody*, another Ashton piece that became one of my favourites, from Lesley Collier, who had created it alongside Baryshnikov. When I danced *Rhapsody* opposite Carlos Acosta the reviews were surprisingly good, with the critics comparing my pas de bourrée, those little skittering steps around the stage, to cascades of pearls,[2] saying my feet barely touched the ground.[3]

I had more mixed fortunes in another Ashton ballet that I danced a lot, the *Thaïs* pas de deux, to an extract from Massenet, which he created for Sibley and Anthony Dowell for a gala in 1971. It looks great when you are paired with someone big and strong, and you feel you are floating around the stage. Because I was small and light, I was often teamed with the less tall men, and its huge lifts, which should look effortless, didn't always work. I've performed it on stages from the grandeur of the Palais Garnier in Paris to a pocket-handkerchief sized space in Dartford where I received some of the worst reviews of my career. Even though there are only two dancers, it is a ballet that works best in a large space. There are lots of runs and you need to get the momentum to make it thrilling.

Stepping into a ballet made specifically to suit someone else is, incidentally, never easy. Every dancer has a side they prefer to turn into and mine is my right. In *Thaïs* Ashton created several left turns for Sibley, so I found it awkward from the start. There's a similar problem for the male dancer, because Dowell was given a slow, unfolding solo which he made look easy but which a lot of men find hard to replicate. As the ballerina, you're kneeling to one side of the stage, mentally encouraging your partner, and sometimes you really feel for him as he struggles through. You then run towards him and prepare for a very difficult, high lift and if they've just blown the solo, the lift can often go wrong too. You definitely need a dancer like Roberto Bolle in your corner to feel entirely confident with the piece. I hardly touched the floor when I was fortunate enough to dance it with him.

What I utterly loved about *Thaïs*, however, was the music—and the way that Ashton used the score. He is the most musical of choreographers. I'm always sad I never performed *Symphonic Variations* to the exciting César Franck music; I learnt it but was injured before my opening night. The gentle drama of *The Two Pigeons* was another miss; I was too junior to be cast when it was in the repertory of Sadler's Wells and had left the Royal Ballet by the time they started performing it.

Back in 1985, after my adventure with Ashton, but while in my head there was still a possibility of dancing *Romeo and Juliet*, I had the excitement of my first foreign tour with SWRB. After making me a soloist, Peter Wright had been extending the range of roles I was performing. I was learning the lead in Hans van Manen's *5 Tangos*, the Bluebird pas de deux in *Sleeping Beauty*, and also getting ready to dance *Giselle* again. In my interview in *Dance and Dancers* magazine I emphasised how keen I was to learn about every aspect of life. 'I do worry when I don't have time to read enough or keep up with what's going on in the world because sometimes in this business one tends to be oblivious of everything else,' I said earnestly. 'I want to keep my brain going and be really knowledgeable.'[4]

The eight-week tour which started in February was a wonderful opportunity to extend my worldview—as well as to catch up with my family in our five weeks in New Zealand. They all came, including Aunty Pat and Miss Hansen, to see my SWRB debut as Giselle at a matinee. A good luck card from a colleague summed up my feelings rather well: 'I sense you feel unprepared at this time but that is the way this company is, and I suspect it will never change. It is something to consider.' The plus side of that sense of always being on the wrong side of an uphill battle was the sheer energy that the constant performing generated—and the thrill of touring. After a successful season in New Zealand, we headed to Singapore for two days of rest, and then on to Seoul, where we danced *Swan Lake* and then *Fille*, which had never been seen in the country before. It was a real culture shock and one I didn't entirely enjoy. Everyone, men and women, spat in the streets, and despite the opulent marble finish of the hotel, it felt dirty. We all had to eat together all the time, from a series of apparently identical bowls all containing unidentifiable foodstuffs. An outbreak of gastroenteritis confirmed my worst suspicions and laid so many dancers low that casting kept being radically changed before every performance. We were driven to and from the theatre by bus, which made me feel claustrophobic and trapped. 'It got a bit much being with everybody all the time,' I wrote to Aunty Pat.

We then flew to Mumbai, which couldn't have been more different. I immediately fell in love with the place. Even though the poverty was shocking, we were given such a warm welcome and felt immediately embraced by the people. We were the third ballet company to visit the city in six months since the Bolshoi and the Paris Opera Ballet had been there before us. But we were the only company to bring a full-length ballet and to perform to live music, and this caused a sensation. Our production of *Giselle* triggered tidal waves of applause, the Indian critics were rapturous[5] and we were feted in the streets. There weren't enough dressing rooms at the Homi Bhabha Auditorium and conditions were taxing, but the impact we made was worth it.

The first night performance was televised and screened by India's only TV channel and watched by more than twenty million people. That entire visit showed SWRB at its absolute best, performing at a very high level given the conditions and opening people's eyes to the wonder of classical ballet. There was a marvellous level of camaraderie; after a performance we'd go back to our hotel and if there was a grand piano in the foyer, the conductor would sit down and play as we all gathered round. There was a real sense that as a troupe we were achieving something, and Peter Wright was in his element. He took ten of us on a day trip to see the temples at Jaipur, where I rode my first elephant, showed us off at receptions and cultural events, where we tried to soak up the unfamiliar intricacies of traditional Indian dancing. Peter was a very approachable boss, unafraid to mingle with his dancers, however lowly, inspiring us with his pragmatic approach. He was a strong director, pulling teams together with his energy and drive, operating against a background of constant worry about money to ensure the company's future.

On a personal level, I was handed another lesson about the life of a professional dancer while we were in Mumbai. I'd danced one matinee as Giselle there, and was only scheduled to dance a peasant at another performance a couple of days later. Trying to explore as much as I could, I went on a boat trip, only arriving back at the theatre at the half-hour call just in time—I thought—to get ready. I was greeted by uproar and was told by one of the principals that my name was mud. The ballerina cast that night had picked up an injury, and the management had wanted me to go on in her place, but I'd arrived too late to prepare. Someone else had to go on instead, and I had to make apologies all round. Looking back, I'm struck by how tired and worn down by relentless travel we must have been that dancers actively didn't want to take on an additional chance to perform a leading role. At the Royal Opera House now, dancers would bite your hand off for the extra performance.

We got back to London and went straight into a very successful season at Covent Garden, where we showed off our new *Sleeping Beauty*, and a triple bill of *Les Sylphides*, *Petrushka* and David Bintley's *Choros*. The company was riding high, especially since this was a period when the Royal Ballet itself, under the direction of Norman Morrice, was seen to be struggling. Galina Samsova, who was one of our leading ballerinas and a superb, inspiring teacher, was singled out for special praise. I was noticed, too, performing a pas de deux in Act III of *Beauty*.[6] It was a good time.

I bought my first flat, back in Glazbury Road, not far from Stella's, and looked forward to spending the summer doing it up. I was fascinated by interior design and property and was already wondering whether it was a world that would provide me with a life and a profession when my dancing days were over. Peter Wright, who was made a CBE in the June honours list, found time to write to my parents, whom he had met in New Zealand, to say how relieved he was that I had finally made up my own mind not to accept the offer to appear in *Romeo and Juliet*. 'It must have been a relief to her in many ways because it can be very unsettling when one is drawn in this way. I am convinced she has made the right decision, and firmly believe she has a great future with us.' It's a kindly letter and he was as good as his word. He was preparing me to climb the heights; the only trouble was that I didn't always feel I had been given sufficient rehearsal time to scale them. The travel, the bad studio facilities, the constant hard floors were all taking a toll on my body, and I felt at sea.

A case in point was being chosen with Roland Price, another Australian dancer, to represent the company at the World Ballet Festival in Tokyo, in August. It was a huge deal. The legendary ballerinas Alicia Alonso and Carla Fracci, Stuttgart stars Marcia Haydée and Richard Cragun, the flavour of the moment Jorge Donn, and Eva Evdokimova and Peter Schaufuss were all on the bill. We were dancing an extract from MacMillan's *Concerto* and George Balanchine's *Tchaikovsky Pas de Deux*, a fresh celebration of bravura dance. It's lively and requires high levels of attack and energy. I got to grips with it later in my career, understanding its style and brilliance, but as a twenty-year-old, I wasn't really up to it. I had a terrible time on the opening night, falling in front of a huge audience and feeling totally out of my depth. The fact that Dad and Madonna were there made it so much worse.

Sometimes my perfectionism went against me, because I put too much pressure on myself, thinking about technique, not delivery. Later in life, I learnt that when I gave a speech the key thing was to concentrate on delivery, not only the words. If I'd grasped that as a young dancer, it might have helped. The other, much more experienced dancers, on the programme were all performing works that suited them. I should have asked to dance something that showed off my abilities better, but I didn't even know that I had a choice. Now I know that if you're dancing in a gala, you need to pick a work with which you're entirely comfortable. Sometimes you don't even have time to warm up except at the side of the stage, so you just need to be able to go on and dance beautifully.

On the plus side, the trip to Japan in the summer meant I could go home for my twenty-first birthday, taking Russell with me to meet my parents. We were photographed in the local papers[7] as we arrived at Rockhampton's postage-stamp of an airport. Being home felt like balm for the soul after an eventful year. At least I knew my family had my back. Walking on the beach at Lammermoor, hanging out in the garden at 62 Agnes Street, catching up with friends and neighbours, I was surrounded by love and unfailing support.

'You're right up there with them now,' my mum wrote on a good luck card she sent to me before the World Ballet Gala. 'You have nothing to prove only to show just what a beautiful dancer you are.' It was time to gather my resources and get ready to face the challenges the autumn season would bring.

CHAPTER 8

PINK TIGHTS SYNDROME

THROUGHOUT MY CAREER, DANCERS WERE called girls and boys by the people in charge. It's a convenient shorthand in the rehearsal room. But it emphasises a problem that big ballet companies are only now beginning to solve, and certainly hadn't begun to tackle when I was dancing. When do dancers grow up? As a dancer, you are institutionalised from a young age. You have been training since childhood; quite often the school you attend is attached to the company you will join. People form a view of you. You might find you are pigeon-holed into being a particular type of dancer because your teachers have known you since you were seven. Your possibilities for growth and change might be restricted by other people's opinion of you and are reinforced by the fact that you begin your professional career so young. Just as most teenagers are setting off on a gap year, or about to go to university, you are joining a ballet company and starting your first job. I was eighteen when I joined Sadler's Wells, seventeen when I was offered a contract. When I looked at my son at the same age, safe at home, studying for A-levels, choosing his path in life, it shook me to realise that at that point I was living on the other side of the world, away from my family, beginning my working life, shouldering the responsibilities of a new job alone.

In those days, our training was supposed to make us obedient. The iconic ballerinas were pinned to our walls: silent, beautifully groomed examples of the people we were supposed to become. In fact, history and biography have taught us that they weren't quite the saintly, sanitised figures we were encouraged to believe. They were flesh and blood women involved in the complexities of living: Markova battled against anti-Semitism to build her career; Fonteyn got involved in an abortive coup attempt in Panama, on behalf of her husband Dr Roberto Arias. But to us they were presented as air-brushed icons, and we had little sense of the hardships and dilemmas of their lives. Most of my female colleagues at that time did what they were told without debate or argument in a pattern of behaviour that I have always thought of as pink tights syndrome, pink being the colour that we most often wore and which best projected both our physique and the traditional image of the immaculate ballerina.

Most dancers in the seventies and eighties were good girls, who were convinced that submissiveness and obedience were part of the way ballerinas behaved. For whatever reason, I wasn't. From my first days in Sadler's Wells, I was regarded as a maverick, someone who was never afraid to ask questions and to speak her mind. I tried to talk things through. Perhaps because I was Australian, an outsider who didn't come from such a deferential culture as Britain, I always wanted to have an explanation of why something was for the best. Anyone who knows me will recognise that what you see is what you get. I am not interested in being compliant in the rehearsal room and then going to the changing room to bitch and moan about something. If I am unhappy, I will say it in front of the person who is making me unhappy. If I don't agree, then hopefully in the politest way I can muster, I am going to have it out with the person on the spot.

This was not always the best strategy with Peter Wright, whose philosophy was very much the old-school belief that ballerinas should be seen and not heard. He described me in his autobiography as 'the most difficult ballerina when it came to rehearsals, demanding time in the studio and on stage and upsetting everybody'.[1] I think I only ever wanted to learn. For me it was always about the work, about what audiences would see, but to do my best, I needed things explained to me.

I remember quite early in my time with SWRB that Peter said to me, 'You can't have your cake and eat it,' to which I replied, 'Why?' That more or less summed up our relationship. I think at some level my ideas were too modern for him. He wanted me to be his next ballerina, to be the successor to people like Margaret Barbieri and Marion Tait, but he also wanted to mould me in their image. I didn't want to be shaped in that way. I believed in Peter and thought he was a great director, but I also wanted to express my own talent. My ability was different from those dancers with a delicate style and a beautiful line. I was more athletic, could raise my leg higher, wanted to make roles seem more contemporary, perhaps less safe. I felt I was being forced to copy someone else, which is not the best option for a young dancer, who should never feel she has to be a carbon copy of someone else. I was only twenty, and probably very naïve but I pushed back against the idea with all my might. Perhaps I was wrong, but it didn't feel that way.

The situation, oddly, was exacerbated by the fact that I was being promoted so far and so fast. Because I was technically strong, I was quickly thrown into some of the biggest roles in the classical firmament. When I took on Aurora in *The Sleeping Beauty* in 1988, for example, I did so after two weeks' rehearsal when someone else had to drop out. 'I don't know whether to laugh or cry,' I wrote to my sister Fiona. 'It's a challenge if nothing else.' The effort prompted a card from a colleague: 'Your coolness in having to learn such a role in such a short space of time has been a lesson to us all.' I could master these things, but I was scrabbling. I needed someone to listen to my concerns, rather than simply telling me I could do it and I should get on with it. My determination to be heard stood out because I rose through the ranks in the last generation of dancers for whom silence was the rule.

I have certainly noticed how different things are for members of the Royal Ballet today. Ever since Kevin O'Hare took over as director in 2012, dancers have felt they can talk to him about their concerns. As they have progressed through the company, he has allowed them to have a say in the shape of their careers and the interpretation of their performances. Dancers in my day were told what they were going to dance and how they would dance it; there was little room for discussion. That's no longer the case in the Royal Ballet and probably in other companies though it is the Royal I know best. In part, I believe, this is because after a long career with Sadler's Wells Royal Ballet, Kevin stepped away from the self-enclosed world of dance and spent a year in a traineeship in company management with the Royal Shakespeare Company. Actors are used to being part of the conversation, speaking to directors, communicating about how and why things happen. I do think the fact dancers communicate with our bodies and not with words is part of the reason so many dancers have historically found it hard to speak up. We are simply not used to it.

For me, the enforced silence was like a red rag to a bull. My main ambition is to know why I am doing something; if I understand that, then fine. But I am unlikely to be quiet if I feel I haven't been given an answer to my question. Sometimes that made full calls and general rehearsals a minefield. These big rehearsals, either in the studio or on the stage, with the entire cast present, have to accommodate everyone's needs, and they are primarily used to help the corps de ballet know exactly what they are meant to be doing at any given moment. But if you are dancing the leading role, especially if you are making a debut, this might be your only opportunity before the performance to run the ballet and get some sense of what it will be like to dance.

I got into trouble in Sadler's Wells—and indeed later in my career—because I would stop the rehearsal and try to solve something that was going wrong. I don't think I was asking too many questions or being difficult, though I do now understand that particularly in a touring company like SWRB, where the pressure was always on, there wasn't enough time to help everyone.

In my early years at the Royal, I was usually third or even fourth cast in a work, behind dancers such as Viviana Durante and Darcey Bussell. Sometimes I went on for a performance without the benefit of any stage call, including one night as second cast in Kenneth MacMillan's *The Judas Tree*, which has a score by Brian Elias that is hard to dance to even after repeated listens. I'd listened to it on a recording and in rehearsal, but the first night I danced with a live orchestra was when I was actually performing it.

One of the oddities of the balletic rehearsal schedule is that you have to be all right on the night, because it's the only night you've got. Actors get endless previews, and eight shows a week to refine their performances. Dancers get one chance to be perfect, and then may have to wait for weeks to return to the stage. In these circumstances, I was always going to wring out every ounce of rehearsal time for myself, but I was doing it in order to improve the performance as a whole. In ballets such as MacMillan's *Manon* or *Mayerling* the society presented onstage is a collective one; you need time as a principal to explore your interactions with the characters around you. It felt illogical to me not to be able to explore something that I needed for my performance, and for the performances of others.

As a principal, many slots would be allotted to practise my pas de deux and solos, but what I most required was time in the short scenes that sometimes get overlooked. If those scenes are under-rehearsed, they can fall flat and as a coach, I always make sure that we go over those tiny moments, because it is in those interactions that characters are developed. It's the nuance of small preparations that make a performance great.

I've been asked whether my reputation for being demanding arose because ballet is patriarchal. I've had five male directors and one female director in my career, and the stagers and coaches I have worked for have been fairly equally divided between the sexes; my sense is that the power balance in ballet is less unequal than many other professions. Historically, dance is full of powerful women, from Ninette de Valois and Marie Rambert, who between them laid the foundations for ballet in Britain, to Lucia Chase, co-founder of American Ballet Theatre, and Peggy van Praagh, founding artistic director of Australian Ballet. More recently, Monica Mason at the Royal, Karen Kain in Canada, and my old friend Tamara Rojo at English National Ballet have been successful directors of companies. I've worked with so many strong women coaches, including Patricia Neary, Maina Gielgud and Loipa Araújo, one of my favourite teachers ever.

As far as I was concerned, I didn't mind whether I was working with a man or with a woman, as long as they were the best person for the job. It's perhaps more relevant to ask whether I would have been regarded as argumentative if I had been a man behaving in the same way. There the answer must be no. I am direct and forceful in how I speak; my mind works fast and I am not afraid to express an opinion. I have seen men throw their weight and their views around and they are often indulged rather than branded as difficult.

Opinionated women need space to speak out if ballet is to grow and thrive as a modern art form. I don't think the problems I encountered in my early years would happen in the Royal or most other companies today, and I have noticed that coaches and teachers are now very conscious of listening to what their charges have to say and allowing them to have opinions of their own. In treating young dancers like grown-ups, we will encourage them to think more deeply and to become better artists. I am not for a moment advocating a lack of respect or saying you need to speak out about everything or speak out of turn, but I do think they must be listened to.

Looking back, I know that particularly when I was younger, I sometimes used to fuss about small details such as my hair or my make-up at precisely the wrong moment and I wish I hadn't done that. But when I teach somebody, whether it's an established dancer or a youngster starting out, I try to treat people equally and to ask them how they are feeling and what they want to achieve. I want to give them agency. They shouldn't be told that they can't ask something that feels relevant and important to them, even if its relevance or importance is not immediately obvious to a wider world. If someone is attention-seeking, that's a different story, but if their query has real consequence for the way they want to learn their role, then it's important, because answering it might reduce their anxiety as well.

Dance companies nowadays are much more conscious, not only of the physical wellbeing of young dancers, but their mental health as well. For dancers to work at their best, they need to feel happy with their coaches and teachers, secure in the knowledge that nothing is off limits in terms of exploring a role. If you go out for dinner with someone and you don't feel confident with that person, you're not going to be totally yourself. You're going to hold back. If you transfer that to the ballet studio, that kind of reticence can affect your performance. What I observe when I go to work at the Royal Ballet is the opposite of that. The atmosphere created from the top makes the dancers feel at ease with being themselves and consequently they are much more fearless. They don't seem to worry about what the director is thinking of them, or whether they've said or done the right thing. A lot of energy can be wasted wondering what other people are feeling about you instead of getting on with the task in hand. I want to encourage dancers to get on with it. In a studio, Darcey Bussell had this amazing ability to be happy, to say yes, and still to achieve. My energy was different. I needed to come at things more slowly, to find out why I was doing something, to explore steps in various ways. Both approaches are valid. I accept when people are difficult or asking a lot of questions, because I remember how that feels.

CHAPTER 9

A DANCER'S LIFE ISN'T MEANT TO BE EASY

A DANCER'S LIFE ISN'T JUST divided into the normal breaks in a year—Christmas, New Year's Day, Easter and so on—but into the rhythm of her company's seasons, the booking periods for the public which tend to begin in September and end in June. They are like a turning wheel of familiarity and difference into which your body falls.

The autumn season of 1985 began with the Big Top in Exeter, where I danced Giselle, and then it was back to London and the pleasure of a week at Sadler's Wells. I was in the premiere of Michael Corder's *Wand of Youth*, a gentle ballet to Elgar, in which Michael O'Hare and I were happy innocent children whose parents were living and loving under the shadow of the First World War. I also danced Giselle again and performed in a double bill of van Manen's *5 Tangos* and the *Tchaikovsky Pas de Deux*, with Roland Price, which still frightened me.

Mary Clarke praised my Giselle for stressing the dramatic possibilities of the role 'although at the same time softening her very considerable technique to the requirements of Romanticism' but she rightly noticed that Roland and I were out of our depth in the Balanchine.[1] In her *Guardian* report, she noted: 'She's a human dancer, not just a technician, by which I mean she uses a very considerable technique entirely to present a character … the high extensions, beauty of line, soft and eloquent arms and wonderful flow of movement all serve her reading of the character.'[2] Clement Crisp was also in the audience to cast his eagle eye. He blamed the fact that I was suffering from a viral infection for some forcing of my performance in the first act but went on to write: 'That she is a Giselle there is now no doubt. What now must take place is the long process of purification, technical and stylistic, which will make this enduring triumph of romanticism clearer and more intense to Miss Benjamin as to her audience. It will be a process worth watching.'[3]

Fernau Hall was more bitterly disappointed. He'd loved me as Grete in *Metamorphosis*, saying my performance had been thrilling in its 'combination of intensity and polish'. But he felt something had gone wrong with my preparations for Giselle. 'She looked as if she had been drilled like a soldier rather than produced as an artist,' he wrote of my overly bright interpretation in First Act. He was kinder about Act 2: 'Now she was mysterious and gentle, using her superb technique with artistry so that it never obtruded.'[4]

He had put his finger on something that I was feeling. I was falling backwards rather than going forward and for all that I was being given additional roles to dance, I wasn't developing as an artist. As the autumn wore on, I began to struggle with small niggling injuries once more and went to work with Monica Mason on class technique. 'It's been very difficult getting back to the basics of plain, simple placing of each step,' I wrote to the ever-attentive Aunty Pat. 'We all tend to get into bad habits when joining a company.' I knew that my technique had been super sharp when I graduated, but I could feel it was dipping with injuries caused by inadequate rehearsal spaces and rushed preparations. Some dancers cope, but I just couldn't, and the trouble with injury is that one can lead to another. You injure something, you take time off, you come back, and then are immediately injured again because you've not been working consistently.

That's why nowadays if I am talking to young dancers, I advise them to work intelligently, listening to their bodies. There's a science to it now, where you balance recovery days with working days, and you shouldn't dance every day but it's good to keep going and not to have too long off. It's like putting money in the bank for the future: if you have a bad day, then fine, but you are going forwards.

I think I let too many days slide when I was at SWRB, and instead of protecting my body, I pushed on in all the wrong directions. There's always the danger of making a short-term decision that has a long-term consequence. For example, I made myself get through a *Swan Lake* rehearsal with a slight injury because de Valois was watching. It meant so much to have her there and I worried that I had been rubbish, although Peter Wright told me she had been impressed. But by November it had been decided that my debut in the leading role of the most famous of classical ballets should be postponed, which was disappointing if inevitable. We were in the midst of another regional tour, and I was nursing inflamed tendons after pulling them in a performance in Canterbury. I was coming to realise that my body couldn't fully function without the stability of a six day a week routine that I followed to the letter. My injuries were as if my body was rebelling against what it knew my mind didn't like. You soon find out what makes you tick. I had realised that my body was not a workhorse, but a racehorse, and by concentrating on performance rather than technique, I was losing my form.

There were, however, many excitements to distract me from the anxiety that fills my letters and was clearly seeping into my thoughts at this time. In January 1986, SWRB set off on a two-month tour of North and South America, including a stop at the Brooklyn Academy of Music in New York, and visits to Boston, Cleveland, Sarasota, Mexico City, Caracas and Rio. It included thirty-two performances of *The Sleeping*

Beauty, which meant we had to borrow extra dancers from the school who were ever-more needed as some of our dancers were injured. A bout of gastroenteritis when we arrived in Boston took out fourteen dancers and five were still missing by the time we arrived in New York. Peter Wright said he got to the point where he had rearranged the cast so often that even he had lost track of who was coming on next.[5]

Worse still, the critics were not impressed either by his production or by the classical standards of our dancing. This was the tour on which the critic Arlene Croce unkindly christened him 'Mr Wrong' for his approach to the classics.[6] Another critic praised the teamwork but admitted he longed for an occasional glint of diamantine brilliance.[7] I was dancing the Bluebird pas de deux, and many different fairies and the tour of North America passed for me in a kind of blur, with photo snapshots of various scenes sticking in my head: a gala in Brooklyn (then a run-down wasteland) attended by Princess Margaret; a visit to New York's hottest club The Palladium, an old theatre in Greenwich Village; the snow as we left Cleveland followed by dazzling sun in Miami, on our first free day, so we could collapse round the pool. Margot Fonteyn, who was by then living in Panama, joined us in Miami to play the Queen in *Beauty*—which means I can always say I danced with Margot Fonteyn.

South America is much more vivid in my mind, where I was dancing in David Bintley's *Flowers of the Forest*, Macmillan's *Elite Syncopations* and Peter Wright's revival of *Coppélia*. I moved from solo roles to performances in the corps; I am always glad I put my time in there, because there's no doubt that dancing small roles helps you to understand what's happening centre stage. You can learn a lot watching from the sidelines. You see the ballet as a whole and understand the great co-operation a ballerina needs from everyone onstage, from the smallest page to your partner. One lesson I never forgot, for example, is that if the principal ballerina asks for her variations to be played too slowly in *Swan Lake*, it causes agony in the corps de ballet who have to freeze in different poses for what feels like eternity.

My favourite cities were Mexico City, full of spirit and colour, Teotihuacan nearby, where we climbed the famous pyramid, and Rio, which was frightening because we were given fierce warnings about the dangers of theft and a man was shot in an alley outside the stage door. But I loved exploring the city, riding the cable car up Sugarloaf Mountain to marvel at the view below, or going up to Corcovado Mountain, topped with a larger-than-life statue of Christ the Redeemer, or onto Ipanema Beach where people showed off their bronzed bodies with an inhibition undreamt of in Australia. I enjoyed the glamour of another gala, attended by Princess Anne, performed in front of an audience dripping in jewels and wrapped in couture, more glittering and grand than any we'd seen in the UK. At the end of it all, Russell and I went on holiday to the seaside resort of Buzios, where we hired a dune buggy and found the most incredible hidden beaches away from the crowds to laze on and swim in. A photograph I still have of me buried in the sand up to my neck brings back happy memories of those days.

Once back in London, I threw myself into the final stages of the creation of another David Bintley ballet, *The Snow Queen*, where I played Gerda, the loyal and loving girlfriend of Kay (Roland Price) whose heart is captured by the icy Snow Queen. When it premiered in Birmingham in April, David sent me a card on the first night: 'Make me cry!' I tried my best. I always liked the ballet, but it was long and slightly over-extended. Clement Crisp's review said Roland and I had charm but not much edge to our characterisations,[8] which was probably fair. Gerda didn't give me much to get my teeth into, as I found her too sweet. We danced it a lot from then on, and it was always popular with audiences.

In May, the disadvantages of performing in a Big Top were revealed when a matinee in Sheffield was cancelled due to gale force winds. We were all so exhausted that it felt like a relief, but there was barely a break before we were off to Israel the following week, on a visit to the Israel Festival. The trip had had been under review in the wake of Britain's involvement in the US's bombing of Libya; there were worries that we would be a prime target for a terrorist attack. A group of dancers and administrators went to Israel to assess the situation and came back reassured.

Eventually, the company voted to go, and the trip was a particularly memorable one. We performed *Swan Lake* in the open air at the ancient amphitheatre in Caesarea with views of the sea beyond and the principals' dressing rooms in the catacombs below, and at Sultan's Pool below the old city walls in Jerusalem to an audience of 8,000 people sitting on the grass around us. Ironically, given the security concerns, we were so keen to explore that I hired a car with a group of friends. We were stopped by armed police for trying to travel unescorted.

For me, nothing beat the Edinburgh International Festival fortieth anniversary concert in late August. One of my heroes, Sean Connery, introduced David Yow and me dancing the Bluebird pas de deux on a bill that also included Ian Charleson as Richard II, Cleo Laine, Felicity Lott, and Tim Rice and Gary Bond performing songs from *Joseph and the Amazing Technicolour Dreamcoat*. I nearly died of excitement at the party afterwards when I found myself talking to 007 over a glass of wine.

As I remember these highlights, it seems strange to remember at the same time how unhappy I often was. All the time I danced at Sadler's Wells I felt I wasn't quite getting the coaching I needed to turn me into the performer I knew I could be. I had quantity but not always quality in my work. This wasn't helped by the way the repertory was arranged in blocks: great chunks of *Beauty* and *Swan Lake* and *Coppélia*, leavened by the occasional historical piece such as *Petrushka* and some more modern triple bills, all prepared while on the road or in snatched spells at Sadler's Wells. We were always packing up at the end of a performance and moving on; getting home at midnight and snatching some sleep before moving to Bradford, or Oxford, or Canterbury or wherever we were expected next. It was exhausting and it wore you down.

There's a slightly romanticised view of the travelling we undertook at that time, driven by a combination of financial necessity and pioneering zeal to take ballet to people who couldn't otherwise get to see live dance. But the need to tour and to attract audiences, combined with Peter Wright's view of preserving a historic repertory, meant the company had little room to experiment. It was also narrow in its coaching staff; there was a small group of hard-working teachers—mainly men—who were often also dancers, such as Desmond Kelly and Alain Dubreuil.

It's interesting to me that when I was coached by a woman, such as Galina Samsova, a ballerina I much admired and who had a wealth of experience, I suddenly felt my horizons widen. A principal and teacher with Sadler's Wells, who had moved there from London Festival Ballet, she was bold as a dancer and had a similar honesty as a person. I learnt more about *Swan Lake* from her than from anyone because she pushed me in the studio. Too much of my time was like an extended warm-up, not a proper workout. Today's dancers are so well prepared to perform at their peak and the repertory encourages them to explore a variety of physicality: dancers in English National Ballet get to explore the work of William Forsythe and creations by Russell Maliphant and Akram Khan. At the Royal Ballet, their minds and bodies are extended by Wayne McGregor, Christopher Wheeldon, Crystal Pite, Pam Tanowitz and Cathy Marston. It means they are stretching in every direction, which is so good for them, filling them with experience and knowledge, literally keeping them on their toes. At SWRB in 1986, I felt starved—bored, hungry to learn more.

By the end of the year, struggling with yet another back injury, I was telling Aunty Pat that I was thinking of maybe moving to a different company 'quite soon'. In December, I was so fed up I actually booked a seat on a flight back to Australia, dreaming of the beach house, the sea and the sun, but finally talked myself out of rushing back to the nest 'each time I am in distress'. By this point Russell and I knew we were soon to go our separate ways; he was about to leave the company to begin his pursuit of his choreographic career. We remained in touch and stayed friends. My next big relationship was with someone who was his polar opposite—a lawyer called Tom O'Brien, who was based in Melbourne. The difficulties of sustaining a long-distance romance added to my homesickness.

On that night, I put my clothes back in my cupboards and turned my nose back to the grindstone. 'A dancer's life wasn't meant to be easy,' I announced, grandiloquently.

Our repertory at this point was full of revivals, including ballets such as Ashton's *Valses nobles et sentimentales*, MacMillan's *Solitaire*, and Cranko's *Pineapple Poll*. My dodgy back kept me away from leading roles, which I found frustrating, but I was still dancing plenty of solos and enjoyed both a revival of *Checkmate* and a new ballet by Jennifer Jackson called *One by Nine*, in which I was one of nine women surrounding the American dancer Joseph Cipolla, who had recently joined the company. His ebullience and lively sense of humour meant I had someone to laugh with, an outlet for my high spirits, which was something I felt I really needed. The six-week winter tour of multiple northern cities also gave me a chance to explore Scotland, hiring a car with friends to drive out on the weekend. 'Gosh it's gorgeous here,' I reported back home. 'No wonder the Scots are so proud of their country.'

April brought a long series of Beauties in a season at the Royal Opera House, in which I danced a lot of fairies, some white cats and some bluebirds. On the tube to and from Covent Garden, I wrote a list of my hates to send to my parents:

1. I hate work (sometimes)
2. I hate being away from you and Tom
3. I hate being so sensitive
4. I wish I could only see the goodness in other people
5. I hate it when I get a spot

6. I'm sick of looking like a rabbit and today I've really got the two teeth look [I accompanied this observation with a drawing]
7. I hate British Telecom for not giving us free calls
8. I hate knowing that within the next two days I have to vacuum the flat
9. I hate the fact that I can't do 32 fouettés with ease
10. I hate my closed in hairline—I look like I've evolved from the apes.

The tone of the list is a salutary reminder that I was still only twenty-one. The mention of fouettés shows that I was beginning to prepare in earnest for my debut as Odette/Odile in *Swan Lake*, and benefitting from Samsova's coaching. Our rehearsals were interrupted by another tour, this time to Eastern Europe, visiting Czechoslovakia, Poland, Bulgaria and East Germany from 11 May to 13 June. The company always printed red books for each foreign tour, full of detailed instructions about what to expect about each place, along with the practicalities of rehearsals and performance, and this one was particularly colourful with its warnings about the currency black market in the GDR, its guide to things to see in East Berlin, and its praise for Bulgarian wines and teas. I was dancing in *Flowers of the Forest*, *Checkmate* and *The Snow Queen* and enjoyed seeing such different countries, even though the hotels were often bad and the conditions difficult.

Lodz in Poland, where I didn't perform, was particularly trying. There were a lot of men loitering around the hotel who bothered me, and a couple of dancers had their rooms broken into while they were asleep. I was deeply affected by a visit to Auschwitz and Birkenau, travelling there alone by plane because I felt it was so important to bear witness to what happened there. But I have good memories too. There's a photograph of me and some of the other dancers lying on a wooden stage in pale sunshine, surrounded by forest. I can't remember which country we were in, but I can still smell the pines, and feel that wonderful sensation of lying on a warm deck with the sun on your face.

At the end of June, back in England, we took the Big Top to the Isle of Wight for the first time and I made my debut in *Swan Lake*. It was 30 June, and my father was in the audience, having come over from Australia to see me perform. There's a picture of me backstage afterwards in the corridor of a Portakabin. I'm clutching a huge bouquet and looking slightly dazed; this was the day Peter Wright promoted me to principal. I was twenty-two years old and had managed to achieve something that ninety-nine percent of dancers never attain.

Until years later, after the birth of my son Thomas, I was always incredibly nervous in tutu ballets, such as *Swan Lake* and *Sleeping Beauty*, and when you get nervous it depletes your energy and your reactions. Your muscles don't fire as well if your mind is playing tricks. These ballets choreographed by Marius Petipa in the nineteenth century remain the ultimate challenge for a modern dancer, because they ask you to master their immense technical challenges while at the same time finding your way into mythical stories, creating believable characters from archetypal figures, cursed queens and bewitched princesses. You've got to make the narrative real. Although I could execute the steps, I could never have gone onstage as Aurora thinking all that was required was the simple ability to hold a balance on one leg in the Rose Adage; I'd want to understand that girl, celebrating her sixteenth birthday, bursting into the world, full of curiosity and life. Yet because of the constraints of time, I was taught the parts in very exact detail, drilled rather than encouraged, asked to copy a formula rather than find my way into the character. It was damaging to me long-term, because although I danced most of those classical roles well into my forties, and danced them well, I know I only rarely felt they belonged to me.

On the other hand, I will always be grateful to SWRB for the way that it gave me an opportunity to learn my craft away from critical eyes. I have no idea how good that *Swan Lake* in the Isle of Wight was—though my feeling is it wasn't too bad—but for all the pressure I felt, I know that if I had been making my debut on the stage at Covent Garden, with a lot of beady-eyed critics and fierce balletomanes watching from the audience, the tension would have been even worse. There was something warmly relaxed about those Big Top performances, the sense of performing to people who, however knowledgeable, were simply glad you were there. There was a very particular atmosphere that grew from the happy juxtaposition between the grandeur of the sets for *Swan Lake* and my glamorous black tutu and tiara, and the sound of children munching their way through packets of crisps while they watched then cheering and cheering at the end. This electricity is something I have only experienced otherwise at schools' matinees at Covent Garden when a new audience of youngsters come in and discover the excitement of ballet for the first time. It's a great feeling and the way those tours gave me the opportunity to make mistakes, experiment and learn was the positive side of my time in the company. It built a resilience and a knowledge that stood me in good stead.

Behind the scenes, however, my relationship with Peter Wright was going through various ups and downs. Around this time, I had the happy experience of filming a BBC Masterclass with him on *Giselle*, which was screened in 1988. On the other hand, just before I made my *Swan Lake* debut, I'd had another confrontation with him about something or other, one small enough for me to forget the details today, but large enough for the ever-supportive Tom—who used to address his letters to Ballerina Girl—to remark, 'He has to know that you're not just a kid who he can put into line at his whim.'

In fairness to Peter, he had other things on his mind than my career. I was making a successful debut as Lise in *La Fille mal gardée* with Petter Jacobsson as my partner on a small, raked stage in Sunderland, worrying about the lack of decent guest houses, which we always had to find and arrange ourselves, and rehearsing a role in a new ballet by Graham Lustig called *The Edge of Silence*; the director meanwhile was struggling to put together a development plan that would ensure the long-term future of the company itself. Discussions were under way for SWRB to leave its London base and accept Birmingham's invitation to have its new headquarters in the city, becoming the Birmingham Royal Ballet in the process. A lot of the dancers were worried when the news began to leak out that we would be changing our name and our centre of operations some time in the next two to three years. I wasn't. I knew in my head that it was time to move on and I was beginning to make plans.

This was not a simple process. British ballet at this point was in a period of flux. The Royal Ballet under its director Norman Morrice had been going through an uncertain time, with falling standards and a loss of confidence that the new director Anthony Dowell, who took over at the end of the 1985–86 season, was beginning to address. My old friend Peter Schaufuss was causing ripples and making waves at London Festival Ballet, assembling an exciting team of dancers and coaches and building an interesting repertory.

In my mind, I still half-wanted to go to dance in America, but I didn't know anyone in the companies over there; Australia was also an option, but homesick though I was, I wasn't quite ready to move back, having spent such a long time getting established in the UK. Pulled in many directions, I agonised. My mother, while saying I should follow my heart, thought I should stay put in Sadler's Wells. She knew how much Peter Wright cared about me, and how much faith he had put in me by giving me starring roles. At Christmas, Miss Hansen wrote from Australia, sympathising with my dilemma but warning me to take care. 'You have had exceptional success with your career so far, I wouldn't like to see you making a wrong move now. You have a big advantage of being you, so to wait a few months wouldn't do any harm.'

Going home for a holiday to Rockhampton in January 1988, and spending time at the beach, helped me feel happier but it didn't stop the turmoil. I was just crumbling inside. It sounds arrogant, but I knew I was becoming a mediocre dancer, giving performances that were good but not great. I wanted to be special and I knew I could be. Over at Festival Ballet, Schaufuss was building a company that seemed to have everything I needed to fulfil that dream: he had recruited terrific international dancers and Christopher Bruce was on board as associate choreographer. They had big new productions of Ashton's *Romeo*, Harald Lander's *Études* and works by Glen Tetley. They had Elizabeth Anderton as one of their coaches, the brilliant teacher Johnny Eliassen as ballet master, and a stream of international guest teachers.

I needed a new challenge and I thought that if I made the change, I would stop feeling in a rut. I made another list to focus my mind. My reasons for being interested in Festival included: 'Partners / Guest principals to watch / Betty Anderton as ballet mistress / Work with Peter Schaufuss: he'll retire soon / Romeo and Juliet, not in SWRB rep and I'm not capable of Swan Lake or Aurora yet / Coliseum and Festival Hall which they work at have bigger stages / In London more often: I hate touring.'

The final sentence I wrote was: 'I want to develop slowly but I don't want to be a potential thirty-year-old as the English like,' a contradiction which summed up my fluctuating feelings. I felt I was being pushed beyond my capabilities, but somewhere in my heart, I also felt I was being held back.

I was still pondering when SWRB set off on another tour of the Far East, from 18 March to 8 May, visiting Thailand, Korea, China, Hong Kong and Japan, where Mum and Dad came to see me perform. I loved the vitality of Hong Kong and the beauty of Shanghai, though I was shocked by the poverty. A bout of flu laid me low and made me miss my debut as the White Girl in *Elite Syncopations*. I sent a long letter to Russell moaning about the need to keep pulling Swan Lakes out of the bag with very little rehearsal, and emphasising how little I was enjoying the work side of the company. I think by then I must have taken advice from two people I really trusted: Galina

Samsova and Lynn Seymour. Galina wasn't beholden to any of the internal politics in SWRB and she was direct enough to give me quiet and confidential advice. I trusted her to give me an honest point of view because she was someone who wouldn't hold back. She agreed that my standards had slipped and told me to follow my instincts, to leave if I felt it was the way to get on. I'd met Lynn a few years before at the pilates studio we both attended; I knew she was a fan of Schaufuss and of his innovations and was herself going to guest with his company. I respected her as someone who had made big decisions in her own life and whose career I had admired. Over tea in her little house in Notting Hill, I outlined my dilemma. I was sure I had more to offer, I just needed to find the place to do it. 'Why not give London Festival a try,' she said. Not long afterwards, I decided to leave in the summer.

But I hadn't yet taken the step of approaching Peter Schaufuss, who had not been at all happy when I'd pulled out of *Romeo and Juliet*. When we returned to London, I finally got in touch and we arranged to meet at the Gore Hotel. As we sat down for tea in a small dark room at the back of the ground floor, I was as direct as I always had been with him, telling him I wanted to join his company.

He was slightly incredulous. 'What on earth makes you think I am going to take you now?' he asked. I persisted, saying I admired what he had done and felt I was ready to join. Eventually, he agreed. It was a massive decision, and I had made it entirely on my own.

I can't emphasise enough how rare it was for a principal dancer to leave her home company at that time, and my own bravery astonishes me. I had weighed up the options, decided what I needed to do and acted. Although I danced Peter Wright's *Mirror Walkers* at a gala at Covent Garden in honour of the retirement of the general director John Tooley on 19 June, as soon as I told Peter my decision, the fall out was sour. According to my letters, he and Desmond Kelly, his deputy, stopped coming to my performances, a source of great sadness to me. But the other dancers were lovely. On 15 July 1988, we had an end-of-year celebration and sang a few farewell songs. I was surrounded by my friends in the company, and felt sorry to be leaving them, but I didn't really have many doubts. I knew that if I stayed any longer, I'd be trapped.

The following night, for my final performance in the company, I was dancing *Giselle*, which felt appropriate, since it was the ballet that had forged my links with Peter Wright in the first place. Perhaps because I felt free of all the worries that had been burdening me, my last run of performances with Petter Jacobsson as Albrecht made me remember why I loved dance in the first place. Suddenly I found that perfect spot where the combination of technique, enthusiasm, emotion and a love of the art of ballet itself came together in a way that made me absolutely sure that what I was doing was worth it—and equally convinced that in moving on, I was doing the right thing.

I was only sorry that Peter Wright, who had been so important to me, wasn't there to see it. But our story has the nicest coda. In June 2013, he came to see my farewell performance at the Royal Ballet, when I retired after dancing Mary Vetsera in *Mayerling*. He paid me the ultimate compliment, saying that the way I managed to immerse myself in the part and forget 'self' was exactly the quality that Fonteyn always said was essential.

'You are a true ballerina and artist,' he wrote. 'Your career has been remarkable, and I do admire the way in which you found your place at the top. I was so sorry to lose you when you decided to leave SWRB; I so wanted and needed you to become a ballerina with us. However, I am now happy that you made that decision and fought hard to reach the top via a different though difficult route.' I was hugely grateful to him for the letter; I knew I had hurt him when I decided to leave. He had invested so much time and so many hopes in me. He was right too to notice that I had chosen a different road to success. The next part of the ascent was about to begin.

CHAPTER 10

'WE BENJAMINS ARE ALWAYS ON THE LOOKOUT FOR A CHALLENGE'

IF I HAD TO COME up with a motto for my entire career, it would probably be 'Be brave!' I have been on so many journeys, and accumulated so much knowledge en route, but I've also had to keep on picking myself up and moving along. My decision to leave Sadler's and join London Festival Ballet definitely fell into the category of feeling afraid but deciding to do it anyway. In the end, to be honest, I just couldn't wait to get out, and my anxiety to be off was compounded by a workload which included rehearsing *Romeo and Juliet* for Festival in spare afternoons and weekends, and then fulfilling my commitments with Sadler's Wells. Also, as if life wasn't complicated enough, I helped out a tiny new company called Dance Advance, set up by former dancers from the Royal Ballet, who were performing *Sea of Troubles*, choreographed by Kenneth MacMillan for their inaugural season. When someone fell ill, I stepped in and learnt the part in two days. My workload at the time possibly accounts for the fact that when the piece was revived at the Royal Opera House in 2017, I felt as if I were seeing it for the first time.

By July, the news that I was leaving SWRB was out in the press.[1] A spokesperson told the *London Evening Standard* they were very disappointed; I said I felt the time was right for a change. In early August 1988, I made my debut with my new company at London's Royal Festival Hall, in—irony of ironies—Frederick Ashton's *Romeo and Juliet*. I was dancing opposite Patrick Armand, a brilliant dancer and a terrific partner. Nicholas Dromgoole of the Sunday *Telegraph* reported that I fitted into the choreography 'to the manner born',[2] which I felt I ought to, given that I'd had the benefit of an evening of private tuition from the choreographer himself.

I also, in that first month, danced Glen Tetley's *Sphinx* and Balanchine's *Symphony in C*, both new to me, before heading out to Aarhus, in Denmark where the company was filming its version of *Swan Lake*, a production devised and rehearsed by Natalia Makarova. The filming took place in a massive warehouse, like a football stadium with a roof. I was so excited to go to Aarhus because I'd loved the movie *Babette's Feast*, and imagined exploring the beautiful countryside; in fact, all I saw was the inside of that hangar, and all I did was dance. I had to learn from scratch the pas de quatre I was performing, in double quick time. Inserted into the opening act, this was also by Ashton and my solo was a little cameo of intricate footwork and crisp turns, tricky but joyful.

I knew Makarova of old—she was the dancer who had been so angry when one of my fellow students had spilt a cup of coffee on her—and even though I was by this point twenty-four and a principal dancer, she seemed terrifying, very much an old-school teacher. 'Vaaat are you doing?' she used to say, in that heavy Russian accent which she has never lost. 'Vaaat is that?'

As the years have passed, she has softened but I always found her a challenging coach; when she taught me *La Bayadère* years later I still found her frightening. She was so focused on perfection that she had a tendency to forget to tell dancers when they did something she liked, and that made me very nervous in front of her. Evelyn Hart, a wonderfully delicate Canadian, who was dancing Odette/

Odile opposite Peter Schaufuss as Siegfried, also got to the point where she started to feel insecure because she was trying so hard to please Natalia, who never seemed very happy. It's a fine line in ballet, balancing perfectionism and anxiety, and Makarova herself came from the toughest of schools, training at the Vaganova in St Petersburg. Outside the studio, her old-fashioned manner was softened with warmth and generosity; she flew from Los Angeles to watch my opening performance in *Bayadère* and turned up in the changing room an hour before the show surprising me with a big bag of beautiful evening clothes from her wardrobe because she thought they would really suit me.

I always think about my different experiences of coaching when I coach others. You are seeking to encourage every dancer to perform to the best of their ability. When I first started teaching, I was so keen that everyone should be phenomenal that I used to get quite exasperated if they couldn't carry out my suggestions. One day when I was getting frustrated, Monica Mason gave me some advice while we were chatting in the tiny teachers' changing room at the Royal Opera House. 'You can't always get someone to the place you have imagined. Sometimes they don't get there,' she said.

That was a big lesson to me. All you can do for a dancer is give them the tools and hope they can use them. I am fascinated by the process, and certainly the coaching was one reason why I was so happy at London Festival Ballet. It took that name on its foundation, in 1950, by Anton Dolin, Alicia Markova and Julian Braunsweg, to reflect the artistic excitement being generated by the Festival of Britain that was scheduled for the following year. Like the Royal Ballet, and SWRB, it grew out of the interest in ballet that blossomed in the Second World War, and particularly from the gala programmes that Markova and Dolin had performed. From the very start the company had a reputation for touring, both at home and internationally, and a reputation for attracting stars such as Nureyev to dance with it. When he took over as artistic director in 1984, Peter Schaufuss had widened its repertoire, and in 1988 founded the English National Ballet School in order to give it a more secure source of talent. In 1989 he changed the company's name to English National Ballet, and to avoid confusion that's what I will call it from now on.

In some ways, there wasn't much difference between the company I had left and the one I had joined. Both were groups of busy dancers, touring constantly, overworked and often tired. But from the very first, ENB suited me better, partly because it put me on my mettle, forcing me to stretch myself and improve. When I first arrived, I was almost overwhelmed by the talent that surrounded me. Among the female principals were elegant Christine Camillo from France, who I had so misjudged when I met her at the Prix de Lausanne, radiant Trinidad Sevillano from Spain, who had joined the company in her teens and caused a sensation, the Australian Susan Hogard, who had worked her way up from the corps de ballet to become an exceptional principal and Janette Mulligan, also from Australia. Lynn Seymour had joined as a dancer and teacher. In the ranks of the men there were Armand, Maximiliano Guerra from Argentina, Matz Skoog from Sweden and the Belgian Koen Onzia. These were world-class dancers, and my desire to reach the same level panicked me at first. In 1990, I told *Dance Australia* that I felt I had improved more in a year at ENB than I had in five at Sadler's Wells, adding that when I first arrived, I felt everyone was better than me. 'But something just clicked one day that it was all up to me. I have got to get there, and I've got to work. I always want to be the best.'[3]

The coaching made the difference. Because Peter Schaufuss was so determined to make ENB the kind of company that could take on the best, and because it was so international, they had devised new methods of teaching that incorporated a variety of different styles. Its basis was the Danish school, in which Schaufuss had grown up, and which is an exceptional training. You learn speed and strength through its footwork, and the way you align and 'pull up' your entire body. Ballet master Johnny Eliassen was a wonderful teacher and my technique improved enormously. Then there was Elizabeth Anderton, who later moved to the Royal Ballet; she'd worked extensively with Rudolf Nureyev and I think he introduced her to ENB. She used to call me her 'pocket Venus' because I was little but could sparkle. There were other exceptional guest teachers, who came in as and when needed, and the whole atmosphere was great, as far as I was concerned, full of energy.

I liked the fact that there were so many different nationalities in the company. It didn't feel like an English company where I was in a minority; I was just another foreigner in a group that was truly international, full of different and contrasting personalities, collectively working towards a goal. Every day we worked on our technique, which was exactly what I needed at that point. The eclectic mixture of coaching I've experienced throughout my career means that now, when a dancer stands in front of me, I know what I need to do for each individual. I understand the exercises they require to build muscles in their legs or their back, for example. In my first six months with ENB, under its arduous regime I completely changed my shape and that wasn't through diet but through work. From that point to the end of my career, class became something that I did with incredible dedication and rigour because it made me strong. I never wanted to go back to feeling weak and out of condition again.

Peter Schaufuss led by example. He worked incredibly hard. He was a tough taskmaster and a complicated personality. Like Nureyev, he had a whiff of glamour about him; his flat in Grosvenor Square was a sophisticated apartment, painted in a fashionable dark green, quite different from my own minimalist accommodation at the time. He knew all the best restaurants and on one occasion whisked the company off to the popular nightclub Stringfellows. When I had to leave early, the owner Peter Stringfellow lent me his limo and driver to take me home.

In those initial, heady days in ENB I was very happy. I loved our rehearsal space at Jay Mews; it felt in the heart of things, near Kensington and Hyde Park, not in Islington like Sadler's Wells.

An extra layer of excitement came from the fact that in the early days of her marriage to the Prince of Wales, Princess Diana popped by for dance classes. She used to arrive quietly in a chauffeur driven car and go very discreetly to a small studio for a private lesson, while the car waited for her outside. No one was allowed to watch, obviously, but I did meet her at events and galas, especially after she became the company's patron in August 1989, and later at the Royal Opera House. You hear everyone saying she was much more beautiful in life than in pictures, but it was true. She was utterly stunning, with perfect skin, and a smile that made you want to beam back at her. We never talked about anything more than the performance, but it was clear she loved ballet and was knowledgeable about it.

Looking back, when more has become known about her since her tragic death in August 1997, I wonder how much her love of ballet contributed to her worries about her own weight. People do come and watch dancers and feel that we are thin, but in fact we are toned and muscular. Of course, there are some dancers with eating disorders, and it was more common in the past than it is now, when everyone has become much wiser about diet and fitness. Anorexia was never common: there was one girl who suffered from it when I was at school, and I have known a couple of professionals who have battled with it. But the truth is that eating disorders make you weak, and dancers need to be strong. Today's professionals understand how to eat the right amount to make their bodies work to their best ability and will adapt a pattern of eating that suits them. I learnt how to tune everything so that my body built the muscles it needed. Outsiders may just look at us and think how skinny we are without understanding any of that.

In terms of physical condition, I was in my prime at English National Ballet. After six months with the company I felt ready for anything, and a lot was given to me. I probably didn't have the profile I would have had if I had stayed at Sadler's Wells, where I knew I was being groomed as a star; at ENB I was dancing alongside a lot of ballerinas who were just as good as me, and I was rarely first cast.

But that didn't worry me. I've never been jealous of other dancers, and shining in a glistening setting suited me very well. The regional touring was still there of course, intense as ever, but we also danced at the London Coliseum and the Festival Hall, both places I loved performing. The Festival Hall is not the perfect dance venue because it has shallow wing space, but it brings you close to the audience; the Coliseum is the exact opposite, so huge you have to project a lot, but the size of the stage is wonderful.

In October 1988, I gave up a chance of going on tour with the company to fulfil one of my dreams—going to Australia to perform the joyful 'Fanny Elsser' pas de deux from the picnic scene in *La Fille mal gardée* at Melbourne's State Theatre as part of Australian Ballet's bicentennial gala. It was such a thrill to be part of the event, dancing this radiantly lovely pas de deux with Roland Price, on a wonderfully nostalgic night, full of legendary dancers from the past, and many memories, not to mention Australian dancers who were still working internationally. From the company's illustrious past, there were principals Marilyn Jones, Marilyn Rowe, John Meehan, Garth Welch, Ray Powell and Gary Norman while dancers including Elizabeth Toohey, David McAllister, David Palmer, Christine Walsh, David Ashmole, Roland and I represented the current era. It was very special for me to perform professionally for the first time in Australia, not only for all my family and friends, but for my countrymen and women too.

The event took on added significance because it was where I met a dancer with The Australian Ballet called Graham Rowe, and we immediately took a liking to each other. He wasn't a typical dancer, having switched to the profession after a period as a tennis player, and beginning ballet lessons at the age of eighteen. Perhaps that was why I liked him; he wasn't too intense about dance. He also had the most wicked sense of humour, which made me smile. What's more, he had just auditioned for Festival and was about to join the company. Six months after we first met, he came to London and we were together for almost six years. We were happy together for most of that time. I'd always been clear in my mind that I wanted a good work-life balance.

I wanted a home and a partner, and Graham did too. He grounded me and it was great to have a partner who was by my side experiencing challenges together.

By early 1989, we were on the road together, touring Scotland and the English regions for nearly two months. I made my debut as Odette/Odile in ENB's production of *Swan Lake* and as Swanilda, the heroine of *Coppélia,* in Ronald Hynd's production, a new role for me and one whose cheeky humour as she pretends to be a doll, suited my love of comedy.

Later that year, I made my debut in Schaufuss's version of the Bournonville classic *Napoli*, which showed off the light, tight footwork that I had been developing under Johnny Eliassen's influence. Watching from the stalls, for her review in the *Daily Telegraph*, Kathrine Sorley Walker praised my 'sustained and unmannered fluency'[4] while Stephanie Jordan in *The Listener* called my footwork 'subtle'.[5] I was pleased they had noticed. In the same season, Lynn Seymour, now aged fifty, was performing MacMillan's *Anastasia*. I watched her, spellbound. She threw herself into the role with complete abandon and conviction. It was a revelation to see up close and personal such a truthful artist perform one of the roles that had been created on her. I treasured the memory when I got my own chance at the part some years later and had the privilege to be coached by her.

In July, a three-week American trip to the Kennedy Center in Washington and then the Metropolitan Opera House in New York became one of the highlights of my dancing life up to that point. New York was always a place I felt happy, and there was something about the city, its audiences and its critics, that meant I received more acclaim there than I ever did in London. Gelsey Kirkland, star of American Ballet Theatre and one of my heroines, came to watch some of our shows, and I was thrilled. But the entire trip was full of excitement, even though on the face of it, my performance in one ballet, *Études*, didn't go to plan.

This piece by another Danish choreographer, Harald Lander, was an important part of ENB's repertoire and its high-wire pyrotechnics suited our dancers, particularly the men who got to show off their technique in great sequences of jumps, like glamorous matadors, strutting their stuff. I had to learn the role of the leading girl quite quickly, because I was replacing someone who was injured, and was determined to hold my own against all this dazzling technical brilliance. The result was that at the beginning of my solo, my own set of chaîné turns from the top wing to the bottom of the stage was so fast that I fell over; in fact, I nearly toppled off the stage.

My embarrassment was soothed by the fact that Stanley Williams, one of the world's most famous teachers, who was on the faculty of Balanchine's School of American Ballet, came backstage to congratulate me. As I hung my head in shame, he said: 'Don't worry, Leanne. I'd far rather see someone take a risk than play it safe. You were just great.' It was amazing to hear such encouragement from him, and I took his compliment very much to heart. Audiences were enthusiastic and the critics complimentary too.

I danced *Romeo and Juliet* opposite Patrick Armand twice, and Anna Kisselgoff, critic for the *New York Times*, who had first noticed me as a soloist with SWRB three years earlier, praised the way we added 'great acting' to our strong technique. '[Benjamin's] dancing was also marked by an exciting streak of flamboyance,' she went on. 'She was not afraid to use her greyhound-sleek line and high extension, especially for the arabesques in the love duet.'[6] Despite these gratifying comments, the most significant eyes on me that night belonged to Kenneth MacMillan, who was also in the audience. He'd spent a bit of time watching ENB on that tour, coming onstage to take a bow when Lynn Seymour danced Anastasia in a triple bill. But I didn't know he was out front and was gobsmacked when he came backstage afterwards to say how much he had enjoyed the show. It was two years before we met again, in Berlin.

I certainly wasn't the only dancer attracting praise at the time. Kisselgoff talked about the company's 'treasure trove of talent' and described us as the surprise dance hit of the season, comparing us with American Ballet Theatre. 'Nonetheless, Festival has a distinctive image of its own. In the end, it looks like an English company simply because its female corps has the soft, refined toe work that produces the lyric style identified with British ballet. But there is also a signature energy. It is remarkable how Mr Schaufuss has knit so many disparate aspects together. The principals are individuals and stand out, but they are also part of an ensemble.'[7] That was how it felt on the inside. I don't want to paint it as perfect, because obviously there were still arguments and bad days. When Patrick Armand left shortly afterwards to pursue his career with Boston Ballet, he sent me a note telling me not to let people scream at me, which indicates that not everything in the garden was permanently rosy.

But I did love the work, particularly since it gave me the opportunity to tackle different repertory. In October 1989, I was part of the creation of a new piece by Christopher Bruce; wanting to work with this choreographer was one of the reasons I had cited as being part of my reason for leaving SWRB in the first place. Bruce by training was a contemporary dancer, and his strongest ties were always with Ballet Rambert (later Rambert Dance) where he had first performed and where he became Artistic Director in 1994. But he was expanding his range and his interests with commissions for ballet companies and Schaufuss was quick to snap him up, later making him associate choreographer. *Land*, which had premiered in 1985, dealt with the tragedy of war, full of despair and desperation. I used to love watching it, and so was delighted when I was chosen to be in the opening cast when he created his *Symphony in Three Movements* to the Stravinsky score of that name. It involved moving in an entirely different, more grounded way than I was used to, and I found him gorgeous to work with, unpretentious and down to earth.

Christmas was full of Nutcrackers, in Manchester and in Bristol. Ballet dancers don't often get Christmas off because we are usually lost in the land of the Sugar Plum Fairy. It was never my favourite role but I danced it often, in many productions, and relished its challenges and its beautiful score. It was, however, the first part I gave up when

I reached the point in my career where I could have some say over my repertoire; it looks dreamy to an audience, but the ballerina only appears near the end of the ballet and then has to perform a pas de deux which seems sumptuous but is testing both in terms of stamina and technique.

As far as I was concerned, everything was all going beautifully. Then it all fell apart. Peter Schaufuss was sacked. During his last year in charge, there had been rumbling disagreements about the direction of the company, and the ways in which it would be most commercially and artistically successful. There were arguments about money. The board itself split into hostile factions and the administrative and artistic sides of the company were not speaking. It was chaos when, with the backing of the Arts Council, a new chairman, Pamela, Lady Harlech, came in, determined to make big changes at board and company level.[8] Peter misjudged the situation. He had a complete falling out with her, calling her bluff, and telling her he would run the company if she got on with running the board.

It didn't go down well. When he turned up for a meeting with her, expecting to meet the new board for the first time, he was summarily fired, with Lady Harlech citing 'irreconcilable differences'. He was locked out of his own office and not allowed back in the building. I remember the shock of it all, but not much more. Since none of us had known anything about the arguments behind the scenes, it came completely out of the blue. I knew that Peter wasn't perfect, and he had fallen out with some dancers, but there was no doubt that he had massively improved the image and standards of ENB and cared passionately about its future. He'd also made it a company that people noticed, so his sacking caused a huge fuss, with stories in the papers, and the paparazzi following him around. I got caught up in that end of things when, a few weeks later, I took up his invitation to go to dance the *Le Corsaire* pas de deux with him at a gala in Spain and discovered Jeffery Taylor, a writer from the *Daily Mail* hiding in the bushes near the theatre, armed with a camera, trying to take photographs of us.

Because I liked Peter and had benefited from his stewardship of the company, I was inclined to be on his side. Later Lady Harlech said that she never intended to sack him, but he had put himself in an untenable position by saying he wouldn't work with her and the board.[9] As a dancer, you never really see inside the politics of a company or completely understand what is going on. I was just devastated that it was all going on around me.

On 6 February, I took refuge in a letter to Aunty Pat, writing in block capitals at the top of the page 'I am really stressed out at the moment.' It wasn't just Peter's departure that had got to me. My flat in Barons Court was falling apart. The builders were due in and I was worried about the endless list of problems they had to solve. I also had an injured hip. That meant that I missed the fortieth anniversary gala of English National Ballet which took place in the presence of Princess Diana at the Royal Albert Hall in March. I wanted to be there and was upset to miss it. The following month, I missed a regional tour because I was having terrible stomach pain and went to see a specialist to find out what it was. (It was later diagnosed as an infection.)

I had also been agonising, once again, about my future. By May, Peter Schaufuss had been appointed artistic director of the Deutsche Oper Ballet in Berlin—and he wanted a lot of the ENB principals to go with him. I lay awake for nights on end wondering what to do, but at that point ENB was still in flux without a new director, the repertory was becoming more conservative again and the money I was being offered in Germany was considerably better. Eventually, I decided to go, even if it was only for a short time.

'We Benjamins are always on the lookout for a challenge,' I wrote to Aunty Pat. 'It seems to be in our blood.' It was a risk, but it was also an adventure.

CHAPTER 11

THE SMALLEST VALKYRIE

MY DECISION TO LEAVE ENGLISH National Ballet and head for Berlin was announced to the world in the *Daily Mail* on 5 May 1990 under the headline 'Top dancers may defect in battle of the tutus'. 'Ballet supremo Peter Schaufuss looks poised to take sweet revenge on Britain's classical dance establishment,' it read, explaining that he intended to poach nearly all ENB's top ballerinas and listing Christine Camillo, Lynn Seymour, Laura Contardi, Susan Hogard and me as the likely leavers. 'All are expected to resign next week.'[1]

The *Evening Standard* had its own version of the same story. 'A big leap in salary lures 10 ballet stars to Berlin', suggesting that annual pay being twice as high in Germany as in the UK at the time might have something to do with our decision and adding Martin James to the list of dancers who were off.[2] The choice wasn't as simple as that for any of us, of course, but there is no doubt that the better money was a factor. A dancer's career is generally a short one and you are always conscious of the need to make hay while the sun shines. Graham had also been invited to join. Schaufuss loved having him around: he was a good dancer and great company.

I had virtually stopped dancing with ENB by that point anyway, struggling with a long-term injury. Over the summer, I had a complicated hernia operation to sort things out and by August, after months away from the stage, I was packing up my flat, and ready to be off. I was fed up with hanging around in London waiting to go, and when gunshots were heard in the night in the road where I lived, I suddenly felt enormously relieved to be leaving as well as excited at the prospect before me.

I couldn't have been making my home in Berlin at a headier time. Just after I arrived, the city celebrated its reunification in a great buzz of festivity. I walked down Unter den Linden, the wide avenue that leads to the Brandenburg Gate, surrounded by jubilant crowds, drinking in the atmosphere. Everything about that day made me feel I had arrived in a different world. If Britain was like a strange country to a young Australian, then continental Europe seemed even more of cultural change. I spoke no German. But I was curious and quite courageous; I really wanted to know what it was like to live in this newly reforged city, and it was thrilling to be part of its story on a day when history was being made. I remembered only too well how it was when I was on tour with SWRB in East Germany and the West was entirely closed to us. This was a new world and I was full of hope.

Graham and I found a modern flat in the west of the city, a twenty-minute U-Bahn journey from the Deutsche Oper, where the company was based, and did it up with colourful, abstract art that we bought in the local markets and hung on the whitewashed walls. It was all very bright, with a lot of glass, an open plan living area and floor-to-ceiling doors that opened out onto a tiny balcony from each room. We had three fish, one gold and two black. A fourth committed suicide by jumping out of the bowl, which in retrospect always felt like an omen. But my early time in the city was very happy. I loved the coffee shop culture, much stronger in Berlin then than it was in London, and the way that people left their apartments to eat, read and think. I spent a bit of time in those early months sitting in cafes, writing long letters to my parents, describing everything that was going on around me. I also signed up for German lessons, determined to learn the language so I could understand everything better. Graham and I invited members of the company back to our flat for dinner, keen to make new friends. We bought a second-hand VW Beetle and buzzed around the city like natives, though I had a couple of mishaps with reverse parking when I was driving on what I thought of as 'the wrong' side of the road.

The problem for me was that many of my ambitions about integration quickly came up against the realities of my daily life as a dancer, mired in bureaucracy and facing a certain amount of antagonism. The Deutsche Oper itself was a shock after the easy-going habits of Sadler's Wells and Jay Mews. It was huge, with two good studios, but stark and sterile, rebuilt after the war to a sober, modernist design, and if the building wasn't welcoming, then the bureaucracy within it was positively off-putting. Even though they were often fluent in English, the staff insisted on talking to everyone in German, which was a challenge for those of us who were beginners with the language, and there were multiple rules that they were keen to enforce. Initially, there was a lot of running around with forms in triplicate, trying to get all kinds of permissions sorted out.

There was also a complex rehearsal schedule, with an enforced four-hour gap for the corps de ballet from 2pm to 6pm, although the principals could continue to work. The weirdness of the hours was compounded because Peter found a loophole in the regulations which meant that if we didn't have a performance, there was nothing to stop us rehearsing until 10pm at night, simply because that was the contractually agreed cut-off point. Some days, he'd keep us working from 10am to 10pm—and all my plans for immersing myself in the life of the city went up in smoke. German lessons were often cancelled because I was in the theatre all day. It was such a difficult, constricting way to work. Even I, with my willingness to dance all day and all night, began to feel it was unproductive.

Peter had assembled a really good company by recruiting new talent to supplement terrific dancers such as Tomas Karlborg, Bart de Block and Marek Rózycki who were already in the company.

Once again, we had the cosmopolitan feel that I had enjoyed so much in the past. But there were two big differences. The first was that at that time the Deutsche Oper was essentially a building for opera, and since the provision of ballet and opera in Berlin was sorting itself out after unification, there was an ongoing tussle between the opera and the ballet company, which only had around eighty performances a year in which to shine. Peter was pushing for more. He was also encountering resistance from some of the established dancers in the company, who perhaps resented the fact that he had hired dancers from abroad without giving them a chance. Some were on contracts that meant even if they weren't performing, they were still entitled to be paid. Others got doctors' notes, allowing them to be off work entirely. You couldn't blame them at all. They felt disgruntled, but it created a strange atmosphere.

My own first performance, after months offstage, was in my view a disaster. I felt out of form, and absolutely thrown by the space I was dancing in. It was like performing in a vast black box, with no connection to the audience. Eventually I got used to it, but it was never a stage I loved, being both deep and wide. Dancing the *Tchaikovsky Pas de Deux* on it was a nightmare, because you never had a moment to catch your breath; as soon as you'd skipped off into the wings, you'd have to start running back on for the next step.

By October, however, I was beginning to settle in, and was certainly back on form. I danced the lead in a full-length August Bournonville ballet called *A Folk Tale*, a very strange and rarely seen piece. I could understand why: it has a plot that might almost be a parody, about an elf girl who is supposed to be a princess but gets swapped at birth and has to live her life underground with all the trolls, until she meets the man of her dreams whom she rescues from an elfish spell before finally they sort everything out and live happily ever after.

By that time my sister Fiona was living in London, pursuing her own dream of a career in musical theatre, which ultimately led her to leading roles in the West End. Madonna was making her way in television, about to direct her first documentary. I wrote Fiona a long letter, describing the ballet. 'It's boring for the rest of the company, but my part is great … and my partner is gorgeous.' It obviously went down well—I won an award from the German critics for my performance, and Wolfgang Lehmann, writing in *Der Tagesspiegel*, was very complimentary. 'Leanne Benjamin is a dancer with a beautiful arabesque and jumps, lightness, a soft line and quick feet.'[3]

Offstage too, there were pleasures and excitements. Suzanne Farrell, muse to Balanchine, arrived to coach us in *Symphony in C*, in which I danced both the first and the fourth movement on alternating evenings and my bête noir, the *Tchaikovsky Pas de Deux*. She was fabulous. Then forty-six, she was beautiful and tall, with a very seventies vibe. She made a massive impact just walking into the room in her high, brown zip-up boots, with her hair flowing; she was such a heroine. I loved being coached by her, relishing the way she passed on the Balanchine style. She was particularly insightful as she translated steps that had been created for a tall dancer onto someone like me.

People often decided that you had to be tall to dance one role and small to dance another. I was tiny, but I danced big and had long legs and there was an entire repertory that I would have loved to take a shot at, which someone thought wouldn't suit me because of my height. This might have something to do with choreographers' estates, who control the rights to historic ballets and tend to cast on the basis of how it has been performed before. Sadly I didn't get to dance in Balanchine's *The Prodigal Son*, for example, where the Siren has long legs which she flashes almost malevolently as she entraps her man. I do understand the aesthetics of it, and why I wasn't cast, but I think it can be revelatory when casting is about the way someone moves rather than dictated by type.

In this instance, and in many others, Farrell was a wise and helpful guide. I had confidence—as I did when I was coached by Lynn Seymour in MacMillan roles, or Patricia Neary who helped me with Balanchine both in Germany and at the Royal, or Monica Mason in the Fokine ballets—that they were going to be able to fast-track me to the place I needed to be. It is valuable to work with the person who has actually danced the role you are learning or has worked closely with the choreographer they are talking about because they intimately understand every detail. Suzanne got the nuance of dancing Balanchine; she could hand on energy hints, how to push yourself up into a lift, how you approach your turns. She communicated the style that was needed beautifully, and my understanding increased exponentially. I felt I was getting every breath of her knowledge in rehearsals, and that's what I most love.

Despite all her care, however, my debut in *Symphony in C*, with Patrick Armand guesting with the company as my partner, was difficult. I loathed every minute of it, struggling because, according to Schaufuss after the performance, the lighting wasn't set correctly. When the stage is too dark, you can't see where the edge of it is, which feels incredibly scary. It's so different from the studio where you've been perfecting your technique in daylight, and it's particularly challenging if you have a lot of turns. If you can't see, you can't 'spot', or fix a point with your eyes to stop you becoming disorientated.

That night I felt engulfed and dizzy. 'I just wanted to be swallowed by the stage,' I wrote to Madonna. 'Peter said it was fine, and that I was overreacting.' He might have been right. Certainly, as I danced the ballet more, I also appreciated it more. I danced a lot of Balanchine's work while I was in Germany, loving the airy pleasure of the solo girl's part in *Who Cares?*, his exuberant piece to sixteen songs by George Gershwin, and the sheer beauty of Terpsichore in *Apollo*, one of his utter masterpieces. Thanks to Suzanne and Patricia's coaching, I felt I improved enormously as an interpreter of his works.

Around the same time, Roland Petit, the French choreographer and another legendary figure in the history of dance, was also in Berlin, restaging his *Carmen*, in which Martin James and I were second cast to Susan Hogard and Peter himself. I don't remember Petit very well, partly because he concentrated his attentions on the first cast, and partly because he wasn't particularly talkative, so I got little sense of what he was like as a man. But I loved that ballet, which Petit had choreographed as a showcase for his glamorous wife Zizi Jeanmaire. It had such style and drama, with a black, figure-hugging bodice and a short-haired wig. It's amazing how a wig and a costume can completely change who you are in terms of looks and confidence.

The end of 1990 brought the arrival of another French choreographer, Maurice Béjart, who had premiered his version of Wagner's *The Ring*, with dancers from his own Béjart Ballet Lausanne at the Deutsche Oper in March, before I arrived. Our dancers were now learning the ballet alongside Béjart's own, and it became part of our repertory from 31 December 1990. Somewhat to my surprise, I was cast as Brunhilde, possibly the smallest person ever to play a Valkyrie in the history of Valkyries. What made it even odder was that the dancer on whom Béjart had created the role, was a statuesque blonde, who couldn't have been more different. For someone like me, who is moved by music, it was amazing to feel the power of an edited version of Wagner's score roaring around us. The opera company was simultaneously mounting their own version of *The Ring*, and I went along for inspiration. But Béjart's *Ring um den Ring* (A Spectacle Around the Ring) was anything but a straight-forward retelling of Wagner's epic story. Instead he took the idea of Wotan as a godlike father figure and *The Ring*'s themes of law, incest, money, power and government and mixed them with the everyday life of a ballet company.

I had to dance with a long stick, tearing up the space in great high-kicking strides; at another moment I had a wonderful pas de deux with Tomas Karlborg, who was playing Wotan, with a barre behind us. The work was athletic, modern, interesting and, at almost five hours, enormously long. I had a two-hour break in the middle where I could just about get home, relax and come back, if I wanted. The whole thing was an experience I wouldn't have missed for the world, and one which emphasised the difference of working in a continental company. Béjart's works have never been popular with English critics, but there's no doubting the scope they offer to dancers. In rehearsal, he was quite literally a massive figure, bristling at the front of the room, with a presence so powerful that he commanded your attention and your effort.

In general, my first nine months in Berlin felt expansive. There were great people coming into the building all the time, and an interesting mixture of dancers too. Despite the burden of the rehearsal schedule and the lack of regular performances, which I found wearisome from the first, I did manage to dance in a lot of pieces that were new to me and which pushed my mind and body in different ways. I enjoyed Hans van Manen's *Twilight*, an erotic pas de deux about relationships to the music of John Cage. The female role is quite fierce: you start the ballet in high heels, which you later take off, which means there's an interesting tension in the steps, and the shifts of speed and attack. It's a conversation that builds to an argument and then gradually resolves. In contrast, I also tackled Petipa's *Paquita*, one of the gems of traditional classical ballet, full of showing off. Alongside these new roles, I was still dancing the classics such as *Giselle*.

In February I made a cross-country dash to Dresden by train, to step into Dresden Ballet's version of *Swan Lake* at a moment's notice. The performance generated one of the funniest press reports about me that I have ever read. 'The news spread like wildfire among the dancers: our swan is pregnant. What can we do? There is a performance of *Swan Lake* on Sunday. Dieter Lösche, ballet director of Dresden, rang Berlin and asked do you have a swan for us? The answer? Of course. You'll get the best one.'[4] I hope my performance was as good as the build-up, in which the writer praised my humility and strong discipline; it was certainly an experience getting used to a new production in just a day.

By then, however, I was beginning to struggle offstage. In March, I suffered another slight injury to my foot, which meant that I was not considered for the opening cast in *Giselle*. I wrote to my mum and dad in frustration: 'You really are made to feel like an outcast if you're injured more than a couple of days.'

My relationship with Graham was also going through a bad patch. Even though I appreciated his easy-going gregariousness, living together was a strain. My life seemed a constant mixture of ups and downs, alternating with roller-coaster speed. An up was undoubtedly a trip to St Petersburg in June, where we performed in the famous Mariinsky Theatre. The powerful Russian dancer Igor Zelensky, who began his career with the Mariinsky, had come to Berlin in 1990 as guest soloist, and now he returned with us to his home stage to perform *Apollo*, attracting enormous acclaim and interest in our performances. On the opening night triple bill, I danced the *Tchaikovsky Pas de Deux* with Bart de Block, and finally it went brilliantly. Every stage has its own atmosphere and I loved dancing on this one, in spite of its steep rake. The theatre felt so full of past glory, with its glistening U-shaped auditorium with the elaborate Tsars' box in the centre.

All through this period, I was coming back to London with astonishing regularity. I made twenty-four return flights to the UK in my time in Berlin, a sign of how unsettled I must have felt. By early August, after a year in the city, I had moved out from the apartment I shared with Graham, at the start of what turned out to be a protracted and messy break-up where we kept reuniting only to separate again. In an attempt to sort things out, I had taken a tiny flat conveniently near the Opera House. It was concrete, soulless and totally depressing. My parents were writing from Australia offering to come to see me because they were so worried about me. Madonna did come out for a visit and spent her time urging me to consider joining New York City Ballet or another American dance company, alarmed by how unhappy I was.

My working relationship with Peter Schaufuss was beginning to deteriorate. When I had arrived in the company, he had been supportive of my talent, telling me that even on a bad night, my dancing was still better than most people's. But now my letters from the time reveal that I felt he was picking on me in rehearsal, showing me up in front of others. Although I tried, I wasn't really happy in Berlin either. It wasn't the vibrant modern capital it is today, but a city still trying to remake itself after its complicated history. It felt sterile and bureaucratic, not a place where a free spirit could be happy. I sent a letter to Mum and Dad. 'Emotional wreck' I scrawled on top, explaining that I was tense all the time. 'I really don't fit into this place or their way of thinking,' I wrote. 'I'm far too emotional to fit into such a methodical way of life and order.'

My disillusion went deeper than the fact that both my personal and professional life were going through a tricky period. I was beginning to doubt whether I wanted to carry on dancing at all. I had been devoted to a daily routine of practice and dance since I was a child. The reward had been my sense of doing something I loved and managing to make a career of it, but I'd never had much time to live life normally, to visit museums and galleries, to soak up the knowledge that I longed for. I had thought Berlin would represent a chance to learn more, to grow. I had come to the city as a young, ambitious dancer, approaching the peak of my ability. But as I reached my twenty-seventh birthday, I was feeling worn down and began to think I had made a terrible decision that had completely messed up my career. The routine didn't suit me, nor did the endless round of rehearsal without performance. I felt like Goldilocks. At Sadler's Wells it had been all performance without rehearsal, here it was the opposite way around. I was looking for something that was just right, for the perfect mixture of rest, training and dancing and if it didn't exist then, perhaps I should give up altogether.

I've always been quite black and white about fixing things: if something isn't working, you should step away. I am also a great believer in reinventing yourself. I knew I was in a rut and had to get out—even a trip to Edinburgh to dance the lead in *Giselle* at the Edinburgh International Festival failed to cheer me up. But I was worried that if I left my third dance company so soon after I had arrived, I would be seen as irresponsible, someone who lacked staying power. I had one piece of good news that kept me going. I had been cast as Marie in *Different Drummer*, a ballet by Kenneth MacMillan, and he was coming to Berlin to oversee rehearsals. The day he walked into the studio, my whole life changed.

CHAPTER 12

'AREN'T YOU TALKING TO ME THEN, BENJAMIN?'

I WAS QUITE SHY WHEN Kenneth MacMillan first came back to Berlin. He had himself been director of the Deutsche Oper for three years in the late sixties, having one of the most testing times of his life. It had taken a bit of persuading on the part of Peter Schaufuss to get him to return, especially since he had suffered a scare about his health in early 1991. His arrival at the company from which he had resigned in 1969 was freighted with expectation, and I was anxious. He was one of the world's greatest dance-makers, principal choreographer at the Royal Ballet, someone I had admired since I first started watching ballet with any understanding. I didn't want to assume that he would want to talk to me. On the other hand, I didn't want to fade into the background either. When he and his assistant Monica Parker first turned up in company class to make their final decisions about casting the production of *Different Drummer* that he was reviving for the company to dance, I distinctly remember them walking in and sitting at the front of the studio. I positioned myself carefully in the second row, not wanting to stand out too much but desperately wanting to be noticed.

Kenneth tended to sit slumped and expressionless, studying everything intently. The studio was a place where he seemed comfortable, somewhere he belonged. He'd been sitting at the front of rehearsals for years and years, watching a lot of dancers, hoping for a new muse to come along, or at the very least that he would see something special in someone. He spotted the potential in a lot of people: Lynn Seymour, Alessandra Ferri, Darcey Bussell, and Irek Mukhamedov among them. He was renowned for having an eye for dancers with spirit and voice; he chose people for how they moved and how they told a story, not for the shape of their legs or the length of their torso. I needed him to see the spark in me that I knew was there—my fear was that he would choose someone else.

Later that day, he walked up to me in the corridor. 'Aren't you talking to me then, Benjamin? You'd better, because you're going to be the lead in my ballet.'

With those few words, the whole balance of my life shifted. He had seen beneath the skin to something in my head and heart, to my longing to be a great dramatic dancer. I can't tell you what it means when someone sees the truth in you in that way. It would have been significant at any point in my career, but the fact that it arrived at that moment, when I was so stuck, felt absolutely magical. I needed inspiration and here he was, offering it to me. Even if I still decided to give up after I had danced *Different Drummer*, I knew I would have climbed to a different level. I felt I was unlikely to let him down, because I had a sense, from dancing in some of his works and looking at others, that I was the right fit for his movement and his stories. His ballets weren't fairy tales but dramas, and his heroines were strong willed, defiant women, who fought against circumstance, and took their lives into their hands. No wonder they appealed to me.

Different Drummer, inspired by George Büchner's play *Woyzeck*, about a soldier and his descent into madness, is not an easy ballet. But as Mary Clarke wrote when it premiered in 1984, 'It should be seen especially by people who think ballet is just *Swan Lake*.'[1] The play was based on a real-life murder case about a soldier who killed his mistress, but its real subject is the exploitation of the poverty-stricken Woyzeck by different arms of the state—military, religious, and medical. The astonishing thing about the ballet is the way it conveys these themes, and Woyzeck's mental deterioration, in expressionistic, agonised movement of twisting, inventive bravery. The female character, Marie, originally created by Ferri with Wayne Eagling as Woyzeck, is a complex creature—both virgin and whore, mother and adulteress, betrayer and victim.

As soon as I heard I was cast as Marie, opposite Martin James as Woyzeck, I rushed out and read Büchner's play. But once we started rehearsing, Kenneth never said very much about what it all meant or asked us to do any research. Perhaps he just knew that if we were the kind of dancers who wanted to work with him, we'd also do our homework. In any case, as far as he was concerned, everything was in the steps, though it was up to individual dancers to find their own way to reach his destination, bringing their own logic and their own style to the ballet.

Being in that Berlin studio with him and Monica Parker was one of the most precious moments of my dancing life. It was intense, but being presented with that incredible choreography felt like something I had to treasure and to deliver to the best of my dancing ability. If you are given a gift like that, you want to maximise all the possibilities; I didn't want to dilute a second of the experience, but rather drink it all up. The days were long, but in this instance I would have stayed in the studio all night. Endurance, and the willingness to work at something, is a quality I have always had, and if I really want to get underneath something, I am happy to stay forever until I get there.

Working on Marie was particularly fascinating because I'd never seen *Different Drummer* and had no preconceptions about how it should be danced. It had been out of the repertory since it had been created, and Kenneth was revising this production as we went along. He worked very closely with Monica Parker, who had all the notations of the original in front of her. She would get up and indicate the steps, and then we'd all work on learning and adapting them. The premiere originally featured a suggestion of an apotheosis where Marie and Woyzeck seemed united in another world while their bodies remained on a mortuary slab; that ending vanished in this revival and did not return when the Royal Ballet subsequently remounted the work. Kenneth was spontaneous, and open to ideas, incorporating movements that we made into his rethinking of some of the choreography.

At one point, I was unpinning my hair at the back of the room when he suddenly said, 'I love that. Let's keep that in.' It was a refreshing reminder of how creative and exciting dancing could be, an escape from the rigidity that I had been feeling before he arrived. By then, I'd danced a huge number of ballets and I was told I'd danced them well. But I felt I'd never hit boiling point. In the studio with Kenneth, I pushed myself to new heights of physicality and depths of feeling.

His choreography asks you to test boundaries all the time, both physically and psychologically. As a dancer, you tell a story with your body, but you must make the jumps of expression in your mind. Once you have understood what you are trying to convey, then you must dig deep into your technical ability, layering the steps with greater expressiveness. In Kenneth's work, every action is an articulation of a mental state. It explains what your character is thinking and feeling. I began to jump further into Martin's arms, extend my legs more, wrap them more tightly around his body. You need to give your utmost, to completely lose yourself in the choreography, particularly with a ballet such as *Different Drummer,* where the darkness and depth of the story requires passionate engagement. If you immerse yourself in this way, audiences start to read what you are saying. For me, it felt like giving myself over to the ballet. The music, played for us in rehearsal on a piano, helped too: its potent mixture of Schoenberg and Webern was so expressive to work to.

I was really in the zone one day, giving my all for Kenneth and for the role, when he noticed that a fellow cast member in one of the smaller parts was sitting at the back of the room reading a newspaper. Kenneth went berserk; I'd never seen him explode like that before. He told the poor boy off: 'How dare you read the paper when you've got a great artist dancing in front of you,' he said, fiercely. 'You should be watching, and learning.'

He instructed everybody to watch how I absorbed and interpreted his choreography, because it was what he expected from them as well. It was embarrassing for me to be singled out in that way, but now I am older I do think Kenneth was right in demanding attention. If you're in rehearsal and someone is using all their artistry and commitment to lift themselves to a new place, giving the room a different momentum, then it is a sign of disrespect to read the newspaper or check something on your mobile phone.

Outside the studio, I began to get to know Kenneth better. With a bit of prompting from Graham, who was completely unafraid and always at ease with everyone, I asked him if he'd like to come out for dinner with us. I started to realise that he was more or less on his own in a city where he'd experienced a bleak and lonely time before. Although the cultural politics of the city were similar to those he had encountered then, the rest of Berlin had changed from his time and I thought he might appreciate a bit of company and some guidance to the best places to eat. He was very quiet, but great fun, entirely without pomp. It wasn't what I had expected from someone I had admired so much for so long, and who was in a position of authority over me. I soon stopped being scared of him and felt completely at home.

I think he was quite tickled that we'd asked him out. I know what it's like when you're working abroad. Everyone assumes you're busy, but sometimes you're just sitting in a hotel room on your own. He was very warm, and quite nosey. We were in a cab together, when he asked me straight out whether I was going to marry Graham. I was so surprised. I hadn't even thought about it before but the minute he said it, I said no, I'm not. Suddenly, I knew I wasn't. However much I adored Graham, we weren't right for each other. Kenneth was perceptive in that way about people; years later his wife Deborah told me he was always the first to know who was going out with who, or who was having a baby, not because they had told him, but because he watched people so closely.

For all that we were spending time together, I didn't feel that I knew him well enough to start telling him my problems or pouring out my worries about my career. But given his powers of perception, he perhaps sensed something all the same. One day Monica Parker came up to me in the corridor—the place where things always happen in dance companies—and asked whether I would consider returning to England. Kenneth was keen to continue working with me. Initially she wondered whether I would return to Birmingham Royal Ballet. I said that was impossible even if they'd have me, but what about the Royal Ballet?

This was quite audacious on my part. I hadn't ever thought about applying to the Royal—all my thoughts of escape had been directed across the Atlantic, particularly to companies such as American Ballet Theatre and San Francisco Ballet, which I thought might suit me. As our conversations progressed, however, it was clear that Kenneth had decided in his own mind at least that he was going to try to bring me back to London. Unbeknownst to me, he was talking to Deborah over the kitchen table about how talented I was and how much he wanted to continue our association. It's always a good sign when you reach the kitchen table; he clearly had a soft spot for me.

All that, however, was in the future. There was the matter of the *Different Drummer* opening to get through beforehand. When he'd been interviewed in the German press[2] about it, Kenneth had been keen to emphasise that he regarded German audiences as having more respect for serious theatre than British ones, and that consequently he expected a more positive response to the ballet than it had received from some critics in England, where it had been seen in some quarters as being part of his 'same old sex and violence formula',[3] though it had proved popular with audiences.

When the new version opened in Berlin at the end of September 1991, the critics did respond to its expressionistic style and understood its intention. The programme itself was a slightly odd mix of styles, containing Balanchine's *Who Cares?*, van Manen's *Twilight*, and Béjart's *Songs of a Wayfarer*, before *Different Drummer* closed the bill. It was undoubtedly the hit of the evening, with the reviewers praising everyone's outstanding dancing. One writer offered 'borderless admiration' for Martin's and my efforts, which 'takes them to the border of physical possibilities'.[4]

In the *Frankfurter Rundschau*, Roland Lander noted that our gestures expressed 'states of the soul'. 'The duets between Woyzeck and Marie grow increasingly entrancing,' he wrote. 'She claws herself like a cat onto him, intertwines herself lustfully to his body, agilely swings herself onto his shoulders and drives him on like a jockey does a horse.'[5]

Different Drummer is certainly gruelling to dance. The ending, where Marie is pulled around the stage by the agonised Woyzeck, is both brutal and extraordinary. You are flipped over again and again in a long circle before the piece finishes, and you end up bruised all over—either from the partnering, which might leave the occasional hand mark, or just from how your body hits the floor. But the pain is entirely worth it for the impact it had; I got completely lost in the role and felt an exhausted but exhilarated high when it was over. The applause was ecstatic; some papers reported there were some angry whistles, but I didn't hear those. I could just feel the rapture of the response. One of the best things about a first night that's gone well is the atmosphere in the changing rooms afterwards, with everyone sitting round chatting, enjoying the moment. Kenneth came round and was so pleased and happy, so I was pleased because making him proud was all I wanted to do. The completely unexpected bonus of the night was that Monica Mason flew over from London. Having her in the audience and seeing her backstage afterwards really lifted my spirits. To have someone watching me who had known me since the start was a big deal.

Dancing *Different Drummer* represented the highlight of my Berlin career, a shot in the arm to my ambition and determination.

Once Kenneth left, inevitably things felt flatter, and I continued to struggle with the unhappiness that I had felt before his arrival. The difference was that now I had his encouragement and support.

At the end of October, Kenneth suggested that I should come over to London to perform in *Dance for Life*, a gala being organised by the choreographer Gillian Lynne, with Princess Diana in attendance, to raise funds for CRUSAID, a charity (later absorbed into the Terence Higgins Trust) that supported people with HIV. It was a very glamorous affair, with Darcey Bussell, Sylvie Guillem and Alessandra Ferri (over from American Ballet Theatre in New York) among the performers, and Moira Shearer and Derek Jacobi as the comperes. Kenneth knew that Anthony Dowell, director of the Royal Ballet, would be attending the gala and he thought it would be a chance for him to see me dance and understand why he was so keen on me joining the company. He decided to create a new pas de deux to the music of Poulenc for me and Stephen Jefferies, who was with the Royal Ballet at the time. I flew back to London on two weekends and we rehearsed in a little wooden-floored studio on the first floor at Barons Court. It was the first time he had created a ballet on me and I felt totally fulfilled, although the partnering was tricky, with lots of off-balance slides across the stage. Kenneth was happy and enthusiastic.

He'd asked Ian Spurling, a designer he'd worked with on *Elite Syncopations*, to design a costume, and we went to the Opera House for my fitting. He'd designed a simple velvet leotard with attached shorts, but Kenneth didn't like it because it made my legs look short. We had to scramble to find an alternative and somebody rushed off to a ballet shop to buy another black velvet leotard. But it didn't fit. On the day before the performance, it was Monica Parker who saved the situation, buying cotton, elastic and some decorative trimming from Shepherd's Bush market, and rushing round to a friend's house to use her sewing machine. I've kept the result and can't believe how small it is—it looks as if it would hardly fit a doll.

Meanwhile, before the gala on 1 December, Kenneth was building me up in the press. 'I was delighted to get two lovely artists like Leanne and Jeff,' he told *The Times*, saying how good it was for the English public to see me again. 'She's astonishing, very, very talented. She has a lovely line and all that, but she brings out the dramatic qualities in the music too.'[6]

On the night, at Her Majesty's Theatre, Haymarket, I was nervous because there was a lot riding on the evening. Anthony Dowell stood in the wings, watching me as I danced, assessing every aspect of my performance. It was quite nerve-wracking because I knew it was effectively an audition. Kenneth was so lovely; after it was over, he came backstage and explained that he was planning to use the duet as a starting point for a ballet he had in mind, and wanted me to star in.

Sometime later, I went into the Royal Ballet to talk to Anthony properly, and to take class with the company, still effectively auditioning despite all I had achieved. It wasn't exactly a triumph since I fell flat on my face while executing a pirouette. I'd danced on lino floors in studios for so many years, I couldn't adapt to the Royal, which was still rehearsing on wood. I was also disappointed about my meeting with Anthony. He said that Kenneth had assured him I was the best thing since sliced bread, so he would 'give me a go' with the company, but only on a senior soloist's contract. This felt like a slap in the face. By this time, I had been principal in three companies for six years, and to come to the Royal as a senior soloist felt like a step backwards. Kenneth wanted me to consider accepting; he was sure that once I arrived and the company saw how I danced, I would be quickly promoted. I wasn't convinced. I went back to Berlin with my head spinning and my future entirely uncertain. 'Basically, I'm in limbo at the moment and things could take any turn,' I wrote to my ever-loyal Aunty Pat.

My next big project—my last as it turned out—was to dance the lead in Valery Panov's *Cinderella* over Christmas. Panov was a former star of the Mariinsky who in the seventies had been imprisoned and banned from dancing for requesting permission to emigrate to Israel. After his release, he come to Berlin as a guest choreographer, and his version of *Cinderella* was full of acrobatic, virtuosic effects. I rather liked it, though it was taxing technically. The critics, while being nice about my performance and full of admiration for my prince, Martin James, were damning about the ballet as a whole, saying it lacked drama and emotion. 'This rotting Cinderella should be left in the urn of dance history,' one wrote,[7] cruelly. It did nothing to improve my mood.

After another performance of *Different Drummer*, in February, I began to have trouble with a second hernia and I went to London for advice and tests. In the end, someone recommended a specialist in dance physiotherapy who was based in Sydney, so I headed off to Australia to stay in a friend's flat, do strengthening exercises, and decide what I was going to do with the rest of my life. I sent a frosty memo to Peter Schaufuss, enclosing an osteopath's report: 'At this point, I am still unable to say how long my recovery will take and as yet have not begun any class work.' I was beginning to enjoy being a lady of leisure, but I was also still mulling over whether to return to the Royal and accept their contract. Kenneth was on the phone regularly, encouraging me to sign, emphasising that he felt I would do well there.

My letters of the time reveal an absolute swirl of emotions. One minute, I am exercising away with bricks, provided by my physiotherapist to improve my stomach muscles; the next I am describing hating the experience of teaching a ballet class at a local dance school. One day I am working hard to get back into dancing mode, the next I am saying how much I like doing nothing.

Under all the turmoil is my sense that I have hit a wall. I didn't want to return to Berlin, but I didn't want to make another mistake. I was still comparatively young, but I had been in three companies and it takes a couple of years to settle in anywhere. Although I loved dancing, I didn't love dancing enough to be performing roles that didn't interest me, or working for a director who didn't inspire me. I couldn't afford to get it wrong again. The Royal seemed like the most obvious choice: I'd trained in its school, knew its repertory and its style. But it was a huge gamble; if I wasn't going to fit in, I'd might as well stop. I was used to being at the top and though I wasn't worried about rivalry or hard work, I did want to know there was a space for me to fit in and thrive. Kenneth was principal choreographer, but he wasn't part of the administrative hierarchy. He was my champion from the side-lines.

Yet the longer I stopped dancing, the more I began to miss it. The space and clarity of time in Sydney, one of my favourite cities, left me convinced I didn't want to give up yet, and if that was the case the lure of working with Kenneth again was irresistible. Sometimes you have to move sideways to get to the point where you want to be. I accepted the Royal Ballet's offer (with a bit of hard bargaining still to come) and handed in my resignation to Berlin. I was lucky that on the advice of Tom, my former boyfriend, I had negotiated a two-year get out in my German contract, and I could leave without any repercussions. That didn't stop Peter Schaufuss being angry at my decision. He said I was making a terrible mistake and that the Royal would only use me in lively soubrette roles, the very ones I was trying to escape from. I spent the next twenty-one years proving him wrong.

Once my decision was made, I realised I couldn't go on thinking that I could get myself fit without an operation. It was time to get my hernia sorted out once and for all, so I had a second operation, this time at the London Clinic, and spent the summer recuperating. Fortunately, I'd never given up my flat in Glazbury Road, perhaps a sign when I think about it, that I had never fully committed to Berlin. That made the process of returning to London relatively simple, and I slotted happily back into London life, reforging links with friends, and seeing a lot of films and plays as well as furthering my recovery with swimming and physio. At the suggestion of the Royal Ballet physiotherapist who was guiding my progress, David Wall, a former principal dancer with the Royal, started to give me private coaching before I returned to general class. I was finally on the mend, physically and psychologically.

At the end of September 1992, I joined the Royal Ballet, returning to the stage on 26 October in the pas de trois in *Swan Lake*, when Lesley Collier and Bruce Sansom were dancing the leads. 'I feel relieved,' I wrote to Graham, who had also left Berlin to join London City Ballet and was again on tour. 'It's so wonderful to be dancing again and feeling good and I am happy with my life at the moment—a truly welcome change to our past couple of years. But if I hadn't gone to Berlin, I'd probably never have had this opportunity.' As I look back, I feel that even more strongly. If I hadn't been in that room the day Kenneth MacMillan walked through the door, then I wouldn't have had everything that followed. He was my mentor.

CHAPTER 13

'BENJAMIN, YOU'RE GOING TO BE FINE'

I DIDN'T SPEND A HUGE amount of time with Kenneth MacMillan. I don't want to jump on a bandwagon and claim I knew him best, or even that I knew him well. I didn't have the same close relationship with him as a lot of other artists of my generation such as Darcey and Irek. But the impact he had on me was huge: he totally reinvented my life and career.

Being back in London immediately made me feel at home. The Royal Ballet then was still sharing its premises with the school at Barons Court, so it felt familiar and welcoming, like being reunited with an old friend. It also felt a little cramped. After the modern facilities of Berlin, I was at first shocked to discover that everyone, from the lowest corps de ballet member to the most august principal, shared a dressing room, with one for all the men and one for all the women. There was a tiny space assigned to you on a bench where you could put your things, but you had to take anything personal or valuable around the building with you all day. It was primitive but I wouldn't have changed it for the world.

After *Swan Lake*, the next major ballet I worked on at the Royal Ballet was *Mayerling*, Kenneth's three-act ballet inspired by the true events surrounding the Habsburg Crown Prince Rudolf, and his double suicide with his young mistress Mary Vetsera at the Mayerling hunting lodge in 1889. It's a dazzling, ambitious epic, built around a series of pas de deux which Rudolf dances with the women in his life, that explain their relationships and their personalities. The critic Clement Crisp, a friend of MacMillan's, once suggested that he acted as a kind of analyst to his characters, forcing them in these pas de deux to behave in a specific way, showing every aspect of their feelings.[1] In none of them is there any suggestion of conventional romantic love.

For my debut, I was cast as two of the key women at different performances: Mitzi Caspar, the high-class prostitute with whom Rudolf escapes his cares, and Mary, the girl whose obsessive passion for the wracked and drug-addled Crown Prince drives them together to their deaths. I was also covering the role of Countess Marie Larisch, Rudolf's former mistress and confidante, who first introduces him to Mary.

I was so happy to be learning *Mayerling*, probably Kenneth's most dramatic ballet, and excited that Mary would be my first leading role with my new company. To walk into a room where Kenneth, Monica Parker and Monica Mason were sitting at the front and work with them for hours, perfecting my performance, was my idea of ballet heaven. Kenneth was incredibly busy at the time because he was also choreographing a new production of *Carousel* at the National Theatre. He had cast me opposite Zoltán Solymosi, a tall Hungarian principal who had just joined the company. He was powerful and dramatic, a man whose stature, looks and temperament all helped him to portray a distinctive Rudolf, and I think Kenneth thought that my strength of character would work well against him. I barely knew him, but instantly in rehearsal I was flinging myself at him, wrapping my legs around his body. It's often like that in ballet. You meet someone, shake hands, and before you know it, you're grappling with each other in the most intimate of poses.

The fact that we didn't know each other added a layer of mystery to those rehearsals which took place in the fishbowl studio at Barons Court. I loved dancing that role with him, because I could dance so big, throwing myself into the extended poses and leaps that make up their three pas de deux as they hurtle towards tragedy. It was insightful of Kenneth to cast us in this way, to make me look vulnerable but strong. Normally people are chosen to dance together according to size; he paired us for our emotional compatibility. The height difference made the lifts very spectacular and I think we made a powerful impact.

Kenneth was always quietly attentive at the front of the studio; occasionally he would get up and make a correction or show us what he wanted, talking in his characteristic drawl. Some dancers found him sarcastic and difficult, but I never saw that side of him, apart from the day he told off the boy in Berlin. We just seemed to have a good rapport. I lost myself in the intensity of going over those steps again and again, developing the closeness of the pas de deux, stretching my body to make the choreography speak as strongly as I could. I enjoyed learning Mitzi too; she's a character whose flamboyance and personality light up the second act of the ballet, before its final tilt into tragedy.

The last time I spoke to Kenneth was on the day I had a stage call with Zoltán to run through the full ballet. There were three casts making their debuts in the roles of Rudolf and Mary: Irek Mukhamedov and Viviana Durante who were to dance the opening night, Michael Nunn and Gillian Revie, then me and Zoltán. Stephen Jefferies and Lesley Collier, who had danced the roles before, were also performing.

At the rehearsal, Kenneth wandered up to say goodbye, just before I had the chance to dance the third and final act.

'Where are you going?' I asked. He explained he was off to rehearse *Carousel*. 'But I need you here,' I said.

I wasn't looking for approval, just to make absolutely sure that he was happy with how we were dancing. Sometimes if someone tells you one thing, it can change your whole thought process about how you interpret a certain part of the story. I was basically hanging off his every word and wanted to be sure he had the opportunity to say everything he wanted.

'Benjamin, you don't need me, you're going to be fine,' he said, with a smile.

It was the last time I ever saw him. Only days later he died from a heart attack, on 29 October 1992, backstage on the first night of *Mayerling*. He'd felt ill, wandered off, and collapsed in a room where nobody could find him. Even though he'd had a long history of ill-health, his death was an absolute hammer blow. The shocking news was announced to the audience at the curtain call, with the cast onstage. I was at home in bed when a friend from the company called me to let me know; it was kind and brave of her to ring because it was awful news to break. I can't really describe how I felt, desperate for his family, for Deborah and their daughter Charlotte, of course, but also devastated on my own account. I had lost my friend and my supporter.

The following few days passed in a blur of grief; everyone was distraught and shocked. The next performance of *Mayerling* was a matinee, with Michael and Gillian making their debuts, and me as Mitzi Caspar. It was decided that the show, and the entire run, would go on as the best tribute to Kenneth there could be. Deborah and Charlotte were in the audience and Deborah bravely came backstage beforehand to assure us that Kenneth would have wanted us to perform. Ninette de Valois took her seat in her usual box by the stage. I can't imagine how it must have been for the people who knew him best and loved him most. I tried to give my performance my best shot: I wanted to do well for him, to thank him, to show that I would always try to keep his work alive.

On 21 November, Zoltán and I danced together as Rudolf and Mary, an extraordinary, searing evening. I was finally there, where Kenneth had wanted me to be, but without him in the audience it was bittersweet. The critics, who watched multiple casts, compared and contrasted our interpretations. In *The Times*, John Percival said that I gave my dancing 'something of the madness with which Lynn Seymour originally filled the role',[2] which felt like a huge compliment. The *Evening Standard* described my pas de deux with Zoltan as 'sexually steamy, a reckless teenage adventuress with a raging bull'.[3] Two years later, when we danced the same roles in New York, Anna Kisselgoff in the *New York Times* noticed our 'electrifying rapport', describing our first duet as 'sensational', 'an image of thrill-seekers locked in an erotic embrace from which each could barely be torn away'.[4]

Mary became the part with which I was most associated in some ways. I danced *Mayerling* a lot down the years; it was the final ballet that I performed at the Royal Ballet at Covent Garden before I retired. When I danced it, and when I coach it, my mind always goes back to those rehearsals in Barons Court with Kenneth. One thing I learnt from him was that as long as you keep the integrity of the steps—and it's incredibly important that these don't get changed by a process of half-understood whispers—then it is possible for a dancer to make slightly different choices, so that he or she looks the best they can when delivering the choreography and, above all, the story. For example, one ballerina might be so flexible that she can bend her back until she hits her partner's bottom where another is less supple and will need to find another but equally expressive route through the movement.

The manner in which I played Mary altered down the years and changed according to who was playing Rudolf. I never had an absolutely set view of the character: different partners would bring out different colours and reactions in my interpretation. Every time I revisited the role, I would find something new. I danced it in many performances over two separate seasons opposite Carlos Acosta, once when he made his debut as Rudolf in 2007 and then again in 2013. Carlos is a partner in whose hands you always feel confident, but the great thing about dancing with him in *Mayerling* was that, as two mature artists, we could develop and explore the roles together. The characters you create are all in the details.

Mary only has five scenes in which to make an impact. In the first scene, she is introduced to Rudolf as an innocent girl, but she glances back at him as she runs off, which to me means she is interested in him and wants to catch his attention. Later, when she is older, she is brought to him by his mistress Countess Larisch. From the moment she steps out from her carriage, she is alluring—she doesn't go to him, she makes him come to her. She has all the instincts of seduction. As she is standing still, waiting for him to move towards her, I would be thinking about how she takes charge of the situation. She's complex; she wants to be a challenge.

The next time we see her is in her own home, when she is dreaming about Rudolf, looking at his photograph, and hiding her feelings from her mother. When Larisch arrives again, Mary knows why she is there: she's probably been eavesdropping on her mother and her friend talking about her future and heard them plotting to introduce her to Rudolf. I was like that as a girl. If I heard a chat starting up, I'd sit at the top of the stairs, listening to what was going on. Afterwards, when Larisch takes Mary to Rudolf's bedroom, she walks in looking demure in a coat, then she rips it off to show that she's basically got nothing on except a see-through black negligee. It's the most thrilling of entrances. She is wise and aware enough to know that sexual fantasy will enhance Rudolf's senses. She understands what she's up to and how to get his interest; he's addled with drugs, booze, illness and women, but she just comes in, bold as anything, and from the moment she takes that coat off, she has all the power. At the end of their passionate, frightening, warped pas de deux, she stands behind him as he crumples to the floor, lifts his head for a final kiss and folds herself into his embrace as the curtain closes at the end of Act Two.

In their final scene together, the climax of the ballet, I think she knew they were destined to reach this point and she is happy to go to her death with him. You can play it different ways, but that's how I've always seen it. There's a moment before their last pas de deux where she just sits watching him, as he dances his final, tortured solo. I feel she is weighing up the situation and the tie between them. At the end of their agonised duet, they kiss, and then you hear the drum beat. Once that sound starts in the orchestra, like a heartbeat, that's the big moment. After it begins, they reach for the gun that they will use to kill themselves. I liked to reach for that gun first, I had decided. If my partner wanted to reach for it as well, he could, but I had made the choice. Rudolf needs to get out of his misery, and Mary needs to fulfil her dream. She wants to go to that place. She's all in. She's not going to leave him, in life or in death.

My thought process as Mary wasn't ever fixed in stone, though. I was always an instinctive dancer. I might spontaneously change my decision about how I was going to react because of the moment onstage. That's why I liked rehearsing so much, because in every rehearsal I would dig away to find something more with the character. Or maybe take something away if I thought it was too much. All the practice that you put in creates space for invention and freedom.

Now when I am coaching this, I am quite adamant that even in rehearsal, dancers don't get used to doing the same things in the same way every day. I expect them to challenge themselves and not get stuck in a pattern, not to be predictable. You can hold a gun, maintain a position, go towards your man, in many ways. You still have the same story in your head but alter your performance. If a dancer tries different things, as a coach, you can say what Kenneth used to say to me: 'Yeah, loved that.' It can be something so small. They might just have decided to look up at their partner at a particular moment, or gone behind instead of in front of a chair, or crawled in a different way in the final pas deux. Those tiny changes will give the dancer their unique interpretation.

What I love about MacMillan's work is how rich and vibrant it is for dancers as interpreters, giving them scope to reveal their individuality while still being faithful to his choreography. As a coach, it's fabulous to explore the ways that contrasting dancers such as the Royal Ballet's

Sarah Lamb, Laura Morera, and Akane Takada can bring the most out of themselves. They all have such different physicality, and I can help them break through their own boundaries. I don't want to say this is what I did, so you should do the same. Instead, I offer them some ideas or explain what I was thinking at a given point. I love it when someone stands up and says that they weren't thinking that at all. It's my favourite thing when someone comes up with something I've never heard said before. When you've danced a role for many years, you think you've heard it all, and then a new dancer takes on the part for the first time and comes up with an entirely new angle. That's what's so refreshing and that's what keeps these ballets alive.

It's essential that ballet develops in this way, but I am there to be a policeman about the choreography, so it doesn't get lost. The story is within those steps and their little intricacies. There are some incredibly difficult passages in MacMillan's works and it's about honouring them, not cutting things out so you can get on with telling the story, but telling the story through those steps. For example, Mary's solo of joy after Larisch reads the cards and predicts her future with Rudolf, is full of fast footwork. MacMillan created it at that speed to reveal her high-spirited emotion. If it's done too slowly it doesn't work. I am not in favour of letting dancers slow the music at that point just because it's easier. You want to keep her excitement.

Sometimes character is difficult to locate. When I first danced *Manon* at the Royal Ballet in 1995, Monica Parker rang me at home to say that I hadn't found the personality of a heroine who is both innocent and venal, on the make and yet curiously giving. 'You just don't get her,' she told me, honestly. It was like the call you get from the headmaster to tell you that your child isn't behaving well and is falling below required standards. I felt slightly humiliated, but it really made me sit up and think. She was right: I was worrying so much about the technique that I didn't feel free enough to develop the role. It was fine, but fine wasn't good enough in my view. The flavours had failed to come out in my interpretation. It took me some time to locate her, though by the last time I danced the ballet in 2011, I was happy that I had. Not that you ever feel you've found out everything about any ballet; I've always gone home after a performance to a sleepless night, thinking of all the things I did wrong, and all the alternative choices I could have made. That's one reason you keep dancing—there's always something new to discover.

By the end of my career, because I knew the steps of Kenneth's work so well, I could put the technique of the ballet together more quickly and concentrate entirely on building layers of interpretation. I think that's what happened when critics said I was dancing better than ever at the end of my career, when I was forty-nine, than at my physical prime. Obviously at some levels that's not true. I wasn't technically better, but I had found that special place where you can start concentrating on interpreting the role. It was a delicious moment.

But that was all further down the road. In 1993, when Kenneth died, I was simply bereft. I had lost my mentor, and I really didn't know which way my career would go. The Royal Ballet was already brim-full of wonderful ballerinas, and Anthony Dowell had a line-up of stars: Sylvie Guillem, Darcey Bussell and Viviana Durante. I just put my head down, took my place in the queue and began to struggle to get out of the shadows.

CHAPTER 14

WORK, WORK, WORK

I WASN'T UNHAPPY IN MY early years with the Royal Ballet. I was back in London, dancing with a company that I had always longed to belong to. I was in the right place. But I knew that its director, Anthony Dowell, hadn't really wanted me there; not surprisingly, initially I wasn't his first choice for anything. I didn't have someone who was unequivocally on my side anymore, as I knew Kenneth had been. Untethered would probably be the best word to describe how I felt. I didn't have a regular partner, or a specific repertory, or a particular period that people associated me with. I was an outsider both by virtue of nationality and because I had only just arrived. I was very reliable, I could fit into any programme, learn any ballet, dance all the major roles and was always in demand. But I felt I didn't fully belong.

It didn't help that I had joined at what became one of the most perilous times in the Royal Ballet's history. The nineties was a decade when the Royal Opera House struggled with financial difficulties and closed for rebuilding. Relationships between the management and board, between the opera administration and the ballet company, were not easy. As a result enormous pressure was put on Anthony Dowell to increase revenue and make savings in the ballet company. Sometimes he was even asked to change programmes at the last minute. In his history of Covent Garden, Norman Lebrecht quotes him as saying, 'The rehearsal time got very tight and we only just got things together.'[1]

In their last five seasons in the Opera House before closure, the Royal Ballet were allowed only half as many productions as the opera, and they were expected to make money.[2] Apart from the personal strain Anthony must have felt as he struggled for the company's survival, the demands meant that there were intense expectations surrounding every production and very few new commissions. Given all this, it's no wonder my own troubles didn't amount to much more than a hill of beans, but I felt I was at the peak of my powers and wanted to be given the encouragement to fly.

When I look back on 1993, however, it was a pretty good year. It began with my debut in *The Dream*, with 21-year-old Tetsuya Kumakawa as Oberon. He was a dazzling rising star, who had joined the Royal Ballet in 1989, and became the youngest soloist in its history before being promoted to principal in 1993. I liked dancing with him, and I enjoyed the quicksilver challenges of Titania. John Percival, in *The Times*, enjoyed it too, saying Shakespeare's fairy had 'suddenly acquired a new capriciousness, humour and sexiness.'[3] Percival had already picked me as one of his stars for the year ahead. 'With so many young women already competing for leading roles in the Royal Ballet it might seem rash of Leanne Benjamin to risk moving there from Berlin Ballet, where she was already a principal dancer. But the small, vivid Australian seems to thrive on this. She has a special gift as a dance actress.'[4]

Those skills were called into full play when I made my next debut in MacMillan's *The Judas Tree*, his final ballet and one of his most controversial. It meant a lot to me. When it was revived again in 1997,

I both danced and filmed the ballet with Irek Mukhamedov, who created the leading role. I later filmed it as a live performance at the Royal Opera House in 2010 with Carlos Acosta. But this was my first go at it. It's a difficult, dark ballet about betrayal, at once naturalistic and purely metaphorical, where a single woman appears under a veil on a modern building site—in Jock McFadyen's designs you can see Canary Wharf in the background—and is gang-raped after the Foreman (a Judas figure) turns his men against her. There's also a Jesus figure who tries to protect her and is lynched by the gang on the Foreman's word. The Foreman then hangs himself, but the woman returns: she seems an unbreakable force. Kenneth's only clue to how to interpret the work is a quote from the Sufi writer Kahlil Gibran: 'As a single leaf turns not yellow but with the silent knowledge of the whole tree, so the wrongdoer cannot do wrong without the hidden will of you all.'

It has always been a ballet that shocked people. I feel that the woman, both provocative and brutally abused, is an eternal figure: both Mary and Mary Magdalene. Although harrowing, it's extremely interesting to dance, as you try to find the nuance of different moments. I felt confident delving into its different aspects—the way the woman is suggestive when she first arrives, the way she tries to provoke a situation without understanding the consequences. It exposes human behaviour, as the men rev themselves up, egging each other on, so the woman is trapped.

It's a ballet that provokes discussion, which is what dance should be able to do. I remember one critic asking me what a little movement of the hands meant, and I hadn't really thought about it, but then I realised the character makes that gesture when she is Mary, good and covered in a veil, as opposed to Mary Magdalene, the flirty, suggestive woman. There is such physicality and strangeness in the solos that Kenneth created, the way they move from a turned in to a turned-out position. Because I didn't work with him on the ballet, I had to make my own understanding of it, but Monica Parker was a brilliant coach and later when I danced it with Irek, I felt I looked into it more and more deeply.

On that first revival, in January 1993, Zoltán and I were second cast to Irek and Viviana Durante, Clement Crisp came to review the performance and recorded the impact I made: 'The revelation was Leanne Benjamin's appearance as the woman, a characterisation of extraordinary sexual and technical pungency. Each pose and provocative movement, the shifts between belligerent sluttishness and invulnerable dignity were superbly understood and stated: the ballet seemed to be about the woman as victim—and ultimate victor—rather than about betrayal. It was a beautiful and piercingly credible impersonation.'[5]

Because Crisp had been one of Kenneth's friends, it was a review that meant a lot to me. I felt I was honouring him as I danced. On the same bill I also danced with Tetsuya in Balanchine's *Symphony in C*, trying to soar just as high as he did, relishing the big, bravura style.

In April, I danced *Gloria* for the first time. This short ballet, inspired by Vera Brittain's *Testament of Youth*, would definitely be in contention as my favourite piece by Kenneth, alongside *The Song of the Earth* and *Requiem*. I never know which I love best, it's like someone putting out all your favourite meals and asking which is your first choice. What I will say is that *Gloria*, which is Kenneth's tribute to the fallen of the First World War and to his own father, who had been gassed in the trenches and suffered the repercussions for the rest of his life, has a unique atmosphere. In Andy Klunder's designs, the men are dressed like soldiers whose uniforms and flesh has been torn off, the women are in shimmering silver-grey all-in-ones, with coiled earmuffs. You feel other-worldly.

My character was a ghost from the far-off past, in mourning for all the loss and sorrow that has gone before. You start underneath the stage, and when the orchestra begins you walk up with your partner, as if emerging from the trenches, onto a ramp of painted yellow earth. The music, which is Poulenc's Gloria in G, just fills you; with its soaring vocal lines, it's sublime to dance to. There was an odd moment when we used to perform in the old Opera House, before renovation, where you had to run off one side, meet a stage manager holding a torch and then run under the stage and up the other side, to make an entrance from the opposite wings. It took you out of character, and is much better now when you can just run around the back of the stage and keep yourself wrapped in that beautiful, sorrowful mood.

I was fortunate because my partner in the central pas de deux was often Christopher Saunders, who I knew from the Royal Ballet School, where we were in the same year. He was a rock through all the complexities of the partnering. It was a pas de deux that never went wrong, unlike my other memorable moment with Chris onstage when I was dancing Aurora and he was one of the four suitors in the Rose Adage. What's meant to happen is that Aurora goes up to each of them, and does an unsupported arabesque penché, leaning forward. What actually happened on that occasion was that as I tipped down, I overbalanced and flung my arm out to stop the wobble. My hand landed on his head—and nearly knocked his wig off. From that point onwards, he made sure to glue it on very firmly.

Another first came that April when the Royal Ballet mounted Mikhail Baryshnikov's production of *Don Quixote*, a version not much-loved by critics but terrific to perform. I was flirty, feisty Kitri, and I was dancing opposite the Basilio of José Carreño, a Cuban dancer who had just joined the Royal from ENB. He was experienced, explosive and sensational to dance with. 'It's just given me the lift I needed—like a gift from God,' I wrote to Aunty Pat. Our dancing wasn't always perfect, but we suited one another's style and sense of fun. 'There was some needling daredevilry between them,' wrote Judith Mackrell in the *Guardian*, after we made our debut on 26 April. 'It was worth the odd miscalculation of timing to see dancers so willingly taking liberties with the possible and the safe.'[6]

On 8 May, Baryshnikov came to watch our matinee, such a red-letter day that I wrote it in the diary I wasn't really keeping at the time. He came backstage afterwards to the square dressing room just off the stage, adjoining Margot Fonteyn's old room. It was tiny and tatty with enough room for a sink in one corner, a mirror surrounded by spotlights, and a rail of clothes down the back, which meant that people coming in always had to push by the chairs ranged along the shelf in front of the mirror. I loved that room—no bigger than a large table—because you walked out of it almost straight onto the stage. The facilities in the new Opera House are much better but the changing rooms are further away; they don't have that old intimacy, that sense of being able to propel yourself into another world. On the day Baryshnikov came round, like a real-life Prince Charming, I was wrapped in a towel and taking my make-up off in the cramped space. It was both terrifying and fantastic to meet an idol in the flesh; he was the great male dancer of my growing-up. He told me I was a very strong dancer, a word that I then analysed endlessly. Did he mean strong in a good way or that strength overpowered my communication? I was always capable of torturing myself about a performance.

Around this time, I made a mistake that I have always regretted. Anthony chose a small group of us to go to Frankfurt to do a workshop with the choreographer William Forsythe, who was due to make a new ballet for the Royal. The ballet never actually came to pass, but that's another story. As it was, I was sent with Michael Nunn, William Trevitt and Deborah Bull to explore possibilities with him. I feel so shocked and ashamed of myself when I look back, because I did exactly what Kenneth had complained to that boy about in Berlin. I didn't concentrate hard enough or immerse myself fully in what we were doing. I had my debut as Odette/Odile in the Royal Ballet's *Swan Lake* coming up, and when there was a break, I'd start practising balances. I can't imagine how irritating that must have been. Here I was, with one of the world's most dynamic and experimental choreographers, the creative heir to the great classical tradition, and I wasn't there for him. As a result, quite rightly, I wasn't cast in the proposed new work—and though in the end the ballet didn't happen, I didn't dance in *Steptext*, the ballet he revived instead. It was devastating and such a lesson.

I learnt something else. Deborah was quite confident with Forsythe in the studio; she realised what an opportunity it was to be working with someone like him, just as I had when Kenneth arrived in Berlin. Perhaps because I was in awe of Forsythe, I backed off, got nervous, kept myself to myself, and let the opportunity slip. I wasn't mature enough to realise how valuable these kinds of moments are, or to recognise that if you miss them, they are gone for good.

I met him some years later when he came to the Opera House. By then I was brave enough to go up to him and apologise for my stupidity. We had a good chat and it stopped playing on my mind as much. The irony of it all was that I was perfectly suited to dancing his work and loved the physical challenge of it. Although I missed that moment, I did dance in three of his works. I danced one performance of *Herman Schmerman* in November, and later, both *In the Middle, Somewhat Elevated*, and *The Vertiginous Thrill of Exactitude*, an exciting roller-coaster of a ballet, with stunning sculptural costumes which, when I danced it, were made of velvet interlined with cardboard, making them so heavy I could barely move. They have since been adapted to make them lighter for today's dancers, which must be a relief because the scintillating choreography is a challenge in itself.

Not creating a ballet with Forsythe was such a lost chance, because he is one of those choreographers who, through the sheer force of his spirit and his personality, can lift dancers to new levels. After I retired, I watched him at work in Canada, preparing an evening of his works for the National Ballet of Canada, and you could see the effect of his inspiration on the room. The improvement in technique and delivery was huge. My own regret at missing out on that experience is one reason I always encourage dancers to seize every opportunity to learn from the greats, to overcome their shyness and show their own personalities in order to make the most of every second they are together. I couldn't quite be myself with people I admired in those days, and I wish I'd been more relaxed and more mature.

The *Swan Lake*, when it came, went well. I was dancing opposite Adam Cooper, another wonderfully calm and generous partner. He was replacing José Carreño, who was injured, but his security and likeability made it as smooth as it could be. Of all the big classical ballets, *Swan Lake* is the most interesting for me because it has such contrasts in it for a ballerina, between the white and the black swan, the good girl and the wicked party animal. Edward Thorpe, reporting on my debut in the *London Evening Standard*, noticed what I was up to: 'Rarely does one see the two parts so carefully and intelligently thought through or projected with such clarity and feeling.'[7]

I liked the challenge of finding two different people within the three acts, registering Odette's despair at the spell within which she is trapped, and the black swan Odile's beguiling attempt to seduce, though I found Odile the more enjoyable role to dance. Her third act may be the one that is full of what people regard as some of the most technically challenging steps, including her famous thirty-two fouettés, turning fiercely on the spot, but I always found Odette's white act more tiring, because it requires such control. It took me a while to get into the groove of a three-act ballet, to find the perfect pacing and the stamina you need to get through it. With *Swan Lake*, Odette doesn't appear until the second scene; there is a big party for Siegfried, and a lot of celebratory dancing, which you have to listen to backstage before you make your first entrance. The music builds up the tension to your appearance and there's a psychological fear and anticipation that starts to grow.

Even now, when I am in a shop or out and about, and I hear the entrance music for Aurora in *The Sleeping Beauty* or Odette in *Swan Lake*, I still feel that same sense of trepidation about what is going to happen and how am I going to perform. There are so many things that race through your mind, and at the same time you are trying to calm yourself down. If you are too uptight, you're not going to make a great entrance, and whereas Aurora has to bound onto the stage, full of lightness and joy, Odette has to fly on and then stand very still. She moves towards Siegfried with a series of controlled balances. You can usually tell how someone is feeling with that first pose on pointe; dancers often stumble.

Swan Lake also brings back happy memories though, because twice in my career I was made a principal after performing it. At the end of my debut on 13 May, behind the curtain, completely unexpectedly Anthony Dowell announced my promotion. It was months after I had joined, just as Kenneth had predicted. I almost felt him watching over me.

It was a busy summer. In June, I went on my first foreign tour with the Royal. We took *Mayerling* to the Théâtre des Champs Elysées in Paris, and I found myself dancing with Stephen Jefferies, who had worked with MacMillan when he created the role. He had been coaxed out of semi-retirement at a day's notice to fill in because Irek Mukhamedov and Zoltán Solymosi were both injured. Something had gone wrong with the advertising for the performances, which were sparsely attended. I found myself taking a curtain call after a Saturday matinee and seeing the first two rows full of nuns, who had been given complimentary tickets. They didn't entirely warm to the sex and violence they'd just witnessed, and applause was very restrained.

I danced Mary opposite Stephen again in Istanbul, which I mainly remember because I bought a carpet in the Grand Bazaar that I still have today. There were so many cockroaches in our dressing rooms at the Atatürk Cultural Centre that the company called in the exterminators. That caused even more cockroaches to be released—when we returned to our changing room at the interval, they were running all over the place. Palermo, Turin, and Frankfurt, our other destinations, were much less dramatic.

In September Madonna married her university sweetheart Lawrence in Devon, which prompted a big family reunion. Aunty Pat came over from Rockhampton, the last time she made the trip to England. In her youth in the 1950s, she had been a great traveller, exploring the world at a time when you had to go to the US Consulate in Canberra to get a visa if you wanted to visit the States.

Rehearsing *Different Drummer* in Berlin with Kenneth MacMillan, sadly my only picture with him.
Photo: Kranichphoto, Photographer Unknown

Performing *Swan Lake* (Black Swan) at Covent Garden.
Photo: Leslie E. Spatt

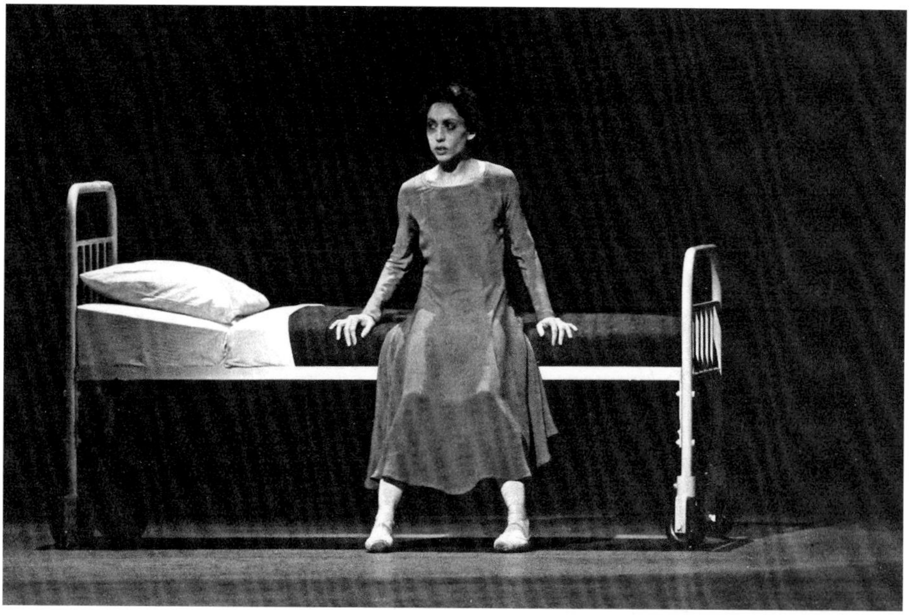

top: Performing Kenneth MacMillan's *Anastasia* Act 3 at The Royal Opera House, Covent Garden.
Photo: Leslie E. Spatt

bottom: My first creation as Grete in David Bintley's *Metamorphosis* at Sadler's Wells Theatre.
Photo: Leslie E. Spatt

top: Guest performing with The Australian Ballet in Frederick Ashton's *La Fille mal gardée* at the State Theatre Melbourne for their bicentennial gala. *Photographer Unknown*

middle: Performing the Young Sister in Kenneth MacMillan's *Las Hermanas* with SWRB. *Photo: Leslie E. Spatt*

bottom: Performing the mad scene in *Giselle* at Covent Garden, age eighteen. *Photo: Leslie E. Spatt*

top: Performing Frederick Ashton's *Romeo and Juliet* with Patrick Armand at Festival Hall in London with English National Ballet.
Photo: Catherine Ashmore

middle: In the second act of *Giselle* with Jonathan Cope: school performance day!
Photo: Leslie E. Spatt

bottom: Lynn Seymour coached me for this performance of Kenneth MacMillan's *The Invitation* at The Royal Ballet.
Photo: Leslie E. Spatt

top: Secret rehearsal for *Romeo and Juliet* with Frederick Ashton and Peter Schaufuss at Festival Ballet studios, Jay Mews.
Photo: Richard Farley

bottom: Rehearsing at Barons Court studios with Sarah Wildor and Coach, Lynn Seymour.
Photo: Sue Adler / ArenaPAL

top left: Rehearsing the adage for my school performance of *Giselle*.
Photo: Royal Ballet School / ArenaPAL, Photographer: Stefano Massimo

top right: Rehearsing at Barons Court with Jonathan Cope for our school performance of Giselle.
Photo: Royal Ballet School / ArenaPAL, Photographer: Stefano Massimo

bottom: Rehearsing Kenneth MacMillan's *Different Drummer* at the Deutsche Oper Ballet studios with Tomas Karlborg.
Photo: Kranichphoto, Photographer Unknown

top: Backstage glamour! Sarah Rendall and I about to perform *Giselle* with the Deutsche Oper, Berlin, 1991.
Photo: Personal Archive

middle: In my changing room at the Royal Opera House post-performance with boyfriend, Graham Rowe.
Photo: Personal Archive

bottom left: Backstage at the old Royal Opera House with my mum and longtime dresser, Elizabeth 'Lizzie' Foyster.
Photo: Personal Archive

bottom right: Celebrating after a performance of *Swan Lake*, a ballet that got me promoted to principal twice in my career.
Photo: Personal Archive

top: Celebrating with Russell Maliphant after being promoted to principal with SWRB following my debut performance in *Swan Lake* at The Big Top in the Isle of Wight, 1987.
Photo: Personal Archive

middle: Chatting to David Bintley in the early years of touring with SWRB.
Photo: Personal Archive

bottom: Signing autographs at the Tokyo Festival in 1985.
Photo: Personal Archive

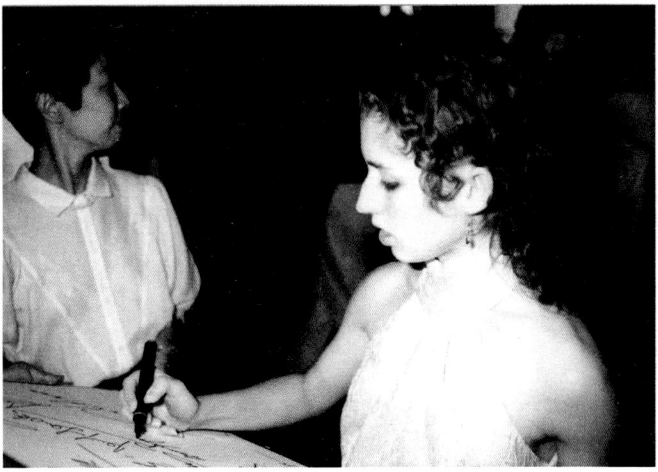

top: On tour in America with SWRB.
Photo: Personal Archive

bottom: Exhausted waiting for a flight with Petter Jacobsson and Russell Maliphant while touring with SWRB.
Photo: Personal Archive

top: A trip to Jaipur, India with Peter Wright and SWRB friends.
Photo: Personal Archive

bottom: The good old days of SWRB on tour in Israel.
Photo: Personal Archive

top: Enjoying the beach at summer school in Monte Carlo, 1981.
Photo: Personal Archive

bottom: In my happy place at Lammermoor Beach near Rockhampton.
Photo: Personal Archive

top: If not in pointe shoes, often in a hard hat doing up a property. Here with Mum at Chepstow Place, 1999.
Photo: Personal Archive

bottom: Painting my first apartment in Glazbury Road, 1987.
Photo: Personal Archive

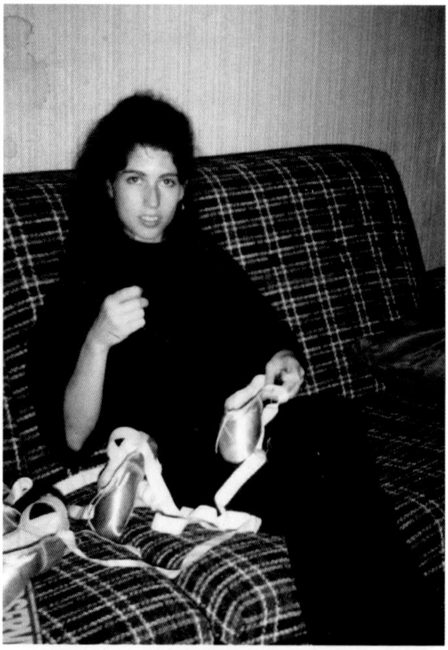

top left: Hanging out in my Berlin apartment, 1990.
Photo: Personal Archive

top right: At digs on tour with SWRB, forever sewing pointe shoes.
Photo: Personal Archive

bottom: With my parents after a performance of *Manon* in Sydney.
Photo: Personal Archive

top: Celebrating my birthday back home in Rocky with Maureen Kerr, Mum, Dad and Aunty Pat (left to right).
Photo: Personal Archive

middle: The whole family together in Sydney in the nineties.
Photo: Personal Archive

bottom: Surprise visit home to see Mum and Dad in Agnes Street.
Photo: Personal Archive

top: Dad playing tourist while visiting me in Berlin. *Photo: Personal Archive*

bottom: Hanging out with Dad in Hyde Park, London. *Photo: Personal Archive*

She'd popped over to support me a lot early in my career, but now she was concentrating her activities and her interests closer to home, with the church choir and the races her main contrasting activities. She was never very active physically. In all our time at the beach together, we never saw her in a swimming costume or anywhere near the water. After a hip operation, her idea of exercise became a walk around the coffee table in the lounge of her flat.

Back in the Opera House for the autumn season, the company revived *Different Drummer* in November, with Jonathan Cope and I chosen as second cast to Irek and Viviana. It was fabulous dancing with Jonathan; he was greatly in demand as a partner to Sylvie Guillem and Darcey Bussell, so it was quite rare we danced together. The reviews were nice too. *The Times* pointed out that the revival had come about because Kenneth had reworked the role around me in Berlin. 'So her first London appearance ought to have been a revelation. It was. The secret of her success in dramatic roles … is that she avoids exaggeration … she shows you a woman responding with an often sad—but sometimes unexpectedly cheerful—openness to whatever life has in store for her. Beyond that she has a gift for comprehending MacMillan's movement imagery and brings out its meaning with special clarity and emphasis.'[8]

When I read a review like that, I felt proud that what I was trying to do had been noticed by a critic. As dancers, we have complicated feelings about reviews. You always hope that you get a positive write-up—it boosts your confidence and your profile. But then if someone says something negative, it can be unbelievably hurtful. It's very difficult reading a terrible review, and I've had a lot in my career. It's also unsettling if you are dancing a leading role and not mentioned at all, because then you tend to think that they didn't like your performance but are just being kind.

I hate reviews that make personal comments, like the one that marked my debut in the Royal Ballet's production of *Giselle* in 1995 by saying that I was 'more Joan Crawford than Cindy Crawford'.[9]

A lot of what the critic went on to write was broadly favourable, but it was hard to climb over that complaint about my looks. I got bored, too, towards the end of my career, when everyone felt the need to mention my age; if I was dancing well, it didn't seem particularly relevant whether I was twenty-nine or forty-nine. On the other hand, I am always interested when someone observes something about me or makes some relevant comment about technique or characterisation. The best reviews, in my view, are—like the best teachers—open-minded. Everyone has favourites, but when a critic allows favouritism to colour what they write and fails to notice the contribution of someone who might not be their preferred pick, that can't be right. I think a critic must be honest but clear-eyed. Their comments shouldn't feel personal. But I do always read them, even if they are.

Christmas brought a run of Nutcrackers, and a couple of galas, including one organised by Wayne Sleep and one where Placido Domingo conducted the 1812 overture. In Australia, my father passed his pilot's licence at the age of sixty-five, which was the cause of much celebration and a letter from him in the guise of Flight Officer B Benjamin. Mum was also busy building Colonial Cottage Antiques into an ever more thriving business. Little brother Tony wasn't so little anymore since he was six feet, one inch tall, in the middle of a business degree at Queensland University of Technology in Brisbane, and on his way to his career as a property developer. Madonna, Fiona and I were all making our way in London and Fiona had met her soon-to-be husband David Malek, a star of musical theatre. We were all as close as ever and my family was brilliant at reminding me there was a world outside the Opera House, where I was so wrapped up in making my way.

In January 1994, I marked another MacMillan milestone, taking on the role of Juliet with Stuart Cassidy as my Romeo. To mark the occasion, Debra Craine interviewed me in *The Times*. 'Funny thing about rising stars,' she wrote. 'Scratch the surface a little and you find they've been hard at work for years.'[10] Never was a truer word spoken. Later in the interview, I talked about how glamorous it was dancing at the Opera House and how frustrated I was at not having a regular partner. 'It's definitely annoying,' I said, in a theme that was to reverberate over the next few years. Juliet was a milestone for me. When I was a student, I'd watched from the upper slips as Alessandra Ferri danced the role, in an interpretation that became one of the most celebrated ever, so to make my own story for the ballet felt like a test. Edward Thorpe suggested my performance, though beautifully danced, needed toning down. Which is probably fair. Less is sometimes more.

There were twenty performances of *Romeo and Juliet* between October 1993 and August 1994, so a lot of people got a chance to reveal their take on the roles. Because it was so popular, it was often in the repertory as the Royal Opera House began to try to resolve its financial crisis. It was the need for a generous dollop of funding from American supporters, that took the company to America in April, for a five-week tour through Washington, Florida, Texas, California and New York. This included the premiere of Anthony Dowell's new production of *The Sleeping Beauty* at the Kennedy Center in Washington DC, in front of President Bill Clinton, Hillary Clinton, and Princess Margaret. It was a weird and stressful time for the company, and the grandeur of the premiere was in sharp contrast to the incredible tension of the rehearsals that preceded it. I was dancing the Bluebird pas de deux, with fellow Aussie Errol Pickford; Darcey was Aurora, with Zoltán as her Prince. The dress rehearsal was a disaster; the scenery and costumes weren't ready when they arrived,[11] and there was a piano in the pit where the orchestra should have been. Darcey was struggling with a back injury but she was determined to go on. She was the great English ballerina of her generation, the incarnation of an English rose, and the company's reputation that night was resting heavily on her. We were sharing a dressing room and I could see she wasn't happy, but she is such a trouper. I really admired her bravery. She didn't complain, just got on with the job and was first class.

Despite all the advance anxiety, that night was incredible. I was always impressed by President Clinton and it was amazing to be in the same room as him for a photograph and at the post-performance party. Given that he was embroiled in allegations of misconduct at the time, he was amazingly relaxed. I couldn't believe how big he seemed. Obviously, he is a tall man and I am a short woman, but it was more than that. He was warm and friendly, easy in his own skin, oozing charisma. When I met him, I understood what people mean when they talk about allure. He exuded a confidence that made you want to be around him. It was a great evening.

When the Royal Ballet returned to New York in July for a season at the Metropolitan Opera House, I performed Aurora with José Carreño and the critic Clive Barnes was in the audience to record that I had 'the makings of a real Aurora'.[12] I was very nervous, though, and it showed. What everyone remembers about that particular production were Maria Björnsen's designs, with huge pillars and slanting perspectives. As Aurora, you had to make your entrance down a perilously steep staircase; it's bad enough coming on and having to dance the Rose Adage as your first big number, but to get down those stairs to do so was a nightmare. I was convinced I would fall. Each tread was about the size of my foot, there was no handrail, and you couldn't see anything over your tutu. The need to worry about the scenery as well as the challenge of a three-act ballet is stressful, and however regularly I danced it over the years, the staircase remained daunting, sucking the pleasure out of that wonderful opening scene.

It was a happy time, however, with a repertory that also included *Mayerling* and *The Judas Tree*. Escaping our troubles at home, the company thrived in New York and I thrived too in repertory that suited me. 'Taken as a whole, it was a lovely, exciting season,' wrote Clive Barnes.[13] I could only agree. That time in New York is ingrained in my heart, though, not because of any dancing achievements but because it was the moment I met the man who would eventually become my husband—and told him to get lost.

CHAPTER 15

'YOU WERE ABLE TO LET THE CHOREOGRAPHY SPEAK'

TOBIAS ROUND IS THE SON of the photographer Roy Round and the British ballerina Georgina Parkinson, who had been a close friend of Kenneth MacMillan and was, by the time I met her, working at American Ballet Theatre as ballet mistress. Georgina was a glamorous figure, staggeringly beautiful, with a slightly terrifying reputation, since she was both revered and very witty. She'd been a principal at the Royal Ballet—she was the first Rosaline in *Romeo and Juliet*—and was one of Kenneth's closest confidantes. Although I didn't know her, I certainly knew of her, and knew that she was in New York initially at the request of Baryshnikov, whom she coached for the film *The Turning Point*. Roy Round was equally famous within the ballet and fashion worlds; a photographer who had been close to Fonteyn, had photographed Nureyev's first performance of *Le Corsaire*, and had subsequently documented a golden age of dance in both Britain and the US, in addition to fashion work for magazines such as *Vanity Fair*. His photograph of Nureyev's first stage call for *Marguerite and Armand* still has pride of place on my wall.

They lived in a loft on West 15th street which doubled as a studio. This was where I was sent in the spring to do a shoot for *Dance Magazine*, in my costume for *The Judas Tree*. Georgina was sitting in the kitchen smoking, her back ramrod straight. I'd heard so much about her sense of humour and her stories delivered in her deep drawl and felt so nervous that I'd scampered through the kitchen, in search of a drink of water, with only a quick hello. Tobias was there too, hanging around, helping his dad with the shoot. I didn't realise that. When I started to hit poses for the shoot, in the skimpy leotard costume, I felt bothered by his presence and asked him to leave. He vanished, but I could tell he thought I'd been rude. He was used to helping his father out with all kinds of photo shoots and he'd never been asked to leave before.

It was, as it turned out, the second time I had been unintentionally abrupt with him. He was at the City of London University working on his MA in arts management, and was renting a flat with my old SWRB partner, Petter Jacobsson. When Kenneth had died, he'd sent me a message of condolence and suggested we should meet up to talk about him. Tobias had grown up with Kenneth as a frequent guest at his parents' home; they were very close, and he thought it would be nice to share our memories of someone we had both loved. For whatever reason, I failed to reply to his message. But a year later, after the article had appeared, I phoned Roy to say how delighted I was with the photographs and happened to ask about Tobias. He said he was well, now working at the classical musical agency HarrisonParrott as a manager of orchestral international touring, but about to be homeless. On impulse I rang him to offer him my flat while I was away on tour. We had a brunch the next day that lasted three hours, and soon after that, we had dinner. I was strongly attracted to this tall, dark, handsome man, with who wore little round glasses and smart business suits.

Conversation between us always flowed. There were never any awkward pauses as we explored our connections in the dance world, our very different upbringings—me with a big family, he as an only child—and our hopes and dreams for the future. I knew he was the man for me when I took him shopping and he didn't blanch at spending hours sitting in Joseph as I tried on everything in the shop, emerging with a white miniskirt which I still have as a memento of a very happy day. That was the start of a relationship that has been through all sorts of winding paths but is still going strong today.

By the time we had brunch, I'd made my debut on the Royal Opera House stage as Aurora, and as Giselle. I'd added the spiky *Danses Concertantes*, Kenneth's first ballet, to my MacMillan repertory, appeared as Irina in his *Winter Dreams*, and extended my Ashton knowledge by dancing Fairy Autumn in *Cinderella*. From May to July 1995, the company went on tour to Japan and Korea and then on to Los Angeles; I was still seeing Tobias and writing to him as the tour whizzed by. Then, over the summer, I had an operation on a bone spur in my foot; this is an injury that afflicts a lot of dancers, and it's always best to get it sorted out, but I was frustrated to be away from the stage again.

My sense of depression—'down in the dumps', which was how I described it to Aunty Pat—was increased by a protracted contract negotiation with Anthony Russell-Roberts, administrative director of the Royal Opera House. He was a quintessentially British figure, the nephew of Frederick Ashton, and a member of English ballet royalty. Tobias, in his role as an agent, was discussing my contract and I wasn't asking for much; just something to recognise my role in the company and the opportunity to guest more widely to increase both my earnings and my reputation. He said that if I wanted to stay at the Royal Ballet, I would have to accept that I would never be prioritised before Sylvie, Darcey and Viviana. I was upset but tried not to feel any resentment as I kept on working.

The financial constraints Russell-Roberts was operating within were real, since the Opera House deficit was running at £3 million[1] and the Royal Ballet, although successful in itself, was intricately caught in the problems. Some of this period in the company's life is caught in *The House*, a fly on the wall television documentary about the Royal Opera House which became a reality TV drama sensation, portraying an institution in crisis, swinging from one disaster to the next. It did enormous harm to its reputation, making it seem out of touch and elitist, an image which has taken years to dispel. I made a fleeting appearance in one episode, dancing in *Mayerling* with Adam Cooper. The same episode shows one of the least edifying moments of a terrible time, where Fiona Chadwick, one of the principals, is sacked because of the need to cut the salary bill. It was a brutal period, and I really did just have to put my head down and plough on.

My foot operation kept me away for five months, but I returned in November 1995 to make my *Manon* debut, with Mum and Dad in the audience. Later the same month I danced MacMillan's *Side Show* with Tetsuya, a short comic duet originally choreographed for Lynn Seymour and Rudolf Nureyev. Further excitement came from one of the few new commissions in that time: the three-act ballet, *Mr Worldly Wise*, to the music of Rossini, choreographed by Twyla Tharp which premiered in December 1995. I was a dancing vegetable. It was that kind of ballet, sprawling, diffuse and unexpected, full of slapstick humour, built around Darcey, Irek and Tetsuya, and mostly disliked by the critics, though the dancing and the inventiveness of the steps were praised. We danced it into January, and again the following year, but it has never been revived and to be honest, I don't remember much about it. I did like working with Twyla, who was intelligent and engaging. Having seen her work on film and with ABT, I wish I had had the opportunity to make more work with her.

I was always happy when I was creating something new. In the next eighteen months, both Ashley Page and Glen Tetley made work for the company, and I was lucky enough to be in both. The pieces—*Two Part Invention* and *Amores*—both had short shelf lives, but there's always something exciting about being in the original cast of a ballet. You hope that it's going to be the next big thing, and even if it's not, the actual act of making it feeds an inner longing to be part of a creative team, instead of just reproducing and interpreting what someone else has already done. I liked *Amores*, which I danced with Darcey, Deborah Bull, Stuart Cassidy, William Trevitt and Michael Nunn. It only had seven performances in 1997, but the experience of working with Tetley, an American choreographer, brought a whiff of contemporary dance into my classical world. His work was exhausting, but I relished the way that he would use the entire expanse of the body, stretching the upper body as much as your legs. You could rest assured that if you were working on a Tetley ballet your physique would change and strengthen throughout the process, because of the physical demands he put on you. *Voluntaries*, which I performed in 2008 and 2011, was one of the most tiring ballets I have ever danced, exposing in a white all in one. *The Firebird* was equally tiring, but it used classical steps that my body knew, a vocabulary that I practised every day. Tetley was something else entirely and I loved him for it.

You want this variety of repertoire as a dancer. It's like food: you don't want to eat the same meal every day of the week. You need the variety to build you up in the right way. As a classical dancer you need to dance some roles to keep your technique strong: *Swan Lake*, *The Nutcracker*, *The Sleeping Beauty*. These are works that make you stand on one leg, turn, keep upright. You gain body strength and keep your sharpness, your standards. I used to think of them as bread and butter, the fundamentals of your diet. They would prepare me to enjoy the ballets that felt like treats—the ones that tasted so yummy to me. This included all Kenneth's ballets, but if you do too many Manons or Juliets and nothing else, it's harder to go back to the classical repertoire that keeps your body in alignment. The classics set you back to neutral and make you a better dancer all round.

In these early years of the Royal I was dancing a good balance of classics, while simultaneously extending my MacMillan repertory. Learning *The Invitation*, which we performed in February 1996, was a particularly rich experience. Lynn Seymour, who had created the ballet opposite Christopher Gable in 1960, came in to coach us in the part. I was dancing The Girl on the opening night, with Stuart Cassidy as my gentle cousin. They are tragically entangled with another couple, played by Genesia Rosato and Irek Mukhamedov, whose marriage is falling apart. The wife seduces the boy; the husband brutally rapes the girl. It's profoundly traumatic to perform, psychologically acute and upsetting, but the rehearsals were a fantastic experience.

Sarah Wildor, who was dancing The Girl in the alternate cast, was a wonderful person to be in a studio with, full of warmth, humour and great energy. *The Observer* featured a photograph of the two of us with Lynn,[2] and I gave an interview to Allen Robertson in *Time Out* in which I said how hard we were working to get it absolutely right. 'Even though I was dying to do this great dramatic role, I've never seen it performed onstage.'[3] In her review Debra Craine said I danced as if I were 'caught up in a rush of adrenalin, the physicality of [the] performance spilling forth like floodwaters … elemental and unstoppable.'[4]

More or less simultaneously, I was tackling another dark MacMillan ballet, the three-act version of *Anastasia*, an examination of the mystery of Tsar Nicholas II's youngest daughter, who was believed to have been executed with her family in 1918. Kenneth took as his starting point the fact that two years later a traumatised woman called Anna Anderson claimed to be her; her belief was later proved by DNA evidence to be false, but Kenneth didn't know that at the time. The ballet was originally one act, made in Berlin, which concentrated on Anderson's recreation of a half-remembered past. When Kenneth returned to the Royal Ballet in 1971, he expanded it into a three-act ballet, which moves from the grandeur of the Imperial Court to the horror of this confused woman, haunted by nightmares about her life.

It's a penetrating study of the psychology of identity and it gives you a wonderful opportunity to move from joyful innocence in the opening act to the unhappiness of the close. I danced it in two seasons in my Royal Ballet career, once in this revival and again in 2004. In an interview with Julie Herd in the *Australian* after of my debut

I said: 'It's my most suitable role to date. I have quite a contrasting personality too—I can be childish at times and a drama queen.'[5] Its gruelling physicality was complicated by the fact that this was the first ballet in which I had performed that made use of film projections; Kenneth cleverly had the dancers sit with our backs to the auditorium, watching real black and white footage of the brutality of the murder of the Romanovs, before unfolding the story and exploring Anastasia's mental state. The counts in that final act, set to the music of Martinů, were some of the hardest I have ever encountered. I tackled learning the role by writing down words that would evoke the movements for me: 'Standing up, forward, across, forward, hands to ground.'

The performance seemed to go well. 'The management and audience were happy, although for me it's difficult to gauge,' I wrote to Tobias's parents, Roy and Georgina. Georgina had danced in the original 1971 production as the Tsarina, so had a particular interest in my progress. 'I still have a headache from Act III. It's emotionally draining.' Christopher Gable, who had also been close to Kenneth, sent me a letter of congratulations, offering great insight.

'It must be quite difficult to find a coherent line through the first two acts because they leave your character very much as an observer and there doesn't seem a lot for you to play other than youth and a kind of outsider gaucheness. I don't think Ken would have done it that way if he had conceived it as a three acter in the first place, but still you did what you had to do splendidly as well as showing some wonderfully accounted for dancing …

'I thought you found a very strongly sustained dramatic line and most impressive of all was the way you were able to allow the choreography to speak through you. This is something of a lost art these days and it might be that Lynnie was able to help you but that doesn't alter the fact that it was a very distinguished and intense piece of work. I think Kenneth would have been very pleased and I certainly felt relieved that there is still somebody at the Opera House who is working for what I consider to be the most important things.'

The performances in London were quickly followed by a tour from May to July to Norway, Denmark, Greece, Argentina, Israel and Italy. In general, touring feels like a privilege; it's tiring but you do get to see the most amazing places, experience different ways of living, meet interesting people, and get a little insight into different countries. Snapshots from each place stick in my mind: the spectacular mountain funicular in Bergen; bicycles in Copenhagen; tango in the streets in Buenos Aires, plus steaks to rival those from Queensland. In Athens we explored the Acropolis and the Parthenon, in Israel we coped with a slippery open-air stage and in Palermo we had the intrigue of discovering that the top floors of our hotel were apparently meeting rooms for the Mafia. In the few days off between Copenhagen and Athens, I even managed to get home to London to do some washing—always an ongoing issue on a long tour. A dancer's life may be glamorous in many ways, but there's a huge amount of laundry. It's in the contrasts that we thrive.

CHAPTER 16

ON THE ROAD, THEN BACK TO THE HOUSE

DANCERS ARE OFTEN ASKED TO name the highlight of their career, but the question is essentially impossible to answer. I couldn't tell you that, any more than I could tell you my favourite ballet. There are so many moments, so many ballets. But it is true to say that in January 1997 I felt on top of the world. I danced the opening night of the Royal Ballet's *Cinderella* at the Metropolitan Opera House in New York and it was as if I had arrived at something special. I was on one of my favourite stages, a place that forms a perfect bond between the audience and the performer. Quite often in my life, when I arrive in a theatre, rather than try and squeeze in an extra bit of rehearsal, I will simply walk out onto the stage, and see how it feels with the lights up, thinking about where I need to look to establish communication with the people who will be sitting out there in the dark. The Met was a place I always felt at home. That night I know I dazzled.

The reviews were some of the best of my career, too, with the critics laying on the superlatives. Anna Kisselgoff said I triumphed through 'the sheer beauty' of my dancing, walking into the ballroom not 'like an ordinary mortal but with the refinement that Ashton's genius defined for the ideal version of Cinderella's true self', praising the natural elegance that both I and Bruce Sansom, who was my Prince Charming, showed in our pas de deux. The review was headlined: 'Once Upon a Time, in a Poetic Land, Lived a Ballerina Who Walked on Air'.[1]

That was just how it felt; I was so happy in New York and it became a very special place for me. I was always busy rehearsing and performing but once I'd met Tobias, I'd make time to see his parents and then visit ABT with Georgina. As I got to know her better, all reserve dropped away; you could quickly see why so many people loved her, because she was genuinely interested you. She drew people to her like a magnet and the New York loft was like an artists' colony, with friends dropping by. There was always classical music playing, and Georgina would make you coffee while Roy settled down for an intellectual chat about whichever composer was on the sound system. He absolutely loved classical music and I have inherited his vast collection of CDs.

New York's energy always sets me alight. I admire the way it conquers nature and is such a tribute to the man-made. There's an air of vitality even walking down the street. I've never minded what people see as the New Yorkers' rudeness; to me it feels as if they are just being direct and it's all part of the city's unique vibe. It's a place where you only need to look up to feel inspired.

In February, I was busy in London. Viviana Durante had taken a leave of absence and I opened the next run of *The Judas Tree* with Irek, and we then committed our partnership to film over three days at the Elstree Studios in March. Apart from the significance of filming a performance of which I was proud, in a ballet I believed in, I got a sudden taste of a different lifestyle. However glamorous a dancer's life seems from the outside, it is fairly mundane when you're living it. Normally I took the tube to and from work and spent my days looking after myself. Filming was something else, with a limousine to pick me up early every morning, before I was pampered in hair and make-up at the studios, with my every whim catered for. I had a glimpse of life as a movie star, though the intensity of the filming brought me quickly back to earth.

In the early part of the year I danced Aurora, Odette, Anastasia again and made my debut as Nikiya in *La Bayadère*, a ballet I never much liked dancing, but which is full of wonderful drama. In May, the company set off on tour again, to America and Japan. Our first port of call was the Orange County Performing Arts Center in California, where I was dancing the Bluebird pas de deux in *Beauty* and in Kenneth's *La Fin du jour* as part of a triple bill. It was a theatre I always struggled with. It had a wonderful stage, but the auditorium was so vast that you couldn't be sure the audience were actually applauding at any point. From there the company embarked on a lengthy tour of Japan, where I danced *Don Quixote* opposite Tetsuya Kumakawa—a series of thrilling performances because he was such a celebrity in Japan. He put a real spring in my step, because he held the audience in the palm of his hand and that lifted my performances as well.

When I wasn't dancing myself, I would rush out to experience the atmosphere of the cities we were visiting. Other nights I'd sit in the wings or in the auditorium, watching the wonderful dancers I was working alongside. One of my favourite things, even now, is to see a performance from the wings, because it's great to get perspective from different angles. As I coach, I like to watch dancers from backstage as well as from every area of the house; some people look incredibly different close up or from a distance, even their proportions seem to change.

I always took any opportunity in those days to watch Sylvie Guillem, wherever in the world and from whatever vantage point I could find. Everyone wanted to watch her. She brought such magic to the stage and her performance was at an unbelievable level. I was compelled by her integrity and always recognised the work she put in.

Because she was a principal guest artist, she had much more freedom than the rest of us, but she was helpful as well as inspiring to me. I remember when I was dancing *Manon*, she looked at me in costume and said, in her deep French accent, 'You need boob cups.' She was right. I disliked wearing anything extra in a costume, but I was so thin, I didn't really have anything to prop up inside *Manon*'s voluptuous eighteenth-century corsets. Sylvie was brilliant at knowing what she needed physically to take on a character. She was also very clear on how she wanted to look onstage, and I admired that.

In my early days as a ballerina you were always encouraged to wear a lot of make-up and false eyelashes, so that your face projected to the back of the auditorium. In the second half of my career, like Sylvie, I wore very little make-up, and definitely no false eyelashes. They made my eyes feel itchy. Generally as I progressed, I realised less was more. I danced my best when I felt most free, so the more minimalist my costume, make-up and hair, the happier I was. I'd have danced without a tutu if I could. Sylvie quite often dispensed with tights for the third act of *Manon*, when the character has been deported to New Orleans as a prostitute. There was a lot of disapproval of her changing things, but I know she was trying to make her performance as real and involving as it could be. She succeeded; I could barely watch that third act without crying. It was a role she was exceptional in.

Sylvie and Jonathan Cope danced a pas de deux from *Manon*, the ecstatic bedroom scene from Act 1, in the gala on 14 July 1997 in the presence of Prince Charles and Princess Margaret that said farewell to the Opera House as it closed for major rebuilding work. I danced the lyrical duet from *The Dream* with Bruce Sansom, and at the end of the evening, Darcey, as the Lilac Fairy from *The Sleeping Beauty*, put the old house to sleep. It was a wonderful but melancholy occasion, streamed both to an audience sitting in the piazza outside, and to the country at large via the BBC. Anthony Dowell had a real gift for putting such galas together, judging the mood perfectly and taking infinite care with quality. I wasn't too nostalgic about leaving the house because I knew they were going to make conditions better. In life, everything eventually needs updating—dancers, directors, buildings. Times change and we have to move on. But I did feel that it was the end of a chapter, and I wasn't at all sure what was going to happen in the next one.

At some point early in the year, I had flown to Melbourne to talk to Ross Stretton, the then director of The Australian Ballet. I felt unsettled, as everyone did, by the multiple crises that were unfolding behind the scenes at the Opera House. A plan to move the Royal Ballet into a single permanent venue for the two-year closure period had fallen through, leaving the company homeless.[2] You could feel the insecurity coming from management and at that point the future of the Royal Ballet seemed to be in doubt. My initial conversation with Ross was about whether it might be possible to go to guest with Australian Ballet for a year. I longed to go home for a time, and it seemed an ideal career solution, enabling me to keep dancing regularly while the ROH was closed. In the end the idea foundered because Ross hesitated, and Anthony wasn't keen on the idea of letting me have a sabbatical. He said he couldn't guarantee I would still have a place at the Royal at the end of the year. I was gutted.

Looking back, I realise this is probably because he was engaged in the early skirmishes of what turned out to be a successful rear-guard action to save company numbers. Despite persistent pressure, he didn't lose a single dancer in that closure period.[3] But from my point of view, I felt I was getting to the later stages of my career (wrongly as it turned out) and I didn't want to have any regrets about not dancing enough. I completely respected the need for management to do what was in the best interests of the company, but my job was also to think about how best to spend whatever time I might have left. It's another sign of how times have changed. Today, dancers seem to be given freer rein over their time and to be allowed to explore different guesting opportunities. Twenty years ago, it was extremely rare to see dancers perform with other companies unless they were Guillem, Nina

Ananiashvili, or Julio Bocca who had guest contracts. Their careers enjoyed the lift they received from international exposure. Most of the rest of us just stayed in one place.

When my idea of a sabbatical was turned down, I explored the possibility of joining The Australian Ballet on a permanent basis. That was a much tougher call, because I loved the Royal Ballet and was happily in a relationship with Tobias, which I didn't think would survive such a move. On the other hand, I would see out my dancing days in front of a 'home' audience and be able to spend more time with Mum and Dad. There's a famous Australian song by Peter Allen called 'I Still Call Australia Home' and that has always been true for me; my heart gets tugged back there. I spent weeks deliberating, writing up lists of pros and cons. In the end, it came to nothing because I found Ross almost impossible to negotiate with; he wanted me to sign up without any idea of either my repertory or my partners. When I queried that, his behaviour became subtly authoritarian. He said I had to accept his offer without any assurances from him. His attitude wasn't that of someone who wanted me to join his company. Then, out of the blue, he wrote me a one-line message saying he was withdrawing his offer. There was no explanation. I realised it was the right decision from the relief I felt and given how events later turned out, I had dodged a bullet.

In autumn 1997 I got on with an itinerant dancing life that was remarkably similar to my SWRB days, except that the theatres we were performing in were usually closer to home and the repertoire consisted of big, blockbusting ballets that would be popular with the large audiences we needed to attract. We danced in September at the Labatt's Apollo, a converted cinema on a roundabout in Hammersmith. I performed Juliet and found myself once more running to Portakabin changing rooms in the pouring rain, just as in the old days.

It was a strange environment and full of problems. Tobias was in the audience on the famous night when Nicola Tranah was dancing Myrtha, queen of the Wilis, in *Giselle* and the dry ice at the start of the second act made the stage so slippery and oily that she couldn't keep her footing in the sequence that marks her entrance. Every time she got up, she fell down again, until they had to close the curtains and mop the floor. It was so dramatic that it made the papers.[4]

For all its oddity, it was nice to be on a different stage in London and the audience felt unfamiliar, as if people who might have been put off by the idea of going to the Opera House were willing to come to sample ballet here. I also broke new ground that month when I made a guest appearance at the Peacock Theatre with Les Ballets Trockadero de Monte Carlo, the company colloquially known as The Trocks. These fabulous male ballerinas send up classical ballet, but do so with such love and finesse that they are funny and immensely clever at the same time. I danced *Swan Lake* alongside them, surprising the audience by my appearance and loving being part of the joke.

Those were, as it happened, my last performances for quite a while. Lady Sainsbury, who as Anya Linden had been a ballerina herself, and who is one of the Royal Ballet's most assiduous and gracious supporters, had asked me to dance in a Stars of the Night gala which she was helping to organise in aid of the Royal Academy of Dance and Benesh Notation at Her Majesty's Theatre, in the presence of Princess Diana. It was going to be a very glitzy affair and I was looking forward to helping raise money for such a cause. The solo chosen for me to perform was from Ashton's *Les Rendezvous*, not absolutely my cup of tea, but very pretty and lovely.

Like a lot of Ashton's work, it is much more difficult to dance than it looks, and on my last rehearsal in a studio at Barons Court, Anya came to watch. The first step is a jump, and as I came down I lost my footing, rolled over my left ankle and landed not on my foot but with my whole body on the floor. I knew instantly that I had done something major. I couldn't move my foot, which was starting to swell, and I couldn't stand up. After much commotion, with icepacks being brought, I was carried to physio by two male dancers. From there, I ended up in hospital, and after several scans was told the bad news: I had ruptured two ligaments completely and partly torn a third. I was going to be out of action for a long time.

Every dancer fears the career-ending injury, and I was terrified by this one. Ligaments are often slower to heal than a broken bone. Awful thoughts ran through my head: would I ever dance again? How many months would it take me to recover? How was I going to cope? Added to all this was the knowledge that even if I could return to the stage, I was facing the lengthy slog of getting back to full fitness. It had happened to me so often and it's so dispiriting. With an injury of this type, there are two options on how to proceed: to operate or to have a long-term rest. After much deliberation, I chose the latter and then, when I could, started exercising once again, pushing one moment, resting the next, doing all the physio, pilates and massage recommended, slowly building strength so that I could travel through remedial class into full class, from tiny exercises to bigger ones and finally to big, expansive jumps. I always say that for every day you miss class, it takes two to get back, and getting back from injury is a process that takes all your powers of endurance, requiring both physical and mental strength to climb the mountain to where you were before. It's like playing chess with your body, making small moves to achieve your aim.

I did what I always did when I felt in need of support, and spent some time back with the family in Australia, relaxing in the sun, walking on the sand at the beach house at Lammermoor. I truly don't think there is better recuperation in the world for me than I have found there. Tobias joined me. He'd met my parents in London, but this was his first chance to get a sense of the city I had come from after two years together. He's a big city boy, used to the streets of New York and London, so it took him a while to adapt to a place where you take a film into the local chemist to be developed, and they look at the pictures and know who you are. My family's easy-going habits took some getting used to as well. He vividly remembers being woken by a bird screeching at five in the morning and finding my mum sitting on the end of our bed, chatting to me while he slept. Chats in bed have always been a Benjamin family tradition. We went sight-seeing, doing all the usual things such as going up in a glider, and visiting a crocodile farm, and he also got a chance to meet all my extended family, including Aunty Pat, who became one of his favourites. He found her authentic, honest and with genuine warmth—and she adored him because he listened to all her stories. We just regarded her as an eccentric and much-loved part of the family, but he came to her with admiring eyes.

As I returned to dancing in February 1998 after three months away, the Royal Ballet was still moving all over the place; we did another Dance Bites tour, which I went on the radio with Anthony Dowell to publicise. I was dancing in *When We Stop Talking*, a new work by Ashley Page, which premiered at the Orchard Theatre, Dartford. It was the first time I shared a stage with Edward Watson, a young dancer who would become very important to me later in my life. I don't remember much about the work, though I do recall one evening when I couldn't understand why everyone was laughing at me from the wings, until I realised that my boob had popped out of the side of my costume. I was so embarrassed.

I've been in a few ballets that haven't quite hit the mark with audiences and it's an odd feeling. You feel you have spent hours and hours building a house and then it collapses at the last moment. It doesn't make the endeavour any less satisfying, but it's disappointing, like putting the final piece in a jigsaw puzzle and seeing it fall apart. The tour felt like hard work. The stages were small, the audiences underwhelmed, and we went on last every evening, which meant a lot of hanging around and late drives back to London, if it was commutable. In March the company headed abroad again, to Turin and Frankfurt, where we danced Beauties and Cinderellas.

April brought a bit of a red-letter day for the little girl from Rockhampton, when I was invited to a Reception for the Arts hosted by Her Majesty the Queen at Windsor Castle. It was quite an affair, with everyone you can possibly think of from the world of arts and entertainment in attendance, both performers and those who worked behind the scenes. Michael Caine, Wayne Sleep, Joan Collins, Shirley Bassey, and me! I was introduced to the Queen as part of a group, and I spent some time talking to Helena Bonham Carter and Kenneth Branagh, at the time, acting's hottest couple. I wasn't blasé about any of it; it seemed thrilling to be in this beautiful castle surrounded by all these distinguished people and meeting Britain's head of state.

We were dancing everywhere that year; a season at the Barbican in June celebrated Ninette de Valois's one hundredth birthday, though I didn't perform; I was at the Coliseum in July dancing the *Don Quixote* pas de deux with Tetsuya in a programme of divertissements. Debra Craine in *The Times* described us as 'a sizzling pair' giving a 'no holds barred performance'.[5] I also danced *La Bayadère* in its entirety. By autumn, we were performing at the newly rebuilt Sadler's Wells Theatre, in a series of mixed programmes. They went well enough, but behind the scenes a story was unfolding that brought the Royal Ballet into a period of maximum peril.

The Royal Opera House was constantly on the brink of bankruptcy; there had been a parliamentary inquiry into the place's future, and a report on the entire landscape of lyric theatre in London. There were union meetings and emergency talks and the organisation got through a general director and two chief executives in two years; Mary Allen, who left in March 1998 after arriving the previous August, later compared her time as chief executive to 'living in a thriller'.[6] Without consulting either Anthony Dowell or Anthony Russell-Roberts, the Opera House, still battling unmanageable debts, had at one point decided that we would become a part-time company, with the dancers offered thirty-six-week yearly contracts.[7] Both Anthonys were ready to resign and the situation was only resolved with the help of private donors who guaranteed our future. It was a deeply destabilising time, and it had repercussions; in October Tetsuya left to establish his own company, K-Ballet, in Japan. In November, five more Royal Ballet men—Michael

Nunn, William Trevitt, Stuart Cassidy, Matthew Dibble and Gary Avis—announced that they were going to join him in January. For those of us who remained, there were fewer performances and the repertory had shrunk, becoming much more conventional.

Around this time, David Bintley called and asked me to audition for the musical *The Pajama Game*, which he was choreographing the following autumn. It was one of those delicious calls that came entirely out of the blue, and I was quite excited about the prospect of appearing in a musical. My entire ballet career had started with 'Animal Crackers', and this looked like a moment when it might come full circle. I took the offer seriously enough to have a couple of emergency singing lessons; although I'd grown up singing in church and could hold a note, I was worried that without professional voice training I wouldn't be able to sustain eight shows a week. Even after that, I didn't really rate my chances, but I thought it would be worth giving it a shot, especially since Simon Callow was directing, and I'd always admired his work.

On audition day, at the old Urdang Studios, so familiar from my Sunday dance classes as a student, I had agonised about what to wear but still looked like a ballet girl compared with all the other prospective talent who were used to musical theatre auditions and turned up dressed in sophisticated, bright, high-cut leotards and proper musical theatre shoes. The dancing part of the audition went predictably well, but I wasn't at all confident about my singing and wasn't surprised when I wasn't asked back. Twenty years later, I went to see Simon performing Oscar Wilde's *De Profundis* at the Vaudeville, when Tobias was managing an Oscar Wilde season. At the opening night party, Simon sweetly and generously said he remembered my audition and that I was 'great'. But he is a wonderful actor, so I am not at all sure I believed him.

Other opportunities were opening up. I was getting interested in renovating properties. I had bought my second flat in 1997, a beautiful apartment in Sutherland Avenue, Maida Vale. It was run-down when

I bought it, its rich period features hidden behind decades of over-painting and sheets of cream plasterboard. Climbing up a ladder with a torch, I found the original cornicing. I remodelled it with an architect, and painstakingly turned it into an airy, elegant living space. In early 1999, I moved again to a flat in Chepstow Place, Notting Hill. It was in a building I'd always had my eye on, an old fur factory that had been used as a tax office and then sat empty for years. One afternoon, when I was treating myself to a cab home from rehearsals at Barons Court, I saw an advertisement in the evening paper about apartments being sold there, off plan. Redirecting the cab, I went to have a look and decided to buy a place on the spot. It was a gamble because I hadn't sold my existing property, but it turned out to be a smart move, since I picked it up just before the Richard Curtis movie *Notting Hill* was released. When Julia Roberts fell in love with Hugh Grant in a bookshop round the corner, the value of my little place soared sky high. It was one of my best investments, as well as a fantastic place to live.

The release of that film and its effect on the London property market is just an example of the biggest lessons I have learnt in my life: always expect the unexpected and be ready to take opportunities when they arise. At the end of April 1999, I had been allowed to book three months away from the Royal Ballet to be a guest ballerina with K-Ballet in Japan on their first tour. Tetsuya, Michael Nunn and I were featured in a big interview in the *Daily Telegraph*, under the headline 'What's so special about K?'[8] In it, Tetsuya explained that he was confident the venture would be a success; 40,000 tickets for the six-week spring tour had sold out in ten minutes. Then fate spun the wheel of my life once again. Viviana Durante had pulled out of the Royal Ballet's planned trip to Japan. With no-one to cover her performances in *Manon*, at two days' notice, the company asked me if I would be prepared to fly out and dance the role.

It's always nice to be wanted and I was only too pleased to help. I flew to Japan early, and performed for a week with the Royal in Tokyo, enjoying my performances of *Manon* with Bruce Sansom as my lover and Irek Mukhamedov as my scheming brother, feeling much more at home in the role than before and encouraged by the warm response from the audience. Then I stayed on for the whistle-stop tour of Japan with K-Ballet that really was something else. Ballet is huge in Japan and Tetsuya was mobbed wherever he went. We made our debut on 5 May in Yokosuka, a coastal town full of American marines, before heading back to Tokyo for a five-day stint at the Orchard Hall.

The bill was a clever mix of mainly new pieces, in which I danced *Cry Baby Kreisler*, by the Royal Ballet's Matthew Hart, 'Concerto in F', a lovely creation set to Mozart by the Japanese choreographer Haruka Ueda, and, occasionally, a Petipa pas deux from *Satanella*. Tobias joined me in Tokyo, and after the performances we'd find traditional sushi bars or restaurants high above the city where we could relax and get to know this breathtaking capital. After this brief oasis of calm, I was off at a breathless pace, dancing in small cities all over Japan, with one performance in each, and the bullet train or bus in between. We once travelled and performed on the same day. It was exhausting but exhilarating, with rapturous audiences giving us standing ovations every night. Japanese audiences rarely applaud during performances, but I have never known anything like the reception you receive when the performance is over, and the endless queues outside the stage door.

Although I sometimes felt slightly excluded from the boys' club at the heart of K-Ballet, I had a lovely time exploring. I was boosted by dancing so regularly and to such warm receptions. I had a long conversation with Tetsuya at one point about whether I might stay with the company permanently or come back to guest again, but my instinct was that I wanted to return to London and that the Royal Ballet was now my home.

In the summer, Tobias and I hit our first rocky patch. He was seven years younger than me, incredibly busy with work, and insistent that he never wanted children. This had thrown me. I knew there was something special between us, but coming from a big, happy family such as mine, I wanted to have the possibility of having a family of my own in the future. We got on so well, but the different pressures on us meant that once a year we tended to split up, and then quite quickly get back together. This time it was a bit more serious and I was miserable. We were living together in Chepstow Place by then, and when Tobias moved out, he used to go to stay with an elderly mutual friend called Richard Bayliss who adored us both and lived nearby. He'd bring Tobias buttered toast soldiers and hot tea every morning; with all that spoiling, it's a miracle he ever came back.

In June 1999 he moved out for a long time, and I thought our relationship was over. By the end of the year, however, we were reconciled, and my mother wrote him a Christmas letter ironically reminding him of the qualities he was taking on in the form of a list: '1. Leanne has lots of antique frames and nothing in them/ 2. She decides in the middle of the street that she is not walking a step further/ 3. Her dinner parties look beautiful with lots of candles and flowers. She forgets food/ 4. She loves big diamonds and little designer clothes/ 5. She throws lots of black clothes away and buys more black clothes/ 6. She has conned her father all her life, so watch out Tobias!'

By the end of the year, too, the Royal Ballet had returned to Covent Garden. Rebuilt at a cost of £214 million, it was ready to open on time, and with a new chief executive, Michael Kaiser, in calm charge. Anthony Dowell had heroically managed to guide the company through the most traumatic time in its history and back into the remodelled theatre where the new conditions were fabulous. Gone were the days of travelling between Barons Court in West London to Covent Garden to perform. Now our studios were on top of the Opera House itself, bright and clean, with beautifully sprung floors instead of the perilous old wooden ones. It was startling to get used to the light in that studio, almost too clean, as if we needed to add a patina of age or a darker shade of paint to bring the whiteness down a little. There were spacious changing rooms, places to relax, a large canteen, and a dedicated area for physiotherapy and rehabilitation, with its own gym and pilates studio. The creation of a second, smaller performing space, the Linbury Theatre, offered the hope of a different kind of programming, with room to make more new work. I felt so proud to be part of this reopening, to have weathered the storm and come out the other side into this revamped building, which contained everything a world-class company could want.

The design by architect Jeremy Dixon also had a new air of democratisation. The front of the building was much more accessible to the public, and the restoration of the spacious Floral Hall made the public areas feel less closed and more available to everyone. Seat prices were also cut to make them more affordable. Given all the charges of elitism that had been levelled at Covent Garden over the previous decade, the rebuilding felt like a statement of intent. This process of opening up has continued in the subsequent years, with a further remodelling in 2018 expanding the public areas of Covent Garden still further and redeveloping the Linbury into a 400-seat flexible theatre. It has been an entirely good thing.

Walking into that new world in 1999, I was very pleased that I had decided to stay, that I was working in this new house, with this amazing company; Anthony Dowell was as happy as I had ever seen him. My first performance on the new stage, which was gratifyingly without bumps, nails or boards sticking up, since it was now covered in a state-of-the-art dance floor, was in Forsythe's *The Vertiginous Thrill of Exactitude*, as part of a programme of International Choreography, a further indication of the fresh air of change sweeping into British ballet. Then on 1 December, there was a historic gala evening, officially to celebrate the opening. It was a huge event, attended by VIPs including the Queen, the Queen Mother, the Duke of Edinburgh, Princess Margaret, the Prime Minister Tony Blair and his wife Cherie, and former Prime Ministers Margaret Thatcher and Edward Heath, and the place was buzzing with excitement.

The Royal Ballet was sharing the bill with the Royal Opera, including stars such as Placido Domingo and Deborah Polaski, but it was our half of the evening that gathered the greatest plaudits. Anthony had put together one of his classiest galas, marking the history of the Royal Ballet in its fifty years at Covent Garden. Featuring many well-chosen excerpts, it ended with a grand défilé to the music from *The Firebird*, and two students from the Royal Ballet School representing the future. It was televised live on BBC2 and broadcast on BBC Radio 3, reaching a wider audience as part of the new policy of wider access. It was also repeated on 4 December, so that members of the public had a chance to enjoy it, too. I danced the pas de deux from *Gloria* with Christopher Saunders, and found it extraordinarily atmospheric and moving to be dancing such a piece on such an occasion. I was ready to turn the page, roll my sleeves up and enjoy this new time. It felt like a rebirth.

CHAPTER 17

LOVE AND MARRIAGE

I WAS THIRTY-FIVE YEARS OLD when I saw in the Millennium, celebrating quietly at home with friends. I'd been dancing since I was three and had been a principal since I was twenty-two. At a point in my career where a lot of dancers would be thinking about slowing down, I seemed to be speeding up. Being back in the Opera House helped; the fact that the Royal Ballet now had a supportive management behind it and an increased number of performances helped even more.

With financial pressures lifted, Anthony Dowell could offer more ambitious, interesting programming, starting the year with a MacMillan triple bill including *Gloria*, which I danced again with Christopher Saunders. The early months of the year also brought me a succession of firsts. With a new partner, the Australian Nigel Burley, I made my Royal Ballet debut in MacMillan's *Concerto*, set to Shostakovich's piano concerto, dancing the slowly unfolding andante of the second movement. I also took on Swanilda in *Coppélia*. In five performances, I had three different partners—Ethan Stiefel and Ángel Corella, both guests from ABT, and Carlos Acosta.

The most memorable of the performances was with Carlos because it was so unexpected. I'd gone into the Opera House on Saturday for an hour-long rehearsal and was leaving to go home when Anthony Dowell called me on my mobile. He asked whether I was free that evening, because Miyako Yoshida, who was scheduled to dance with Carlos, had injured her back, and they were filming the performance for live broadcast on BBC2. How would I feel about stepping in?

I jumped at the chance, though even as I said yes, a few other thoughts were running round my head. At this point, Carlos and I had not danced *Coppélia* together, though we had performed in a revival of MacMillan's *My Brother, My Sisters* the previous year. I knew how brilliant a classical dancer he was, with a jump that seemed to hang in the sky, and a sunny, charming disposition, perfect for the role of the rascally Franz in *Coppélia*. I loved dancing Swanilda too; she's such a little minx, by turns sunny and sulky, charming and manipulative, and always on the lookout for fun, but ultimately tender-hearted. But if it is going to work its magic, it's a ballet that depends almost entirely on the comedic rapport between the two lovers. Would we be able to find that without a chance to rehearse?

There were practical problems too. Had I got a pair of shoes prepared that would be suitable for dancing the role? Would we be able to find any time to go through everything? In the end, after the briefest of chats in a studio, where we worked through a couple of the more complex moments in the pas de deux, we found ourselves onstage. We delivered a performance that to this day I am proud of—and wonderfully it was saved for posterity. When you hear about movie stars wanting to do something that their children will admire, this was the balletic equivalent. More than 1.4 million people watched it on the night and when it was released on DVD, it made me incredibly happy that my son, my cousins, and the children of friends loved watching this ballet about a doll who came to life and that their children will also be able to see it as well. It's a little sliver of immortality.

In general, my practical problems nearly always revolved around shoes, which play such a big part in a ballerina's life. The men are lucky.

They just pull on a pair of flats and away they go. For the women, pointe shoes can take up a huge portion of time, mental and physical energy. I had a lot of trouble with them, perhaps because I had such pain from my toe early on and perhaps, I now think, because I didn't measure my feet for two years after I arrived at the Royal Ballet School.

My shoes were made by the world-famous Freed of London. By the time I was a principal, they were created personally to my specifications by an individual maker, and if one retired, I had to find another who could make a shoe that felt the same. You would think that having hand-made shoes would mean they always fitted perfectly, but consistency was difficult, and because I was such a perfectionist I might only like five out of twenty pairs in any given batch and so would have to send them back to be redone. Freed worked painstakingly on them until I was happy and were wonderfully patient with my requests. In later years, I got what I needed down to a fine art: the pointe had to be a certain size and I insisted on a heel pin that would bring the heel up a little. I needed space for my long toes, but couldn't have the heel moving down too much.

I also developed a formula for the preparation of a new pair of shoes. I'd break the arch and then shellack the toe area, to harden the top and the toe. Once I'd treated them, I'd wear the shoes lightly, so that they didn't go out of shape, maybe just wearing them while I was at the barre, and then I'd shellack them again. I didn't want to be able to feel the floor too strongly. Tamara Rojo darned the toes for me once, a traditional way of protecting the satin on the tips, but I didn't like the way they felt, thank goodness, because I'd have found all the extra sewing almost impossible. I just chopped mine off. When I was happy with the feel I'd sew the ribbons on, and place two pieces of transparent elastic across the front of the shoe, so that I could flex my feet without feeling that they were in danger of popping out.

I'd keep different shoes for different ballets, writing on the bottom of each pair so I knew what to expect when I put them on, and hoarding them in huge piles (never very tidily) in my dressing room. There would be softer shoes for dancing in the ballets of Kenneth MacMillan, where I wanted my feet to be more pliable and expressive, and sturdy, virtually unworn pairs for the classical repertoire, so that the strength of the block could support the complicated pointe work, often on one leg, that those ballets involve. That's what I mean when I say that I had to check I had a pair of shoes to dance *Coppélia*; you get into the habit of preparing different pairs for different ballets. Sometimes I would even change a single shoe in the middle of a ballet, so that the pointe felt harder or softer depending on what I needed. For the hops in the first act of *Giselle* you might need a tougher tip, for example. Even though I was particularly pernickety about what I put on my feet, all ballerinas take great care of their shoes. It's like a violinist having a Stradivarius as opposed to a normal violin, or a rider being given the best horse. You're only as good as your instrument, and for a ballerina, that instrument is bound up with their feet.

If a dancer asks me advice about her shoes now, I say start with a factory-made shoe and see if you can find one that's comfortable before going down the hand-made route. Hand-made is a luxury, but can be inconsistent. There are lots of brands of pointe shoes now, and the same thing applies. It's important you are comfortable and that they enhance your feet. If my shoes felt great, I knew I was going to give a better performance—which meant that I ended up in my changing room, trying on three or more different pairs thirty minutes before a show, because suddenly the shoes I had chosen to dance in felt different than they had the previous day.

I had one other idiosyncrasy too. To protect my toes I used to pack the inside of my shoes with a particular type of absorbent paper towel, which became increasingly difficult to find as my career went on. At the beginning, I used to buy it in supermarkets. Then it only became available in one particular supermarket, so I bought rolls and rolls of the stuff, thinking that it would get me to the end of my career. Then I kept dancing, and my supply ran out. By the time I retired, I could only find something similar in the restaurants of posh hotels, and in order to achieve the desired effect, I would have to mix a paper serviette with a little of my diminishing stock of paper. I would have paid £10,000 to find the perfect roll, but it wasn't available, so I ended up smuggling napkins out of hotels. Costumes mattered a lot to me too. I'd ask the wardrobe to make sure they fitted loosely so that I had room to breathe. A lot of dancers like a tight waistline but I was the opposite—I wanted to be comfortable.

My next new role in that 2000 season was *The Firebird*, which I learnt under the guidance of Monica Mason, and which became one of my favourite ballets. At some level this was counter-intuitive. I didn't like wearing elaborate make-up or a tutu, and Firebird calls for both. But I loved wearing that particular tutu; it's cut quite low at the back and so cleverly designed that it really does make you feel like an exotic bird. *The Firebird* had been one of Monica's most famous roles as a dancer; she had been taught it by Fonteyn, who in turn had been coached by Tamara Karsavina, on whom the role was created by Mikhail Fokine for Diaghilev's Ballets Russes in 1910. Monica taught it to me with the enthusiasm and respect that unbroken lineage deserves, standing at the front of the studio, putting so much energy into her arms as she demonstrated the wild movements the Firebird made, that she danced every second alongside me. She was completely absorbed and committed; that was what I loved about being coached by her. The sessions were filmed for a masterclass on BBC and brought the ballet magically to life.

Stravinsky's music is such a treat, especially the overture, which is very long. It gives you a bit of a chance to jump around on the stage to warm up before her very first entrance. When the moment comes, you arrive like a ball out of a canon and then go straight into a long solo as you appear outside the enchanted castle. It's the most tiring role I've ever danced, the only part of any ballet that made me feel sick through sheer physical exhaustion. You've got all these big, masculine jumps while you're also flapping your arms in an elaborate and heavy double bounce, which would be shattering even if you weren't having to do anything with your legs. You have to use every single part of your body, alone and in unison. I had always loved jumping so I knew if I could get through the physical endurance test, I'd be fine. Although it's so clearly a descendant of nineteenth-century ballet, this dramatic work still feels fresh because Fokine was so ahead of his time. I loved it. In *The Times*, Debra Craine described my interpretation as 'wild and turbulent'.[1]

I danced *The Firebird* opposite Nigel Burley and in summer, Nigel and I took our partnership to the Vail Dance Festival, an annual two-week outdoor festival at a ski resort in Colorado, which has a unique atmosphere as it gathers performers from round the world. We performed *Manon*, the andante movement in *Concerto* and *Elite Syncopations*. It was always fun dancing with a fellow Aussie. In May 2000, there were more thoughts of home when I was included in a photographic exhibition called *Australians* at the National Portrait Gallery, which featured the Australian photographer Polly Borland's portraits of fifty-four Aussies deemed to have made a significant contribution to British life. As I took my place on the gallery walls alongside Kylie Minogue, Robert May, Cate Blanchett, Barry Humphries and Germaine Greer, I felt a blush of pride, tempered only by wondering how my Catholic Bishop Uncle Ray would have reacted if he could have seen how many items of clothing I took off before Polly got her shot of me in a black tutu, with red pointe shoes (that I had to dye) in a boldly provocative position, knees drawn up to my chin.

It was a year full of happy memories. In August, my sister Fiona married David Malek in his Canadian homeland. The whole Benjamin clan flew to White Rock just outside Vancouver to celebrate their big day. Tobias came too and immediately ran into trouble; he got a speeding ticket for driving at twenty-five miles an hour in a twenty-mile an hour zone. The following month, I went to Epidaurus for a gala, dancing the second movement from *Concerto* with Nigel. The legendary Italian ballerina Carla Fracci was also performing, along with an all-star line-up including Aurélie Dupont, Nicholas Le Riche,

Paloma Herrera, Maximilliano Guerra and Nikolaj Hübbe. Dancing *Concerto* in that stunning open-air amphitheatre was a moving experience; the setting enhanced the calm and serenity of the pas de deux. Our hotel was on the water, and we all had a fantastic time, swimming at midnight and staying up to watch the sun rise.

Then I nearly died. Again. Back in London, I'd been out for dinner and a movie with Tobias and eaten sushi. After a lovely evening, we went to bed in our flat in Chepstow Place at around midnight. I don't really remember what happened next, but Tobias does. At 2.30am he woke with a start, discovered I wasn't in bed, and went looking for me. I was lying in the spare bathroom, unconscious, surrounded by a pool of vomit. I was stone cold. He called our private doctor who came rushing round; by that point I was semi-conscious, so white you could see through me and cold as ice despite being covered in duvets. He decided that I must have had food-poisoning, gone to the loo to be sick and passed out, hitting my head on the sink as I fell. Tobias was seriously worried, and even more so when the doctor explained that because I was so slim there wasn't much margin in my body to cope with sickness. I was dangerously dehydrated, so Tobias had to spend the next day pouring electrolytes, fluid and clear soup into me. After about three days I felt fine again, but I'd been incredibly lucky. If Tobias hadn't woken up, there was a chance I would have died.

As it was, I just got on with things, dancing happily through a nicely mixed autumn season of Swan Lakes, Nutcrackers, and *Gloria* and *Concerto*. I picked up a slight injury early in the new year, which kept me out of a run of *Romeo and Juliet* that I was meant to dance with Johan Kobborg. Alina Cojocaru, just promoted to soloist, took my place and was wonderful. A new generation of ballerinas was now emerging, not only Alina, but also Marianela Nuñez, who spent a year at the school before beginning her career. Tamara Rojo had also arrived as a principal and was making her mark. We shared a dressing room, and you could see our personalities from the separate sides of the room. Hers was immaculate, full of carefully lined up make-up, and neatly piled shoes. She was meticulously organised, and always had everything a dancer might need. My side of the room wasn't like that at all; I'd tidy everything up before I went onstage, so I could find things easily, but the rest of the time it was a tip. I'd always be asking to borrow things. We got on very well and had a good dressing room friendship.

The season of 2000–1 was Anthony Dowell's last, and he filled it with ballets from the Royal's history that he had most loved. This farewell season ended with a double bill of *The Dream*, by Ashton, and *Song of the Earth*, by MacMillan, a tribute to the company's two most significant and loved choreographers. I danced both on different nights, making my debut in *Song of the Earth* alongside Johan Kobborg as the Messenger of Death and Johan Persson as the Man on 25 May 2001. I can't really begin to express what that ballet feels like to dance—it's one of the most beautiful, atmospheric, exhilarating, overwhelming experiences I've ever had.

It's set to Mahler's immense piece for orchestra and two singers, a setting of ancient Chinese poems which deal with the themes of beauty and transience, the joy of living and the sorrow of parting. Kenneth's ballet, which sets the singers on either side of the stage, is one of his most luminous works, full of unforgettable images and emotions. The music is so powerful you feel it resonating through you as the Woman faces the loss of love through death. The final song is a long journey from grief to acceptance to a tentative hopefulness; it culminates in a sequence of bourrées, running backwards on pointe from side to side of the stage until you almost reach a point of collapse. Just then, the Man she has lost reappears, now wearing a mask that symbolises death, and he holds her as she folds down onto the stage. The Messenger appears and the three of them walk slowly forward as the curtain falls, as if stepping into eternity. You can't catch the impact of that final section unless you have worked yourself almost to exhaustion. It wouldn't have the same impact if you were to dance it fresh. On my debut, Jann Parry in *The Observer* said: 'Benjamin pares away all passion, her small, gaunt frame transfigured by her acceptance of fate. It is a remarkable, ruthless performance, Noh-like in its simplicity.'[2]

The reason *Song of the Earth* is such a masterpiece is that it seems to sum up the whole of human experience, all our longings for love and permanence, all our fears of loneliness and death. They'd all been on my mind more than usual that year in any case because my relationship with Tobias had reached a critical point. When we first started seeing each other, we never thought it would last; our age difference meant we were at different points in our lives and aspirations. But because we enjoyed each other's company and never ran out of things to say, we couldn't ever quite tear ourselves apart from each other. In early 2001, we split up. I was at an age when I was starting to think about my life beyond the stage and what I wanted that to look like. I was thirty-six and I knew that I wanted to have children, but I was in a relationship with a man who clearly wasn't ready for that, who in fact was insistent that he didn't want to get married or have kids.

It felt like a terrible situation, to be with the right person but at the wrong time in our lives. It was made worse by the fact that ballet itself can be a trap for women, in that they keep going with the work because they think it is their only opportunity to shine, and then miss out on life's other gifts, such as a parenthood, as a consequence. It's tricky for women seeking any kind of career, but particularly difficult in an athletic arena such as dance. There's nothing wrong with choosing not to have children, of course, but I didn't want to miss out. I wanted a family of my own. If Tobias didn't, then I was going to have to break up with him.

But that separation in early 2001 triggered something in him. He realised that although in theory he didn't want to get married or have children, he did want to be with me. Whenever he thought of his life in the future, he discovered I was part of it. Without me knowing anything about it, he went to Miami to talk things through with his closest friends, and returned with a Tiffany box containing a small diamond ring. That night, he took me out to dinner at a posh restaurant in Ledbury Road, but I was in a mood, and quite grumpy with him all through dinner. Then just before dessert, he took out the box, popped it on the table, and asked me to marry him. The four girls sitting next to us went very quiet; I looked at the box suspiciously, opened it and shut it very quickly. Then I opened it again and started to cry.

That was in April and it was immediately full steam ahead with planning the wedding, because we realised that both sets of parents were due in London in the summer, and that would be the perfect moment to hold the ceremony. There was only one problem as far as I was concerned: I was quite busy dancing and it seemed an awfully short time in which to get everything arranged. In Tobias's view, I was making a big fuss about nothing. He was executive director of a theatre management company by this time, and entirely used to organising international tours and West End shows. How difficult could it be to stage a wedding in two months? To him, this was something you could sort out in about three hours with a mobile phone and a credit card. My view was that it was hard to rush things, particularly since I was off on tour to Washington and Boston in the weeks before. I wanted to look gorgeous for Tobias and since *Hello!* magazine was covering the wedding, that was extra pressure on us all. In the end, it came together, but I found it stressful.

Darcey suggested going to the designer Neil Cunningham for a dress, and he made me a stunning sleeveless number, with a corset bodice in French beaded lace that fitted long, before flaring from the hips into a full, tulle skirt, so thin it was almost transparent. Flowers were simple; I went to my old friends from SWRB days, Stephen Wicks and Mark Welford, who owned a wonderful flower shop called Bloomsbury Flowers in Great Queen Street. I wanted to conjure my memories of the white hydrangeas in Grandma Mulhern's front garden in Rockhampton, so I went for a mixture of those and white roses. One hydrangea would be tied at the end of each pew; a mixed floral arch would make a stunning entrance to St Paul's Church in Covent Garden, known as the Actors Church, where we were getting married.

The rector of St Paul's, the Reverend Mark Oakley, who also held the title of Deputy Priest in Ordinary to the Queen, made the planning of the service easy for us. Tobias was a non-practising Jew who doesn't really do God, and I was Catholic, but he found a way of fitting us easily into the Church of England for our wedding. We had a lovely dinner with him where I voiced some of my worries about marriage; the seriousness of the whole thing sometimes overwhelmed me. I wanted to be sure I was doing the right thing. After a small silence he told me we were definitely ready to take such a significant step. 'Most couples begin marriage imagining that everything will be perfect and don't foresee the possibility of any problems,' he said. 'The fact that you sat here and voiced them is refreshing. I give you my blessing.'

Before I could even contemplate getting down the aisle, however, I had to go on tour to Washington and Boston, where I was dancing *Swan Lake* with Johan Kobborg. I remember Boston quite vividly, because ironically it was the only time I remember being on tour and getting chatted up in a bar. He was a nice man, Princeton-educated and obviously quite rich. He even invited me up to the family house in Long Island, but I had to tell him I was very firmly spoken for.

Then it was back to London, to make all the final preparations for the big day on 30 June. I was staying at the Savoy with my parents, while Tobias was at our flat with his friends from New York. It was a tense time for me, as I worried away about getting everything just as I wanted it. I had terrible trouble with my hair and arrived back in the hotel in tears after the hairdresser had been through a practice run. But as so often, everything was all right on the night—or rather the afternoon, though there was one embarrassing moment when my brother Tony, who had arrived, late, was changing his trousers in the vestry, as the priest walked in.

For me, walking down the aisle with my father was profoundly emotional. I was so grateful to have him there. I have always been a daddy's girl and he has always been my rock. The only sadness of the day was that Fiona and David couldn't make it over from Sydney, where they were then living. But Mum and Madonna were there and Georgina and Roy, and I was surrounded by friends from the Royal Ballet: Tamara, Johan, Adam Cooper and his wife Sarah Wildor, Michael Nunn and his wife Belinda Hatley, Nigel Burley and his wife Rachel Rawlins, Nicola Tranah, Elizabeth McGorian, Joshua Tuifua, Ricardo Cervera, Emma Sandall and Jenny Tattersall. I walked up the aisle to Handel, out of the church to Carillon-Sortie by Mulet and in between we had my favourite Adage Cantabile from Beethoven's Pathétique sonata. It was all quite perfect and after the ceremony we strolled over to the Reform Club where Darcey, who had just given birth to her first daughter, and other friends joined us for an evening reception.

Tobias sailed serenely through the entire day, a broad beam on his face. The only thing that had worried him about the entire enterprise was the first dance. Perhaps because he had grown up around dancers—he shared a room with Gelsey Kirkland at one point—he had an almost pathological fear of dancing, convinced that whatever movement he made would be clumsy and stupid in comparison. Now he had to dance in front of a room full of dancers, including his mother and Monica Mason, by then assistant director of the Royal Ballet.

We'd chosen the Bond song 'Nobody Does It Better'—and he swayed manfully from side to side. I think it went as well as it could and the whole event, full of old-fashioned elegance and a lot of warmth, felt like the perfect start to our married life. We spent the first night of our honeymoon at the Savoy and Elizabeth McGorian took one of my favourite pictures of the whole day, of Tobias and me walking slowly away from the reception, back to the hotel. My left hand is in his, and in my right, I am carrying my high-heeled shoes as I stroll on the pavement barefoot.

Our six-day honeymoon in the South of France had two unusual qualities. Firstly, because I was dancing both *Swan Lake* and a gala to celebrate Anthony Dowell fairly soon afterwards, I wanted to keep in shape, so I had to do some form of training most days. Secondly, Tobias's parents came too. He's always a bit embarrassed about this, but it was lovely to spend some extra time with them. They stayed in Beaulieu-sur-Mer, while we booked into the Château de la Chèvre d'Or, a luxurious hotel perched on the cliffs above, nestling in the medieval town of Èze. It was a heavenly setting with a pool where I would work through some ballet exercises every day before either lazing around in the July sun, or setting off to explore.

We didn't see Roy and Georgina every day, but we did have dinner together occasionally, visited the casino in Beaulieu and went on a day trip to Monaco where I went to the Academy Princess Grace, the world-famous ballet school, to do a proper class. We drove back to Èze past La Turbie, full of memories for Georgina because it was where Nureyev had owned a villa and she, Roy and Tobias had spent time there.

One day when we were sitting side by side in physio in the Royal Opera House, Sylvie had recommended that if we went to the South of France for our honeymoon we should drive to La Colombe d'Or, a famous restaurant in St Paul de Vence, which had been a meeting place for artists and performers since the 1920s. It was an enchanting, dreamlike setting, showing on its walls paintings by masters such as Picasso, Matisse, and Léger and photographs of the film stars such as Yves Montand and Simone Signoret, all of whom used to hang out there. We ate in the garden and loved it so much that two years later we returned with our baby son and Georgina and Roy, who hadn't been allowed to join us for that moment on our honeymoon.

After this fairy-tale break, it was back to London for the gala in celebration of Anthony, in which I danced the first act pas de deux from *Manon* with Johan. The second performance of the bill, on 4 August, coincided with the Queen Mother's 101st birthday and she came along to the Royal Opera House as part of her birthday celebrations. I was invited to a small private party at the back of the

Royal box after the performance. My strongest memory is how tiny she was; at five feet, two inches, I towered over her. The whole occasion felt very special. The Queen Mother's presence on the opening night of the Royal Opera House after the war, with the two young princesses peering over the edge of the box, had been part of the continuity of the place ever since. She had seen so much change and now the Royal Ballet was about to undergo another period of upheaval with Anthony Dowell's departure. Entirely unexpectedly, Ross Stretton, the head of The Australian Ballet, had been hired to replace him. It was a shock for everyone, but particularly for me. After everything that had happened in our conversations about my joining The Australian Ballet, and how badly it had ended, it was hard to swallow the idea that he would be my new boss. He didn't say anything to me, and I didn't say anything to him. He was polite, and I did what I always had. I put my head down and did my best.

CHAPTER 18

NEW ARRIVALS

AS ROSS STRETTON ARRIVED IN London, I went to Australia. I'd been asked by his successor at The Australian Ballet, David McAllister, to guest with the company in Melbourne in *Giselle* and *Études* when the Royal Ballet were on holiday over the summer. I jumped at the chance to spend a little time back near Mum and Dad and to dance in Australia. I felt I owed my homeland so much and it was always a particular pleasure to be back in front of audiences who had been so supportive and proud.

It was also a chance to experience a new *Giselle*. I was so used to Peter Wright's versions for SWRB and the Royal, and it was refreshing and interesting to fit into Peggy van Praagh's production, which cast a familiar role in a different light. The second act is always more or less the same wherever you dance it, but different producers change the flow and feel of the first act quite considerably. Van Praagh was another balletic pioneer who traced her knowledge back to the early twentieth century; she danced briefly with Anton Dolin's company in London, learnt mime from Tamara Karsavina and repertoire with

Lydia Sokolova. She danced with Marie Rambert's Ballet Rambert and taught company classes at SWRB before becoming a teacher at the school in the immediate post-war years. With the backing of Ninette de Valois she became the founder director of The Australian Ballet.

Her 1965 *Giselle* was one of the milestones on the way to the company becoming acclaimed internationally, and it had just come back into the repertory. There was a lot of dancing in the First Act, so I had to learn a new pas de deux and that suited me because I was moving more. In the Royal Ballet production, the dancer playing Giselle has to sit on a bench on the sidelines, watching the action for a long time, and I don't much like sitting before having to dance, particularly since the solo you're waiting for needs control, so like a lot of ballerinas I used to nip off to warm up, have some water and retie my shoes before the solo.

But when you're sitting in the auditorium as a spectator, you often notice the character's absence. With my coaching eye on, I realise there's something lovely about having Giselle absorbing the action with the audience, as it were. In ballets such as this and *Coppélia*, the ballerina has to do a lot of sitting around, watching other dancers. You're not really needed but you are colouring the scene. When a ballerina remains onstage, your eye still leaps to her reaction, to her animation, to the way she interacts with the story. I really value that. If you do need to sneak off, you've got to find a way to get back on seamlessly, otherwise it just looks ridiculous—and you have to know what you are doing in order to slip back in and get yourself absorbed in the story.

I was dancing with Steven Heathcote, a brilliant principal and one of the strongest partners and nicest people I have ever met. He performed Albrecht in such a natural, easy way that it turned my experience of the ballet around. I found it easier to react to such a warm presence opposite me, and I think my performance became more naturalistic and engaged as a result. Certainly, the reviews were pleasingly appreciative. In his review for *The Australian* the critic

Lee Christofis said the night belonged to me.[1] When I returned to Australia to coach *Giselle* in 2019, Steven sat next to me as a coach as we helped a new generation understand the ballet. It was another moment when my life felt as if it had come full circle.

Those performances together, however, were overshadowed by the terrible events of the September 11 attacks in New York. I walked back to my rented apartment in Melbourne from the State Theatre, and like the rest of the world, turned on the TV to find myself confronted with the horror of the bombing of the World Trade Centre. I didn't know who to call. Tobias was in Los Angeles as the executive producer for the opening of Matthew Bourne's *Car Man*, Georgina was in Japan with ABT, but Roy was in New York. I was terrified by what was happening, frantic with worry and relieved when I eventually discovered he was safe. Although he had only been a mile away from the towers coming down, he found all the fuss about him bemusing and slightly irritating, since, as he kept pointing out, he had survived the Blitz in London as a child. The next performance of *Giselle* in Australia was dedicated to the families of those who had died.

Coming back to London, I faced a difficult period in my own life. Almost as soon as I returned, I was elated to discover I was pregnant. Then, just as we had been out for drinks—a sip of champagne in my case—to celebrate, I had a miscarriage. It was very early in the pregnancy, but it was still a complete roller-coaster of emotions and a sad and horrible time. Like most people who don't know how to grieve, I went back to work the next day.

Tamara was the only person I confided in, and she was lovely; when I was rehearsing with Carlos Acosta later, I told him too and he was equally sympathetic. It was particularly unsettling for me because there was a history of miscarriage in our family and Madonna had miscarried three times before giving birth to her first child. I began to worry that I would struggle to have the baby I so longed for. I hadn't always felt that way; in my youth, I was fairly relaxed about whether I had a child or not. But then I met Tobias, fell in love, and everything changed. Suddenly, I realised I didn't want to miss out on the experience of having a child or building a family in the way my parents had. I was already thirty-seven and time seemed to be slipping by. I didn't talk about my feelings to anyone.

Professionally, it was a fraught time. Ross Stretton had been appointed as a new broom, but in his thirteen months in charge, he didn't so much breathe new life into the company, as virtually blow it apart. It quickly became apparent that he had favourite dancers who he would work to the point of exhaustion while demoting others. Principals were suddenly relegated to the matinees while soloists took the evening slots. Some people danced all the time, some barely at all. Sarah Wildor, a principal, resigned when she discovered she had no leading performances; Irek Mukhamedov, loved by audiences, was unceremoniously dropped without being given a chance to say goodbye. I felt trepidation about Ross's arrival because I thought he had behaved so oddly when he suddenly withdrew my invitation to dance with Australian Ballet; I was also conscious that I was an older, established dancer when he was looking to make his mark with new stars who caught his eye. I felt vulnerable, but as it turned out we had an amicable working relationship and I managed to make things work.

At the start of his directorship, because of the schedule, I had a long patch away from the stage, only returning in December with a set of Nutcrackers that ran until January, opposite Johan Persson as my prince. Tobias and I celebrated Christmas with our friends in London, while the entire Benjamin clan, including Madonna, Aunty Pat and Uncle Ray, were in Rockhampton. It was the first time they had all been together for Christmas—without me. Our tight extended family had been stretched across the world, physically apart, but emotionally together. My mum joked in a letter about the cooking, which had never been my forte. I wrote back to assure them that although I was in charge of ambience—candles, champagne and flowers—Tobias was in charge of food. Perhaps strategically, I have never really learnt to cook and have been known to forget to serve a main course.

In January 2002, Ross introduced the first of his mixed bills, called *Memories*, which included a new work called *Beyond Bach* by the Australian choreographer Stephen Baynes, for which I was in the second cast. Created in 1995 for The Australian Ballet, it was a pretty, neo-classical work that I rather liked because it gave me a new vocabulary of steps to learn, but though it had been successful in Australia it didn't translate to the UK. That sometimes happens—different countries have such varying tastes. It mainly remains in my memory because I was dancing with Johan Persson and at one performance in February, he had an injured knee that he was reluctant to put weight on before we even ventured on to the stage. There were a lot of injuries during this period. By the end of the summer season, the principals who were scheduled to dance only appeared in two out of twenty-two shows.[2] In this instance, there was no cover for Johan in the ballet and he went on; it was terrifying and awful. He hopped off into the wings midway through partnering me, leaving me to improvise. He never danced again, though he has since forged a career as one of the best ballet and theatre photographers. The other reason I remember that bill is that it marked the first time I danced with a young soloist called Edward Watson, in Antony Tudor's *The Leaves are Fading*.

In June 2002, the Royal Ballet set off on a tour of Australia. I was so excited. I was going home with the company that had been my adopted home for so long. There was a buzz about the visit, because it was the first time the Royal had visited Australia in fourteen years, the first time Stretton had taken his new company abroad, and it was billed as the most ambitious ballet tour to Australia ever. There was quite a lot of advance publicity about my homecoming in the papers, including a proud piece in the *The Catholic Leader* headlined: 'Star role for Bishop's niece in Royal Ballet.'[3] As far as I was concerned it all began very well: I danced *Swan Lake* at the Lyric Theatre in Brisbane with Johan Kobborg, and then in Sydney and Melbourne with Robert Tewsley, a tall, elegant dancer. I also performed in *The Leaves Are Fading* with Ed.

In Melbourne, on the morning I was due to dance *Giselle*, disaster struck. I woke up feeling incredibly dizzy. The whole room was spinning and there was nothing I could do to stop it. I was distraught. Many members of my family and my friends had booked tickets to see me performing the role that had launched my career and were flying in from across Australia, and I couldn't even stand up. Apart from letting down the company and my partner, I felt so guilty that all those people were waiting on me and I was going to disappoint them.

I was also very, very frightened. I rang Monica Mason in a panic, and she was wonderful, calm and reassuring. Initially I wondered if the dizziness had been triggered by the pressure on the plane. Tamara had got off the same long flight with a toe swollen to twice its normal size which stopped her dancing for most of the tour. But I had been fine at first, really in my groove, dancing at the peak of my power. Suddenly to wake up with an injury I couldn't see was terrifying and I didn't know what had hit me. The acute dizziness vanished as quickly as it had arrived, and tests in Australia couldn't reveal the cause, but it has never entirely gone away.

Eventually it was diagnosed as benign paroxysmal positional vertigo, which is a condition where the 'small stones' in the inner ear, which help the body sense what position it is in have been displaced. Doctors thought it might have been caused by my fall on the bathroom floor the previous year, but I will never absolutely know. I have tried all kinds of treatments, including one where they threw me from side to side in an attempt to recalibrate the crystals. That just seemed to make it worse. It's never been quite as bad as it was that first day, but I have still had many moments of dizziness when I was dancing. It was like having an injury I had to work around. Edward Watson was always incredible about it. If I turned upside down, or went into a backbend for too long, it sometimes brought it on. He'd make sure I was all right and help me plan my movements in advance to avoid triggering it.

After that day in Melbourne, when Miyako Yoshida stepped in to dance Giselle in my place, I retreated to Rockhampton to soak up some family love before coming back to London. I wrote to my parents on my return: 'You have been incredible as ever with your love and generosity and I feel so lucky to be your daughter.'

Back in London, I didn't dance in the infamous gala that Ross mounted at Covent Garden for the Queen's Golden Jubilee on 23 July. Where previous galas had been so carefully chosen and curated, he had decided to stage ten excerpts from ballets in the current repertory, and add a section from *Birthday Offering*, Ashton's 1956 celebration of twenty-five years of the Royal Ballet. It was flung together with no real thought or care and no sense of history; I was glad not to be part of it.

By this point Ross's time at the Royal Opera House had turned very sour,[4] and unbeknown to me, the dancers were considering a vote of no confidence in him as director and had complained to Tony Hall, who had succeeded Michael Kaiser as chief executive in April the previous year. There was unhappiness about casting decisions, and profound concern about his failure to appreciate the history of the company he was running. There were also rumours beginning to reach the press of inappropriate relationships between him and younger dancers.[5]

Ballet is a physical art form, and dancers spend most of their working day in close proximity to others. Sometimes the touching, the portrayal of intimacy and being emotionally, professionally and physically vulnerable, can bring about situations which require experience and maturity to handle—not always easy if you are young, and new to negotiating your professional life. Indeed, you could be as sophisticated and worldly as possible, and still find certain things difficult to cope with. In 2016, the world began to take a good hard look at some huge, urgent questions about how women (and sometimes men too) are treated, particularly in the workplace. Looking back on my entire career now, there were situations I found myself in that would not be tolerated today, and rightfully so. The acceptable orthodoxy of the time needed to change. Without going into any details, the 'Me Too' movement could have been a reflection on behaviour commonplace in ballet, going back a very long time, in many parts of the world, and there are unquestionably people whose lives have been harmed because of it. I think the ballet world, while still not perfect, has never been a safer and fairer workplace than it is today, in no small way thanks to the courage of those who have stepped forward to challenge the status quo.

I was away on holiday in Sardinia when matters with Ross Stretton came to a head. The Board intervened, and in September 2002 he left without clearing his desk or saying goodbye. He tragically died of melanoma in June 2005, at the age of fifty-three, having been ill for some time and I wonder now whether he was already ill when he took on the job and whether that affected his judgement. Looking back, it's clear that he tried to do too much too fast; he wanted to modernise the company, but he did so without any appreciation of traditions that were worth keeping. There were moments of excitement in his time: both Sylvie and Tamara scored personal success in Mats Ek's *Carmen*, a ballet I would have loved to have danced. Christopher Wheeldon created the lovely *Tryst*. *Onegin* was also a hit. But too often the ballets he brought in were not well received, because they were not a good fit with the traditions and training of the company, and those he omitted by Ashton and MacMillan were too valuable to lose. It was an unhappy period, though it was also one that affected me less than some other dancers. I did my rehearsals and went home, keeping very much to myself. If there's one thing I am proudest of in my career, it is that I have survived so many ups and downs, making the situation work however dark it may seem.

Things got back on track when Monica Mason stepped in, first as acting artistic director and then confirmed in the role. From my point of view, there couldn't have been a better choice. The company was now in the hands of someone I respected and who understood its repertory intimately. One of her first acts was to alter the 2002–03 season to include tributes to Nureyev and to Kenneth MacMillan on the tenth anniversary of his death. *Mayerling* was the first of his ballets programmed, and I was cast to dance Mary again, this time with Robert Tewsley.

One morning, in class, just before our rehearsals were due to start, I began to feel a bit strange. I was sweating during barre, which I didn't normally do and felt as if something was subtly different. I had been trying to get pregnant ever since the miscarriage a year before, so I was very aware of my body. When we went into rehearsal and were practising the big lifts, I fudged them a bit because all I wanted to do was to go home and do a pregnancy test. Robert was shocked. I never didn't give my all in a rehearsal, and here I was refusing to repeat a lift to get it right, shirking from trying new things. I was so sure I was pregnant, but I didn't want to say anything until it was confirmed. I went home, did the test and I was. It was extraordinary to me that I had felt it so quickly in my body.

Shortly after, I went to see Monica Mason in her small office. She wasn't aware that I had lost a baby the year before, as I had kept the trauma of that time close to my chest. But she was understanding and accommodating, particularly when I told her that I wanted to stop dancing immediately. Some dancers carry on performing in the early months of their pregnancy and most continue to exercise throughout. But I didn't want to do anything that might risk another miscarriage. I was also, immediately, extremely nauseous, a condition that continued for most of the early months. I went right off coffee and red wine. I couldn't even bear the smell. It took me fifteen years to start drinking coffee again, and I now always choose white wine over red. I would never have thought that having a baby would put me off two of my favourite things.

I was terribly excited but also nervous, worrying that something would go wrong again. I was lucky to find an obstetrician in the person of Jeffrey Braithwaite who looked after me and helped to make my pregnancy both happy and calm. He had the most perfect, confident manner during my many check-ups in Harley Street; when I was with him, I could never imagine anything going wrong. I needed that reassurance, because I was so sure it might, and trying to be so careful that it didn't.

On that day in September, I walked out of Covent Garden and went home. I've no idea what Monica told everyone about where I was, but a few months later, when I felt more confident about not having another miscarriage, I walked back into the studio for a social visit. I was greeted so warmly and with a fair amount of teasing: I had breasts and a tummy and no one had ever seen me with curves before. Around that time, I also started to do a tiny bit of pilates in the gym underneath my apartment block in Chepstow Place. I would stretch out on the mats and let the world pass me by; to this day, I can't listen to Coldplay's *Yellow* without a feeling of nausea, because that was the most popular CD in the gym at the time. It brings it all back.

In November, the press office officially announced my pregnancy, saying my baby was due in the summer, and added, 'She intends to continue her dancing career after the birth of her baby.' To be honest, that was by no means a given. I was enjoying my time away from the stage. There's such a difference in voluntarily stopping dancing and not taking class because you are injured. With an injury you are always anxious, working your way back towards something. With pregnancy, I could let myself go and begin to enjoy the changes that my body underwent. I had been dancing professionally for so long that this absence for such a positive reason felt like a revelation and a luxury, something I had never had the opportunity to enjoy. Over Christmas, I went back to Rockhampton with Tobias and was pampered as I soaked up the Queensland sun and enjoyed my Mum's home cooking. It was entirely without pressure and full of joy. I loved being with my parents at that time. They have always been my role model as a happily married couple and as parents. To be able to share the early months of my pregnancy with them felt inspirational.

There were other advantages to this break as well. Getting away from dance helped me to realise it was only a part of my life, not all of it. It was a part I adored, but having a child was always going to come first for me. Enforced relaxation gave me an opportunity to open my eyes, to see the world around me, to pursue my interests in theatre and art. Ballet became one strand in a multi-coloured world. I learnt a lot from taking my seat back in the audience. Watching Irek Muhkamedov, for example, by then forty and coming to the end of his career, taught me a lot. He had so much energy, such commitment, and I suddenly realised that dance wasn't always about perfection but about impact. He gave himself completely on that stage, lost in his role, and seeing him woke me up. My battle as a ballerina was always about doing everything just right; he understood performance, didn't get caught up in trivialities, was careful with his partners, and so full of life.

In late spring, I popped back into the Opera House for a meeting, and to take some photographs outside with Tobias, showing off my bump. Wayne McGregor bounced up to me as I was queuing in the canteen. I didn't know him that well then; he was very much a new face at the Opera House, better known for his experimental contemporary dance work than for creations for ballet companies, but he was friends with Ed Watson, who had worked with him on new pieces seen in the Linbury. I liked his vibe, the way that with his shaven head and lanky frame, he was so different from everyone else.

He was smiling and enthusiastic as we met. 'Do you want to dance the lead in my new ballet?' he asked.

I looked down at my bump and we both laughed. But he was entirely serious. Even though I hadn't done any contemporary work, he wanted me to dance in the first work he was making for the main stage at Covent Garden. The contrast between the athletic, taut movements of a McGregor piece, the knotty partnering, the skimpy costumes and my current appearance seemed an unbridgeable gap.

There was only one possible response: 'Yes, I'd love to,' I said.

I had no idea how it was all going to come together, but it was too exciting a chance to let go.

In May, Tobias and I returned to the South of France for a few days, knowing that life would soon be about to change for ever. We wanted to have a last, romantic break in a place that we had always been happy. Until that point, despite Tobias's doubts, Mr Braithwaite had been confident that even though I was so tiny, I would be able to have a natural birth. I was keen to try because I knew it would give me a faster recovery time, but eventually everyone decided that an elective caesarean would be safer, and 2 June was scheduled as birth day. The events of the morning are confused in my mind, but I know that I did my usual faffing around about leaving the house, procrastinating over whether I had what I needed for my hospital stay. I looked on the whole event as a performance: I'd been through nine months of rehearsal—now I was ready for the show.

The whole thing went wonderfully smoothly; I've had more pain dancing with a blister. I had no idea what kind of baby I was about to have—I'd never peeked at Christmas presents as a child and I saw no need to know the sex of my baby in advance. This meant that we hadn't finally decided on names either. I come from a family with three girls and one boy, so I'd convinced myself that I was having a girl, and we had quite a few options to choose from. For boys we only had two: Evan, in honour of my grandfather, or Thomas because we thought it sounded good both long and shortened, and because I'd been completely smitten with Steve McQueen who played Thomas Crown in *The Thomas Crown Affair*. Thomas Round had a good ring about it, but we hadn't decided.

I was crying with happiness when my seven pounds and three ounce baby boy was born, with a full head of dark hair. The moment that Mr Braithwaite said, 'It's a boy' and handed him to me, Tobias said, 'Look Leanne, it's Thomas.' That was that. I was so emotional, elated and overwhelmed, that I didn't have strength to discuss it, even if I'd wanted to. Tobias says it was the quickest acquiescence he's ever won from me, and I suppose it was. Every mother knows how you feel immediately after childbirth; you're exhausted but just so happy to hold this tiny, trusting bundle in your arms, all eyes and limbs, who is all yours. I felt such a sense of joy and fulfilment.

Tobias went in to work later that day; he's never been able to shake off his puritanical American work habits. He was by this time general manager at the Donmar Warehouse, and his colleagues thought he had taken leave of his senses and sent him away with a big bouquet for me. I was in a private room at the Portland Clinic, battered and sleepy, but triumphant with Thomas by my side. I was due to stay in hospital for five days but escaped after two. I was desperate to get home, where we had, very wisely, given that neither set of parents was around in London to help us, employed a maternity nurse called Margaret Evans. She was brilliant, a complete cliché of the Welsh mother, with a big bosom and a bigger personality. We were such newbies and she knew everything, guiding us through the first two weeks of parenthood with consummate ease, and teaching us all we needed to know. Tobias had never held a child, apart from holding Madonna's infant daughter, Miriam, for about two minutes, and we both had such a lot to learn. It always amazes us that you need lessons and a licence to drive a car, and you have to fill in a questionnaire if you want a dog, but you're packed off with your first baby without any kind of manual. We weren't even sure we knew how to keep Thomas alive, but Margaret did, and she saved our lives too.

Luckily, Thomas was a really good baby. He was healthy and happy, and never suffered from colic or sleepless nights. I breastfed him for almost three months, before switching to a mix of breast milk and bottles so I could leave him for a time. Those early months with him were blissful as we learnt how to look after him: changing nappies and bathing him on a wooden table in the middle of the living room, feeding him in a big chair by the window, and taking him out in the summer sunshine in his pram.

After four weeks, however, I walked up the road ready to start pilates with Dreas Reyneke. Dreas has probably improved the posture, health and strength of more dancers than any man living. A Rambert dancer himself originally, he has worked with Lynn Seymour, Gelsey Kirkland and Russell Maliphant, not to mention people such as Christopher Lambert, Tilda Swinton and Martin Amis. He's wise as well as knowledgeable, someone who makes you feel better by his presence as well as his training.

I'd first met him through Russell and had been going to see him since my earliest dancing days. He had got me through difficult injuries, so I knew he was the man to help me post-pregnancy. That first morning, he sent me home again, saying it was much too early to begin any form of training, however gentle, after a caesarean. Two weeks later, I went back and began, starting just with feet exercises, then slowly working my way up and around my body. I knew it would be a slog to get back to full dancing fitness, and although there was an amazing team of rehab specialists available to help me at the Opera House, I devised my own programme, feeling I knew what my body required. I found a studio at the ROH, and worked my way back to strength, pushing myself in increments: ten minutes ballet barre on the first day, fifteen minutes the next, then twenty and so on until I was strong enough to join company class again and then go to rehearsals.

The idea of dancing in Wayne's new work dangled before me like a carrot of inspiration. I'd also been cast in Christopher Wheeldon's *Polyphonia*, imported from the New York City Ballet, and in my beloved *Romeo and Juliet*—all things I longed to dance. I worked day-to-day and made plans week-to-week. I was thirty-nine years old. It was getting to the time to call it a day. But after Thomas's birth, my career was reborn.

CHAPTER 19

A CAREER REBORN

AFTER THOMAS WAS BORN, I thought I would return to the stage for a year, that I would see how it went with juggling a child at home and a career as a ballerina. Then I went back and he was fine, and I was enjoying myself, so a year became two, then three. My body felt great, and my repertoire was expanding. All of a sudden it was another ten years.

I think if I hadn't had a baby, I would have called it a day much sooner, retiring in my early forties, which is already later than most dancers hang up their pointe shoes. I'd always had a horror of hanging around; my mother and I had seen Fonteyn at the end of her performing days, when her lustre had vanished. We were watching a memory of a legendary dancer, not the real thing. I remember my mother whispering to me, 'Why do they go on so long?' I didn't want that to happen to me. But I really felt rejuvenated after Thomas arrived.

A lot of factors played into that. One was luck. Anthony Dowell once said that dancers are forced to retire just as they reach their peak artistically. Their bodies fail them at precisely the moment their knowledge has increased to the point where they will bring new perceptions to their work. It's not always true. Sylvie Guillem famously built a second career when she retired from the balletic stage, forging a new world in more contemporary work. I had similar good fortune on the ballet stage. My body allowed me to carry on dancing at my peak; if anything, the absolute break from dancing my pregnancy had enforced seemed to strengthen me. I didn't feel worn out. I felt refreshed and ready to go.

The second quality that helped me was my mental attitude. I never got bored. I saw dancers younger than me who had lost interest, but I was happy to challenge myself physically at all times. It became a virtuous circle. Because I was interested, I wanted to push my technique and so I kept up my standards. I would have felt a failure if I hadn't pushed myself and I didn't want to fail, I wanted to keep doing what I loved. That meant I did everything to the best of my ability, with the best of intentions, and with the most rehearsals I could squeeze in while still giving plenty of attention and love to Thomas. What's more I was mature enough to know how to manage my time and my dancing to sustain myself. I regarded every show as a bonus and danced each as if it were my last. That makes a difference.

In the last decade of my career, too, a terrific new generation of choreographers was emerging, and they were interested in seeing what I could bring to their works. They kept my mind as pliant as my body, by allowing me to explore more contemporary ballets alongside a band of much younger dancers. It was thrilling for me to give myself over to them, to make the decision to stay current and to embrace the new, not just to stick with the classics. As a result, I helped to create more new works in the last decade of my career than I had in the previous two.

I jumped in at the deep end as soon as I went back to the Opera House. Wayne McGregor's *Qualia* was like nothing I had danced before; to be truthful, its sci-fi, twisty vibe wasn't like anything most people had seen before, either. Wayne's background was entirely contemporary. He had come into the Opera House at the invitation of Deborah Bull, who had been charged with bringing new talent into the building. He'd made a couple of small works in that context before Monica Mason asked him if he'd like to try his hand on the main stage. That piece was *Qualia*, which had been cast mainly from the up-and-coming members of the company. I was one of only two principals in the room—and the only person who had just returned from a maternity leave of more than a year.

It was an incredible shock to the system, like learning a new language. It felt so fresh. Wayne himself is invigorating—bouncy, exciting—and he brought a blast of energy into the Opera House. His entire attitude was so different from everyone who had come before. It was a place that felt enmeshed in its classical lineage of pink tights and pointe shoes. I love that side of ballet very much, but it was just fabulous to feel the contrast in Wayne, in his manner and his appearance, in his tracksuits and zany pants and different music and dance language choices. Three years later, Monica Mason showed extraordinary vision in appointing him resident choreographer after the success of his next ballet *Chroma*. By his commitment to the Royal Ballet, he has made himself part of its great tradition, his innovations guiding it towards the future.

But when we were all making *Qualia*, his presence still felt experimental. My main memory of that first encounter is my aching limbs and sore muscles when I went home every night. Everything hurt, including my brain, as I struggled to get my head and my body around a vocabulary of movement that was totally unfamiliar to me. Wayne stretches you in ways you can't describe, asking you to imagine steps that seem impossible, and then asking you to perform them at high speed. I was lucky that I was working with Edward Watson, who has been in every ballet Wayne has made for the Opera House, bar one (when he was injured). He was really helpful to me, offering ways of remembering the complexity of the steps. He already had the same understanding with Wayne that I felt I had with Kenneth in that brief moment with him in the studio. Ed was on the same wavelength as Wayne's intentions. I would watch him attack the choreography without asking too many questions, and began to stop querying things and adopt the same approach of just getting on with it.

Dancing Wayne's work keeps you nimble. Sometimes ballet can become a bit rigid and you get into the habit of sitting down on your legs. With Wayne's work you never get the opportunity to do that, as you're on the move all the time. He's also rapid in the way he thinks; he is cerebral and his interests in science and maths shape both his themes and the way in which he creates. You never quite know where the section you are creating will fit. I remember once making an entire passage with Steven McRae that took ages but was eventually dropped. Steven and I were gutted. Wayne cuts and pastes like that all the time, making changes until the last minute, and it's amazing to be part of that process. Finding success as a dancer isn't just about staying fit, or even about being talented. It's also about how you are as a person, how you behave in the studio, and whether you have enough to give. You need to be interested and curious. Someone like Wayne encouraged both of those things, and that fed me, giving me the chance to stay relevant.

Although *Qualia* was the first piece I made when I returned to work, it wasn't the first I danced. That was *Polyphonia*, choreographed by Christopher Wheeldon, another ground-breaking choreographer who became significant in shaping the latter stages of my career and the modern face of the Royal Ballet. Chris, who is now Artistic Associate at the Royal Ballet, had been trained in the Royal Ballet School and danced with the company before going to New York and forging the early part of his career with New York City Ballet. He'd made *Polyphonia* there in 2001, and I was chosen to be in the first Royal Ballet performances in November 2003, taking on a role originally created for Wendy Whelan, a muse to Chris, and a dancer I had always admired. It was the first time I had worked with Chris who brought great energy and honesty to the studio. His choreography is uniquely sophisticated in structure, and comes directly from the heart.

He also has a very intense response to music, often setting his movement against complicated, atonal compositions, and I had to learn to navigate those demands. *Polyphonia* took its title and its texture from the music of György Ligeti and is probably one of the scores I found most difficult to dance to. The first movement asks its four leading couples to dance in unison, which is a struggle because unlike a corps de ballet we are not used to that. It switches between order and disorder, and there's no melody as such to give you a clue to the music's shifts, but there was also no possibility of fudging because you need to be in time with the others. The YouTube film of Chris rehearsing this section, which was filmed on World Ballet Day some years later, shows how phenomenally tough it is.

Music is massively important to me as a dancer. Some people learn a role through counts, but I tend not to use them. Wayne's choreography is the exception to this; he rarely plays the final score when we are making the ballet in the rehearsal room, deliberately choosing other pieces to work to at the start of the creation. I learn steps quite easily, using the music to remind me of a phrase or a pause. When that's not there, it's difficult for me to remember sequences. The idea of changing the rhythm of my body to fit the music Wayne knew he was going to use, but didn't have playing, was testing.

Having a range of choreographers making regular work for the Royal Ballet is such an asset for today's dancers. They like to create with a variety of people, and choose dancers from every stage of their career. To know that you could be in the first year of the corps de ballet and yet end up working with one of these great choreographers is a phenomenal opportunity that I don't think would have happened in the past. When you arrived at the Royal Ballet in my time, you had to wait your turn and creep through into what opportunities were available. The repertory now gives youngsters a greater chance to express themselves. Without that kind of experience, it's much harder to develop.

When I stepped back on to the stage in *Polyphonia* on 15 November 2003 it felt like a mixture of a homecoming and a new adventure. To add an extra layer of significance, my partner was Jonathan Cope, who had accompanied me on my first great venture at the Royal Opera House in the school performance. We had a long, sculptural pas de deux in the second movement, which Debra Craine described as 'startling, knotted into intricate connections yet yearning for simple intimacy'.[1] A lot of the critics noticed my return to form after maternity leave, with one saying that I looked 'softer and gentler than we are used to'.[2] The applause was thunderous.

Before *Qualia*, I also danced a *Romeo and Juliet* with Viacheslav Samodurov. It was such a pleasure to return to a role I had always loved, and one that I felt from the very first fitted me like a glove. It wasn't just the choreography that suited me, but the high-waisted costumes designed by Nicholas Georgiadis that were perfect for my frame. The first time I danced it, as is customary, I went to the costume department for a fitting and was given a range of previously worn costumes to see which one was closest to my size. Each had a cotton tag stitched in the bodice, recording the dancers who had previously performed the role in that particular garment. The one that fitted me perfectly had Natalia Makarova's name inside; I have never been more pleased to wear something second-hand. By this point in my career, I had my own name stitched inside a costume specially made for me. Hopefully one day a young dancer will feel as happy as I did when she puts it on for the first time.

'It's exciting to see a young dancer triumph in a role for the first time, but it's just as exciting, if not more so, to see an older dancer come back from a long absence and triumph in a role we thought was behind her,' wrote Debra Craine. 'On Monday night, Leanne Benjamin was determined to prove that Juliet, that slip of a girl, was still hers. Benjamin is a 39-year-old woman who gave birth in June, but you would never know it. She looks young enough to be a teenager in love and she sailed through the demanding role with an impetuosity and lightness that made the years fall away.'[3]

The performances made me feel so alive. I tended to view them as a night off from the ritual of feeding Thomas and getting him to bed. I loved that too, of course, but there was something so glamorous about being back on that stage. By then, like every working mother, I was beginning to get adept at the daily time management that goes on when you're trying to combine a career and a child. I was much helped by a Latvian nanny called Irina Gladun, an inscrutable character with her own firm view on how things should be done. The first time she turned up for an interview, I was barefoot, and she was horrified; she felt it wasn't good for the baby. I knew instantly that her loving instincts would make her the perfect person to help us and we never had a moment's hesitation about leaving Thomas in her care. For the next two years, she was an essential part of my life. After she left, Thomas was a pageboy at her wedding, and even though she now has children of her own, she never forgets to send him greetings for his birthday.

Qualia opened on 3 December in a quadruple bill of new work, that also featured Russell Maliphant's *Broken Fall*, starring Sylvie Guillem with Michael Nunn and William Trevitt, who were by then universally known as the BalletBoyz. If I felt my life was beginning a new chapter, this felt like a new beginning for the Royal Ballet itself, containing Russell's first piece for the company where he had trained and for whose touring arm he had danced, Wayne's first main stage work, plus a piece by William Tuckett and American choreographer Mark Morris's *Gong*. Judith Mackrell wrote in her *Guardian* review: 'It's widely rumoured that ballet companies are dying for lack of new ideas … but on Wednesday, the Royal raised a defiant finger to that notion by programming a quartet of works that flaunted fresh blood.'[4]

It was bold and exciting, with not a tutu in sight, and there I was in the centre of it all, in short shorts and a tiny, figure-hugging bodice. The conclusion of *Qualia*, which had an electronic score by Scanner, was a lingering, slow duet for me and Ed in which, as Clifford Bishop remarked in *The Sunday Times*, 'they seem to stretch each other like elastic bands'.[5] That pas de deux, more emotional than anything that had come before in the ballet, became one of the works I performed most often in my final decade; an obsessive exploration of what two bodies can do, that is both beautiful and endlessly inventive.

January brought a night of exceptional offstage excitement. I was dancing Cinderella when the whisper suddenly ran round backstage that David and Victoria Beckham were in the audience. If you had asked me who in the whole world I most wanted to meet at that point, it would have been English football's superstar David Beckham. I wasn't much into football, but I was completely smitten with him and watched every England game he played. When he and Victoria came round to see us all after the show, they were ushered on to the stage to a burst of applause and for once in my life I was awestruck and tongue-tied. Victoria was very gracious, standing back so we could all cluster round her footballing husband. He has incredible charisma and always seems very genuine; I managed to get a photograph taken of me and him. Nowadays, we go to the same grocery store, and I sometimes run into him. I always want to ask if he remembers seeing me as Cinderella, but though we have had little chats while queuing for the cash register, I've never plucked up courage. I admire his career; he has done so much for England, for football and for sport in general.

The same month, I danced *Giselle* with Jonathan Cope, which felt like a closing of a circle. Sitting on the same bench as we had done when we were teenagers, picking daisies and gazing into one another's eyes, made me realise how far we both had come. Sometimes it can be hard to play Giselle and Albrecht when you are more mature, but I tend to think that the most difficult time to engross yourself in these classical parts is in the middle of your career. Certainly, there was a point in my thirties where I was almost embarrassed to be playing a sixteen-year-old on the threshold of love. It's so easy when you are young, but actually I think my performances as an older dancer were probably better. I approached my early performances in the classics with so much energy. Later I had more refinement; I could say more with less. But you couldn't get to that point if you hadn't first gone through the process of flinging everything you had into the production. At nineteen or twenty, you are usually more athletic, and you think bigger is always better. You learn that that's not always true; perhaps because you have less power when you are older, you find something less gestural and more truthful.

It was the same with Juliet. I felt a bit of a fraud clutching a teddy bear in my forties, but once I'd climbed over that sensation, I could bring different strokes of understanding. At twenty, you're colouring the role from your first-hand, recently-felt knowledge of being a teenager in love, and your interpretation is full of vitality. At forty, you conjure a romantic ideal from your memory, and fill it with more nuance. You begin to understand the balance of Kenneth MacMillan's ballet. I always found Act III the most interesting, because there is more opportunity to act as you spring off the character artists surrounding you. In this way, I think my performance had greater freedom the more I danced it. I certainly discovered more depth through moments of stillness, which perhaps I didn't when I first performed.

In early 2004, I was re-exploring a lot of the MacMillan repertoire. I returned to Mary in *Mayerling*, dancing with Carlos as Rudolf for the first time. When I returned from maternity leave and was discussing my repertory, Monica Mason suggested I drop the role as someone had replaced me when I was pregnant. I put my foot down and insisted; I knew Mary was a character I danced well and I would never willingly give her up. This was quickly followed by a revival of *Anastasia*, which I had last danced eight years before. The critics struggled with the differing tones of the three sections of the work. Luke Jennings wrote in the *Observer*: 'As Anastasia, Leanne Benjamin seems to be featuring in two completely separate ballets and it is a tribute to her brilliance that she extracts something like a star performance from both of them.'[6] It always seemed coherent to me as I danced it, trying to bring the young girl of the opening acts into the traumatised figure of the third.

One of the reasons my post-birth career went swimmingly was that I was more involved in what roles I would dance than I had ever been before. I could have a conversation about what would suit me and what I wanted to do. This didn't prevent some missteps—I had one glorious moment in full dominatrix mode, high heels and a red wig in a quickly forgotten tribute to Diaghilev. But it meant in general that I could combine a repertory I loved with a happy home life with Thomas and Tobias. The range of what I was dancing also expanded in interesting directions. I collaborated with the dance historian Millicent Hodgson on *Akhmatova, Dance Poems*, a tribute to Isadora Duncan; I flew off to dance *Manon* pas de deux with the fabulous Julio Bocca at a gala in aid of the First State Ballet Theatre in Wilmington, Delaware. In July, I enjoyed another season with the Royal Ballet at the Met in New York, celebrating my fortieth birthday onstage while dancing a pas de deux from Ashton's *Voices of Spring*. When I repeated the performance in the Ashton 100 programme at Covent Garden in November, one critic suggested it was as 'effervescent as champagne',[7] so it was a perfect birthday celebration.

In September, the principals of the Royal Ballet were invited to Paris to dance alongside the Étoiles of the Paris Opera Ballet for a gala to mark the one hundredth anniversary of the Entente Cordiale between Britain and France. This was a more mixed experience for me. I had got into the habit of always joining tours or engagements abroad at the last possible moment, so I could maximise my time with Thomas. On this occasion, I arrived in Paris and discovered that the organisers had allocated me a terrible hotel room on a stairwell, with a single bed and a small window. I rang Kevin O'Hare, then company manager, and told him I was changing hotels, which he took very well. For every tour afterwards we would joke about finding the right hotel room for me.

The gala was a spectacular event. The Opéra Garnier, built in the time of Napoleon III, is such a staggering building, the setting for the novel *The Phantom of the Opera*. Performing there felt like stepping into a Degas painting. I loved the well-proportioned rehearsal rooms, the big corridors which you reach through unexpected doors and hidden staircases. We changed in the grand eighteenth-century dressing rooms, with wooden floors and shutters, scenes of faded glory and rich memory. I made a new memory of my own, dancing the *Thaïs* pas de deux with the phenomenal Manuel Legris, one of that amazing generation of dancers, cultivated by Nureyev when he was in charge at the Opera, which also included Sylvie and Laurent Hilaire. Looking out across the grandeur of the ornate auditorium, I felt as honoured and terrified as a Catholic visiting the Pope. The Opéra Garnier is the Vatican of the ballet world and it took my breath away to be performing there alongside these amazing artists.

In November 2004, a letter in a heavy envelope arrived out of the blue, asking me, very confidentially, whether, if the Queen offered me an OBE, I would accept the honour. I virtually hit the ceiling as I jumped up in surprise and joy. I was totally gobsmacked: 'Does that mean I will actually get an honour?' I asked Tobias, quite overwhelmed.

It was such a mark of respect, especially since I had been born outside the UK, and I had never imagined it happening to me. After the initial excitement, I had all the agony of deciding what to wear for the ceremony the following year. Colour, style, dress or trousers, hat or no hat? I agonised endlessly, deciding eventually on a pretty navy blue and white cotton dress from a shop close to the Opera House, which was formal without being too stuffy. It was strapless, so I had a simple navy chiffon top made to fit over it and put a little chiffon flower in my hair at the back. You're allowed to take three guests to the Investiture, so I asked Mum and Dad if they'd like to fly over to attend with Tobias.

On 27 April 2005, we drew up to Buckingham Palace with Tobias at the wheel of our second-hand Ford Focus, which was definitely a few steps down from most of the cars driving through the gates that day. After security checks were completed, we parked in the grounds, which was in itself both a complete novelty and a lot of fun. As we walked over the loose stones of the forecourt, I was in agony about what they were doing to my new pair of Dior high heels. We all entered together, but then the family was taken into one room, and I was ushered into another with a lot of other people who I'd never seen before. Everyone's a little bit nervous because none of you really knows what to do, until an official from the Palace explains the formalities of the day, in a humorous way that instantly puts you at your ease.

The instructions are quite precise: 'When you approach the Queen, do not speak unless she invites you to, and as soon as she nods, don't linger, immediately step back, bow and move off to sit with your family.' The guests are given equally detailed instructions, and my dad was chuffed that having been told the Queen would arrive at 11.07am, she turned up at that time on the dot, with the kind of military precision that thrills him about the British.

It felt like a very long walk in my perilous heels from the holding room to a waiting position in the main hall before my name was called. I had to walk up to Her Majesty, who was raised on a little platform, armed only with her signature handbag, and stand with my back to the audience—an unfamiliar position. I felt doubly special because it was the Queen who was holding the investiture. She offered some lovely words of congratulation, though I do remember thinking what a shame I wasn't a horse trainer or a jockey, because it's well known the Queen is more interested in racing than in ballet.

Others who received honours on that day included General Michael Jackson, Ellen McArthur, the round-the-world yachtswoman, Anna Massey, the actor, and most memorably, Private Johnson Beharry, who received the Victoria Cross for two acts of heroism in saving the lives of his Warrior crew while under sustained fire in Iraq. His bravery made me feel so insignificant; he had done so much, and here I was, a pretty little ballerina. What I did suddenly seemed unimportant. But I did feel immensely proud, and I was very emotional that my parents were there to witness it all. It wasn't really about me, it was about them, their trust and their sacrifice—proof that they had spent their money well in sending me to London all those years before. I felt the day was a small way of giving back to them and Tobias who had seen me through so many ups and downs.

After the formalities were over, and we had our pictures taken in the forecourt of Buckingham Palace, we went to the Wolsey Restaurant for a family celebration. Madonna joined us and we talked about the old days back in Rockhampton and the fact that without those early performances in St Andrew's Hall, I wouldn't be here today, being honoured by the British establishment and the Queen.

I received a lot of letters; the whole of Rockhampton seemed to know my news and sent greetings and memories. Some, like the one from my Aunty Fay, were intensely personal: 'I won't say this is our proudest moment because I have always loved you and been proud all along your life's journey.' Barbara Fewster and Jean Bedells, who had both taught me, sent congratulations, as did the critic Mary Clarke and the Culture Secretary, Tessa Jowell, who said my work had been 'enormously influential to successive generations of young dancers.' Tony Hall, chief executive of the Royal Opera House, sent a warm and complimentary note, and Michael Berkley, the composer and, at that time chair of the Royal Ballet governors, wrote: 'You have been and are still very much a tremendous credit to the Royal Ballet and it is so good that the pleasure you give and the part you play in the life of the company has been acknowledged in this way.' I was particularly pleased with a letter from Prince Charles, offering 'warmest possible congratulations.'

Onstage too, life was full of interest. I danced Odette/Odile for what turned out to be the last time, and Ashton's *Rhapsody*, with Carlos, for the first. At one performance in March 2005, Carlos twisted his ankle at the very beginning of the ballet.[8] Ivan Putrov, who was sitting in the audience, was called to come to take his place, but I was reluctant to dance with him because we'd never rehearsed together and the pas de deux in *Rhapsody* are fiendish. One of the other dancers remembers me sitting at the back of the stage, on the little steps that form part of the set, refusing to go on until something was sorted out. In the end Ivan nobly stepped in and danced the solos, while Carlos and I danced the duets.

In June, I was coached for the only time by Georgina, when she returned to help mount *Les Biches*. I learnt a lot from Georgina's manner as a coach, honed over years of working with dancers at ABT. She was totally in charge in the studio; she managed to give insightful corrections without ever offending anyone. The dancers always felt she had their back and she treated the rehearsal room as a sacred ground. Nothing said inside the room was ever carried outside it and she brought both honesty and a rich humanity to the way she talked to people. Over the years, she'd developed a knack of explaining a lot about a character in a very short space of time, and she'd communicate her thoughts with intelligence and great warmth. She had a way of saying 'What *are* you doing?' that I can hear in my head today. It would crack everyone up, and they would fix whatever was wrong instantly. She was a fabulous teacher, balancing friendship with discipline.

Balance was the thing I was striving for, on stage and off. Dancing isn't the worst career to combine with childcare, though it does pose particular challenges, and Tobias was sometimes literally left holding the baby when I jetted off for galas across Europe. These events aren't just a boost to a dancer's bank balance, they are also an opportunity to burnish your reputation and to meet other dancers you admire. One happily close to home was held at the Royal Opera House in February 2006, to celebrate the eightieth birthday of the sumptuous Russian ballerina Maya Plisetskaya. I was dancing the bedroom pas de deux from *Manon* with Federico Bonelli, which was always a delight. I'd performed on the same stage as Maya in Athens some years previously when she was still dancing *The Dying Swan*, and felt that excitement you feel when you meet someone who has actually progressed the art form you are working in, making it live and breathe for everyone who sees it. I felt a similar excitement some years later when after dancing at a gala in Perth, I met Lucette Aldous, the Australian ballerina I'd always admired who had been chosen by Nureyev as his partner when he filmed *Don Quixote*.

When I wasn't flying round the world, I tried to shape my day so that Thomas, Tobias, and dance all fitted into it, going off in the morning for class, then returning to spend time with Thomas if I wasn't rehearsing. Evenings were free, unless I was performing, so most nights I got to tuck him in and read him a bedtime story. But I do feel I missed lots of little moments in his early years because of my dedication to dance. It's what a lot of mothers feel, I know; we all do the best we can, but sometimes you just can't avoid a clash.

By 2004, we had moved to a larger house in Shirland Mews in Maida Vale and hired a live-in au pair. On the day that Thomas started school, at a little Montessori nursery at the end of the road, I realised I was going to miss collecting him after his first day because I would be rehearsing at just the moment he was coming out of the school gates. I walked to school with him, hoping I could at least settle him in. But the school's rules meant that only one person could walk in with him. Since Kristin, our au pair, was collecting him, I felt it was better that she took him through the front door. I was upset but the headmistress was adamant, so I tried not to show it. As I waved him off, clutching Kristin's hand, I was amazed how emotional I felt. I knew it was a milestone that I would never get back. But it never occurred to me to use him as an excuse to miss rehearsal, or to ask for the afternoon off work. I just sat on a bench at the bus stop across the road, had a little cry, and then got the underground to Covent Garden.

CHAPTER 20

'DON'T F*** IT UP'

IN APRIL 2006, I WAS cast to dance *Giselle*—and I asked if Edward Watson could be my partner. This is one area in which ballerinas have a major impact; once they get a certain seniority, they are usually consulted about who they dance with. There was some surprise about my request. Ed wasn't your typical Royal Ballet man. He excelled in some aspects of the repertory, but he had waited an unusually long eleven years to be promoted to principal. He had never danced Siegfried, or Florimund; the only prince he had ever played had been in *The Nutcracker*. In the big classical ballets, he tended to be the sidekick, or a friend, and he had never tackled a role like Albrecht. I knew him well at that point, so I was quite direct. 'I've done this a lot,' I said, jokingly. 'Don't f*** it up.'

People talk a lot about perfect partnerships, but truth be told, they're as rare in dance as they are in life. For every Fonteyn and Nureyev or Astaire and Rogers, where two contrasting dancers seem to spark something thrilling, or Sibley and Dowell, where two complementary styles blend beautifully, there are about ten ill-matched couples, struggling to make it through to the end of a performance.

And probably about twenty more where you just rub along and do your best and it's fine—not sensational. There are also partnerships which look wonderful when you are sitting in the audience, yet are boiling with personal antagonism when the curtain falls. Mikhail Baryshnikov and Gelsey Kirkland were apparently fighting like cat and dog while giving some of the most memorable performances of their careers; Marianela Nuñez and Thiago Soares managed to get married and divorced without most people in the audience knowing. Onstage chemistry is both mysterious and elusive.

I really struggled to find the right men to dance with. It started at school; as I was tiny and light, I would always be given the small boy to dance with because we looked good together, and because they had some chance of being able to lift me when they might struggle with a taller, heavier dancer. But partnerships aren't just about appearance. They are as much about an emotional connection as a physical kinship, and it was hard for me to find men with whom I could create that elusive dancing attraction.

In my early years at the Royal Ballet, the lack of compatible partners felt like a real problem—and not only for me. At that point, the company had Sylvie and Darcey in its principal ranks, stunning, tall ballerinas who needed a strong, tall man to dance with. Jonathan Cope was first choice for almost everyone, being both an amazing partner and a wonderful presence with whom to share a stage. I loved dancing with him from the moment I was cast opposite him in the school performance of *Giselle*, but I always knew I wasn't his first choice, and we weren't that well suited physically. Zoltán Solymosi was also much in demand, but he walked out in 1995, citing irreconcilable differences with Anthony Dowell and senior artistic staff. The much-adored Adam Cooper left the same year to find huge success as the Swan in Matthew Bourne's radical version of *Swan Lake*.

Principals often danced with guest stars, rather than forging long-term partnerships although Viviana Durante had a famously successful partnership with Irek Mukhamedov. When five of the company's men, including Stuart Cassidy, who I had danced with quite regularly, and Michael Nunn and William Trevitt, who had been my more occasional partners, walked out to join Tetsuya Kumakawa when he started his own company in Japan in 1998, the partnering ranks looked even more depleted.

All of which goes some way to explaining why between 1992, when I joined the Royal, and 2002, when I paused for a moment to have a baby, I had danced major roles with more than twenty different men and hadn't forged a stable, long-term partnership with any of them. Early on, I had a terrific professional bond with José Carreño, who was exciting to dance with because he was so technically confident. We had some success together and were beginning to build a real understanding, egging each other on to high standards, and discovering that we had a similarly committed attitude to work. We were both determined to make the virtuosic side of our performance really shine, but as chance would have it, he left to join ABT soon after we started building that relationship. From a technical point of view, Tetsuya was also great fun to share the stage with; he was young and a big star in the making. But then he too vanished.

After that, I seemed to get paired with whoever was left. Sometimes it worked, and sometimes it didn't, yet if I didn't feel inspired by the person I was dancing with, I doubted the audience would be either. It's not just a question of temperament or physical compatibility. It's to do with how you approach work, and how you respond onstage. It's difficult to find a rhythm with a partner if you don't hear the music in the same way. A lot of the men I was paired with were quite grounded, while I responded best to someone who was fast on their feet.

After Johan Kobborg joined the company, we danced a lot together and that worked very well, because he was a phenomenal partner. He wasn't very tall, but he seemed to be ambidextrous, holding you as well with his left hand as his right. Often you feel that someone is stronger in the hand he writes with but Johan had great dexterity. He made me feel very safe and I sensed an equality of experience when we worked together. But then I was injured, and Alina Cojocaru began to dance with him. She loved dancing with him, and she loved him. They fell in love and I would sit with her in the changing room and watch her eyes lighting up when she spoke about him. They became one of those fabled couples who are in absolute synchronicity onstage and off.

It was a pleasure dancing with Carlos Acosta too, particularly in *Mayerling* and *The Judas Tree,* where our familiarity with the roles meant that we had plenty of scope to dig deep into our interpretations of the story. He was a confident partner for a lot of dancers, with remarkable strength and power; he could lift a ballerina from the floor as a dead weight. He and Tamara Rojo, in particular, had a perfect physicality together. As with Jonathan Cope whenever I danced with Carlos, I knew that this would be an occasional partnership rather than a double act that could grow with time.

The right man for me, the person I felt happiest dancing with, turned out to be Ed. It was Ross Stretton who brought us together in June 2002, in a period during his short, unhappy directorship when the company was struggling with a high level of injuries. He called me into his office and said: 'I haven't got any boys left for you to dance with, so would you want to dance with Edward Watson?' I was a little taken aback. I'd been a principal for nine years and Ed was only a first soloist but given the situation, I thought I'd give it a go.

The first ballet we worked on together was a revival of Antony Tudor's *The Leaves Are Fading*, a piece for nine women and six men which is full of lifts and awkward holds that need to look effortless if the ballet's delicate nostalgic mood is to be preserved. After the first day of rehearsals, I realised Ed had not yet done much partnering, but was keen to expand his knowledge and his range. He worked hard and didn't look at the clock. Like me, he just wanted to get things done. He made me laugh, and it was a pleasure to be with him. That was all very good news.

It was after I returned from giving birth to Thomas that we began to dance together much more regularly, although not exclusively, and working with him on *Giselle* was a turning point. I knew I was giving him something; he had wanted to dance Albrecht and wasn't being cast because he wasn't seen in that way.

In an interview he gave in 2020, he acknowledged this. 'Without her, I wouldn't have done all the roles I have,' he said. 'I literally wouldn't have been able to do them with anyone else because she was tiny and I'm not a great partner and I'm not that strong.'[1] But it went beyond that. If I asked for him, we could break the typecasting that had kept him away from the classics—and hopefully create something special, building on the understanding we had developed in more contemporary works. My feeling was that he doubted himself because he had never had the opportunity to try those classical roles at a young age; the longer you don't get to dance them, the bigger that hurdle of standing centre stage begins to feel.

I was convinced he would be great. I would never have teased him about messing things up unless I had absolute confidence that he wouldn't fail, and he didn't. On his debut, he fell in one set of leaps and thought it was a catastrophe, but I knew it was a beautiful solo and that he had produced an extraordinarily interesting interpretation of Albrecht as an arrogant seducer, who learns humility and seeks forgiveness after Giselle's death. The critical response agreed with my assessment.

In *The Times*, Debra Craine said: 'Lucky Watson to have his debut performance paired with Leanne Benjamin's Giselle. She has been dancing the role for years, but I can't imagine she's danced it better ... Most importantly there's a real dramatic connection between the two of them that makes their story come alive so vividly, and there's never a moment when their emotional intentions aren't absolutely clear.'[2]

What we had hoped to achieve had come off; in that context a fall was neither here nor there. Sometimes, as Stanley Williams had pointed out to me when I went head over heels in *Études* all those years before, what looks like a mistake shows the level of your involvement. My worst moment onstage in *Giselle* with the Royal Ballet was when I was gracefully bourée-ing backwards towards the grave, right at the end, and was so bound up in saying farewell to my lover that I found myself falling over the gravestone. I ended up sitting ungracefully on the ground. It was a lesson. You can only allow yourself to be carried away so far; you also have to be aware of everything around you. Getting round that grave without looking over your shoulder is a particularly difficult manoeuvre and if you start travelling when you are too high upstage, you don't leave yourself enough time beautifully to make the adjustment to slip behind it.

Something similar happened when I was dancing opposite Ed in *Romeo* and slipped in the abandon of the balcony pas de deux. Such adrenalin floods through you that you get up faster than you can possibly believe. But eagle-eyed Thomas, then aged around six, was in the audience with his father. When he came to collect me at the end, he got embroiled in a conversation with Monica, who said, with a huge smile, 'Wasn't your mum wonderful?'

'No,' he replied firmly. 'She made a mistake. She fell over. It wasn't good.'

It is shocking when you hit the deck, but it's perhaps better than not being fully engaged, which Ed and I always were. He and I had advantages as partners. We both danced slightly ahead of the music. When I watched him move, I understood how people described me. We were both dynamic, with an early take off, so that we danced absolutely on top of the notes. But it was our dramatic sensibility, our shared vision of communication, that was the basis of the rapport between us. The more we explored our partnership, the more we drew out of each other. With his slim, ultra-flexible physique, he's different from your average principal, but you can't use a cookie cutter to create a dance company and it's vital that not everyone is the same. What Ed had in bucketloads was the ability to tell a story, and that's what audiences come to the ballet for. They want to be drawn into another world, whether it's an abstract piece where the movement is creating the atmosphere, or a narrative ballet where every step conveys a thought or a feeling. If you don't come across the footlights as a dancer, there's not much point in having the highest technical standards in the world. Your ability to convey meaning is the most valuable thing you possess.

I think the day when we knew we would dance together as much as possible came when we were rehearsing *Different Drummer* for its 2008 revival. We had a meeting of minds when it came to rehearsals, because we just believed in practising until we couldn't practise any more. Those rehearsals left a strong imprint on me; I was so impressed with the way that Ed picked up the pace, unafraid to delve into the characters. Every time we rehearsed, it felt as if we were pushing the boundaries, finding new qualities and taking more risks. Such explorations make ballets more interesting and understandable for audiences, but you need them as a dancer as well. You stay involved because you are willing to challenge yourself. I always needed energy in a room to work, and Ed responded to that energy.

You can't be intense and in the zone all the time, however. Ed is very witty, and we spent quite a lot of time in fits of laughter. In one of our final rehearsals for *Different Drummer*, he completely forgot the next step and I was dancing around shouting 'Kiss me, Ed, kiss me!' at the top of my voice because that was what Woyzeck had to do to Marie at that hugely dramatic moment. We both collapsed in giggles, not entirely appropriate for such uncomfortable subject matter. For ages afterwards, people who were in the rehearsal at the time would greet me in a corridor saying, 'Kiss me! Kiss me!' It took a while to live it down. Our performances were fantastically well received. Ed's was described as 'career-defining'[3]; I was said to show 'yet again why she is the foremost interpreter of MacMillan's often hidden agendas'.[4] It felt like a very special moment.

In terms of helping each other out, Ed later repaid the favour, rather more quietly, when I lost my way in *Machina*, a ballet by Kim Brandstrup and Wayne that was commissioned as part of a programme inspired by Titian's three famous paintings of the myth of Diana and Actaeon. All were on display in the National Gallery in London in

2012, and we had been filming an extract in front of the paintings for a documentary about the gallery being shot by Frederick Wiseman. The shape of the pas de deux and the directions in which we turned were altered for the cameras, and we spent a lot of time adjusting it to fit a different space. That night, when we performed the full work at Covent Garden, for the first and only time in my life, my mind went blank, and my muscle memory vanished. I literally didn't know which way to turn, and Ed had to talk me back into the ballet, doing so with amazing calm. I think if it had happened with anyone else, I would just have freaked out, but Ed was so comfortable in Wayne's work that he could steer me through without any fuss. That's quite unusual. You don't often speak to your partner during a performance; there might be a tiny bit of hissing if you really know them well but generally it's too distracting.

It wasn't all plain sailing between us. I had a reputation as a demanding partner, apparently. Erico Montes, a younger dancer who became a friend, remembers that partnering me in Alastair Marriott's *Children of Adam* felt like a rite of passage, even though it was much easier than he feared. Ed and I definitely had our moments of tension, because we both wanted the best out of a performance. The reason it worked so well between us was because we could laugh about things, and we saw ourselves as a team. It wasn't a case of one of us propping up the other; we succeeded or failed together. There were times in the studio where we behaved like an old married couple, bickering and sometimes even ignoring each other. We were both highly-strung perfectionists, which meant we could combust; we nearly always sent each other good luck cards before a first night, in which we each thanked the other for putting up with a mood or a moment when the other had been a nightmare.

I was never deliberately rude but sometimes I would forget that you need to compliment your partner as well as tell them what they're doing wrong. With limited time in the studio, you don't always have time for the conversation that begins, 'That was great but ...' You end up talking in shorthand—'You're hurting my ribs when you're lifting me'—and sometimes you end up annoying each other. I always apologised to any partner if I got tense in the studio. I never really meant it. I was just trying to be efficient. When I was working on a ballet, I didn't want to waste any time and I expected a partner to put in as much effort as I was. In dance as in life, you can't always assume that everyone is going to have the same level of willingness, and you shouldn't expect it because people operate in different ways.

Ed and I found a way of working that suited us both. He was never as confident a partner as someone like Jonathan or Carlos, but the dividend was that we got so far inside different roles. We built the foundations for new discoveries, not a copy of anything anyone else had done, but a completely authentic interpretation that was all our own, particularly in ballets that were created on us, or in the MacMillan repertory. There's a balance in dancing between spontaneity and planning that you only really achieve after long years of experience. You can't throw yourself into every step, you have to be controlled and abandoned simultaneously. Even at your most dramatic, you must align yourself into perfect positions, because by making tiny adjustments, you are creating the best visual impact for the audience.

By the stage in my career when I started to dance with Ed, I had refined my process before a performance, learning from all the mistakes I had made down the years. Your body is the equivalent of a musician's instrument: you need to tune it to make it produce the finest possible sound. I had a regime like an athlete, where I would train and train for a particular ballet until I reached peak form a few days before the actual performance. Then I'd take it a bit easier until the actual day, always doing class, but trying not to push too hard in rehearsal. The night before, I'd always be slightly agitated. Tobias described me as coltish, wanting to make sure everything was ready, and then go to bed early. The house fell as silent as a church as Tobias and Thomas tried not to disturb me. When I woke in the morning, I'd nervously try to eat a bowl of muesli, and then take myself into class.

After class, I'd start my pre-show run in, trying on several pairs of pointe shoes that were contenders for performance, marking them in order of preference with comments on the base, checking the ribbons were clean. If I was going to wear pink tights, I'd cut them under the ball of the foot and then on the heel, being careful not to ladder them, for better friction. I'd fuss about my hair; if it was washed, I sometimes felt it was too flat, and if it was too dirty it might be stringy and not take the best shape. Despite my reputation for untidiness, I'd then organise everything in my dressing room in neat rows, so it was all ready for my return. As I got older, I tried not to rehearse on the day of a show, instead taking myself home to get away from the building. I'd eat something stodgy like a chicken or cheese sandwich around 2pm—it is a nutritionist's nightmare but it worked for me. Then I'd have an afternoon nap, before returning to the theatre two to three hours before the performance

I'd always do my hair and make-up first and then warm up, so I didn't have to sit for too long before the show. I preferred to warm up alone, so that I could concentrate on running through the sections I wanted to check without any distraction. By the half-hour call, I'd be in my tights and putting resin on the soles of my shoes, for further friction. I was always paranoid that my shoes would come off. I didn't have any specific pre-performance rituals—dancing is complicated enough without giving yourself superstitions to worry about. My main aim was to leave it as late as I dared before going to the wings, usually to the point where I would be called over the tannoy. It drove the stage manager nuts. I wanted to explode onto the stage, in character, but also be confident that everything I had prepared beforehand would stand me in good stead.

All of this was to create a mood onstage where it was possible, within the constraints of knowing what you were doing, to find the spontaneity that can take a performance to electric heights. That's why I loved working with Ed, because every time I danced with him, he surprised me. There are certain dancers who are brilliant in rehearsal, but you feel slightly let down once you hit the show. I don't mean technically, but emotionally. You feel you are dancing alongside them, rather than with them. They look slightly past you. With Ed, it was as if we were having a conversation. It was real for us. I would look into his eyes and I would know what he was thinking and feeling—and react entirely to that in the way I danced the part. It always felt like an experience and it meant that anything was possible.

None of this means that I didn't value dancing with other people. But Ed and I were a proper partnership, supporting each other in life and finding a real rapport when we performed.

'People ask me what I remember about a show,' Ed said in an interview. 'Well, I remember seeing Benji's face.'[5] It was the same for me as well. He opened something inside me that I wouldn't have discovered without him. I am grateful to him for some of the best nights of my life, and for helping me to enjoy a truly golden era at just the moment when most people are planning to stop.

CHAPTER 21

SPREADING MY WINGS

IN 2006, THE ROYAL BALLET was marking its seventy-fifth anniversary. On 29 April, the *Telegraph Magazine* devoted most of its pages to a series of photographic portraits, a history written by Sarah Crompton and interviews with dancers. There I am, in the striking, black and white photograph by Christian Witkin that opens the last photo section of this book, a 41-year-old mother of a three-year-old, looking strong and fierce. Rupert Christiansen, the interviewer, described me as 'an endlessly brave, thoughtful and versatile dancer, with a vivid stage presence, springy jump and the gift of surprising even her most ardent fans with the originality of her interpretations'.[1] I answered a series of questions: my dressing room essentials were hot chocolate, lip balm and a sense of humour; my dream job was 'luxury hotel inspector'; my dream dinner date, the tennis player Pat Rafter. My best moment was 'the point at which I have the audience in my hand' and my indulgence, 'a husband seven years younger than I am'.

In the same year, Her Majesty the Queen was celebrating her eightieth birthday. The two events came together in a glamorous gala at Covent Garden, with a grand party in the Floral Hall afterwards.

Some dancers don't like these events, but I love them. We spend so much of our lives in tracksuit bottoms and leotards that I enjoy the opportunity to put on my glad rags and my lipstick, dress up and live a little. The final ballet that evening in June was *Homage to the Queen*, a revision of the work that Frederick Ashton made for the Queen's coronation in 1953, to music by Malcolm Arnold that conjured the four elements. Our new production retained Ashton's final section, Air, then three new choreographers each added a piece. I was the Queen of the Earth in David Bintley's contribution, the first time I'd worked with him since our Sadler's Wells days. He'd taken over Birmingham Royal Ballet when Peter Wright retired and we hadn't seen much of each other in the intervening years, but I always enjoyed the musicality of his choreography. He sent me a good luck card saying I'd been difficult but was worth every minute. I guess I'd been asking a lot of questions in rehearsal again.

Royalty and new work ran through the rest of the year. On the royal front, I went to a reception at Buckingham Palace that the Queen hosted for Australians working in the UK. Incidentally, I returned to the same setting in October 2011, when I was one of the 350 high-profile Australians in London invited to Buckingham Palace to meet the Queen before she set off on a tour of Australia. Hugh Jackman was another guest, which made my evening complete.

In September, a group from the Royal Ballet were invited to see Prince Charles at his home at Highgrove, where we toured his lovingly nurtured gardens and had a delicious buffet in the Orchard Room. It was a great day out, and I was really taken with Prince Charles. He was charming, warm and welcoming, and seemed to appreciate ballet. He'd been patron of the Royal Opera since 1975 and had taken over as President of the Royal Ballet in 2004, after the death of the previous president Princess Margaret two years earlier. In 2015, he became patron of the Royal Opera House in its entirety and has been constant in his support. To walk around Highgrove and spend time chatting to Prince Charles was one of those moments where I felt like pinching myself as I thought back to the rural streets of Rockhampton and the simpler times with family and friends thousands of miles away.

In terms of new work, I performed two short pieces in the Linbury and then, in August, was in the premiere of a production of *The Fall of the House of Usher,* commissioned by the Bregenz Festival, which mixed an unfinished opera by Debussy with a dance interpretation of the same Edgar Allan Poe story. It was an interesting idea, with opera singers dressed to look like the dance cast. Conceived and directed by Phyllida Lloyd and the choreographer Kim Brandstrup, the ballet section featured four of us from the Royal Ballet—me, Gary Avis, Johannes Stepanek, and Steven McRae, who was my partner because Ed was injured. It was the first time I had worked with a theatre director as well as choreographer and I found it interesting to be in a show that was being created by artists from so many disciplines. We worked separately to begin with and then it all came together in front of the massive grey sets, with the dancers entwining themselves around the singers. It was great to work with Phyllida. She is such a visionary, direct, modest and unassuming. I'd relax after a long day of rehearsal by sitting and talking with her and I loved being with that group of dancers from the Royal Ballet, the musicians, singers and creative team. It was a precious time.

The collaborative atmosphere was enhanced by dancing with Steven, who became a principal in 2009. He was someone I took under my wing; we had a kinship, both being Australians in London, and we always had a terrific time dancing together. He's an amazing virtuoso dancer, but he also, admirably, made sure he was a good partner as well. The creation took a few months, so I'd nip over to Austria and then back to London. I also managed to perform Alistair Marriott's *Tanglewood* on tour to Washington, and *Romeo and Juliet* in Madrid, challenging the Royal Ballet's planners to get me there and back as fast as they could, so I never spent too long away from Thomas.

Autumn brought my debut in Balanchine's *Stravinsky Violin Concerto*; Ed and Darcey danced the acrobatic first movement, while I danced the more tender second with Johan Kobborg. Judith Mackrell's review noticed 'the dangerous sensuous energy' that we managed to convey.[2] What I remember most about the night is that Antonio Pappano, the Royal Opera House's music director, was conducting the orchestra. He didn't often conduct the ballet, but to have him in the pit was phenomenal. For someone who loves music as much as I do, his conducting really spoke to me. Every dancer has a slightly different relationship to music. Some ask the conductor to alter the pace to suit how they want to dance; others ride serenely through, dancing to the tempo in their own head, whatever is happening in the orchestra. I always asked conductors to play at their own speed and let me react, rather than the other way around. I hated it when a conductor tried to follow me; I wanted to be the one who did the adjusting. If I was holding a step, I didn't want them to wait for me. I was eager to respond to the sound rising from the orchestra pit, to play with the music.

I am no connoisseur of the nuances of balletic conducting, but I always liked to discuss the music with a conductor in rehearsals to give them an idea of the tempo I needed. It's like having the right pointe shoes on; if you know where a conductor is heading with his phrasing it makes your performance feel better. But it's also wonderful to hear a magnificent sound swelling around you, and simply go for it. That was how I felt that night with Tony.

At that time, I was deep in the creation of DGV: *Danse à grande vitesse*, another new ballet from Christopher Wheeldon that opened in November and once again paired me with Ed in a super-speedy pas de deux. The ballet was made around four leading couples and a corps de ballet, set in front of Jean-Marc Puissant's metallic shapes, to music by Michael Nyman that had been commissioned to mark the opening of a new TGV rail service in France. It took its inspiration from that idea of speed and propulsion, and the pas de deux for Ed and me was an exhilarating blast of vitality and life. There had to be a lot of trust because Chris challenged us with some unique partnering, where Ed kept flipping me over, mimicking a wheel turning at high speed.

When I was cast in one of Chris's ballets, it always seemed like a blessing. I felt on his wavelength and could be myself, without filters. I like to think that he felt he could push Ed and me to our limits. There was a huge level of trust and respect between the three of us, which I hope was reflected in the outcome. Not that it was ever easy, and *DGV* posed some particular challenges, the most difficult of which was counting myself onto the stage in the first place, because the music is deliberately full of repeated phrases. I'd be standing in the wings asking, 'Ed, is it now?' and he'd pull me back, saying, 'No, Benj, one more phrase.' After I had done my bit, I would sit at the side and watch Darcey (in the premiere) and then Zenaida Yanowsky (in the revival). I loved watching that ballet unfold and I adored the big finale, where we are all onstage, in intricate patterns of coordinated arms and legs, with the rolling movement that is so much a part of the work's character. In the good luck card he sent me on the opening night, Chris wrote: 'I am so glad we got to create together this time.' The feeling was entirely mutual. I always felt I was flying as I jumped through that piece.

I was spreading my wings in other ways as well. I'd been invited to speak at Cambridge University, talking to the Australia and New Zealand Society about my career, and even though public speaking is about the most terrifying thing a dancer can do, I did it. In December, I was invited to Sydney for the inaugural Advance 100 Leading Global Australians Summit, which brought together 'a diverse group of 100 of the best international minds in business, science, education, research and the arts'.[3] I couldn't quite believe that I had been chosen to be part of such a prestigious gathering. As my mum told the *Morning Bulletin*, proudly: 'It's wonderful to show what someone from Rockhampton can achieve.'[4] Before my arrival, I gave an interview to *The Australian*, explaining that I felt growing up in a small town had made me strive harder. 'Being from a small place you didn't expect that you would be good enough. Then I arrived in London and realised I was quite good. Probably because I had a bit of individuality and character thrown in with a bit of talent.'[5]

The Advance 100 was special because it meant I was being recognised as a significant Australian in my own right. The day-time events, where people swapped ideas, were held at Sydney Opera House, where I noticed that the arts didn't, in my opinion, get enough attention. The conversations were all about business, science and sport and although I found them fascinating, I felt disappointed that culture wasn't higher up the agenda. Nowadays, I'd have said that. Then I very much viewed myself as being on a learning curve and I settled in to enjoy the richness of conversation on offer. It was amazing to go to Kirribilli House and rub shoulders with Prime Minister John Howard and the writer Clive James, who gave the after-dinner speech at the gala evening. He was one of my all-time heroes: I loved his books, his wit, and his humour. I also introduced myself to another of the speakers, John Eales, captain of the Australian rugby union team and a hero to all Australia, who knew my brother Tony from their Brisbane days. He's six foot seven, so we must have made a very odd couple as we stood and talked.

I stayed in Australia after the conference in Sydney to do the photo shoot with Jason Bell for the Royal Ballet's *A World Stage* series, with me flying across the outback in my red chiffon. Thomas and Tobias came out to join me for a while and there was a big family reunion with Fiona and David, and Tony, all by then living in Sydney. By this time Aunty Pat was very frail and living in a care home. I still kept in close touch with her. In August the following year she died in hospital, sadly at a time when Mum and Dad were away in London. My family had meant so much to her and as she got older, her world had shrunk. She was unwavering in her support of us, living her life through our doings. To the end, she was helped and guided by her own religious faith and the strong community of the church. Her absence was keenly felt, and the stories about her live on. Going back to Rockhampton was never quite the same without seeing her.

Back in London, life had settled into a pattern of sorts. Our new nanny lived with us in Shirland Mews, which made life easier in the sense that I wasn't always filling in the complicated diagram of knowing where everyone was at any given moment. We were lucky that she took the shape of a German student called Judith, whom we all loved and who loved Thomas. The great news about being a dancer is that it isn't like being a lawyer. Class isn't until ten-thirty every morning, so I could always take Thomas to school. As I changed my repertoire, and took on a little less, occasionally I'd be there in the afternoon and evening too. The disadvantage was the travelling, but Tobias was brilliant. He grew up with his mother doing major touring, three months away at a time, so he understood the pressures and how to manage them so they didn't affect Thomas. We were pretty good at the organising, but like any working mother I did feel that sense of being pulled in conflicting directions, of trying to do everything well and not always succeeding.

Around this time, the critic Ismene Brown wrote 'what a rewarding ballerina [Benjamin] has become as she's passed forty',[6] and I think it was because I understood things much better. I'd been a prodigy, someone who could do almost anything technically, but age had brought wisdom. I was refining my art every day. I had learnt to concentrate on burnishing my interpretations of a role, and I was working within a repertory that precisely suited me: returning to parts I had loved and felt I could deepen, while simultaneously always taking on the challenge of new works.

The year of 2007 brought a perfect mixture. In March, I opened in Alistair Marriott's *Children of Adam*, his second main stage work for the company, one that had allusions to Cain and Abel and the Garden of Eden. He was a home-grown choreographer, entirely trained in the Royal Ballet, and I always enjoyed working with him and liked his movement style. He scored a much bigger hit two years later with *Sensorium*, for two couples and a corps de ballet. I was one of the couples with Thomas Whitehead and one of our pas de deux was utterly beautiful, a gentle expression of feeling to Debussy's 'Footsteps in the Snow'. 'It's in the style of a modern reverie with the pair hinting at love's tenuous bonds as they manipulate their bodies in an elegant show of flex and stretch,' said the *Standard*.[7]

I also returned to *Mayerling*, dancing with Carlos for the first time, and finding more in the role of Mary each night I performed it. *The Times* was particularly complimentary: 'With her astonishing physical spirit and wild, unfettered emotions, she embodies everything MacMillan's choreography stands for, a Mary so dangerous that no reason can contain her.'[8]

I returned to *Song of the Earth* too, in June that year, dancing alongside Edward Watson as the Messenger of Death and Valeri Hristov as the Man. Valeri, who has gone on to become an excellent teacher at the Royal Ballet School, was a first soloist then, and I insisted we talked before we danced a step. I didn't want there to be any nervousness or tension between us. I just said, straight out, that I would be tough because the partnering in *Song of the Earth* is so difficult, but I didn't want him ever to be offended. It would all be about the work, never personal. It was another sign of my newfound wisdom to communicate in that way. Perhaps it did help, because working with him and Ed at that time was one of the best moments in my Royal Ballet life. He was fantastic and the entire experience was fulfilling.

We were the alternate cast to Darcey Bussell, Carlos Acosta and Gary Avis, in what were Darcey's final performances with the Royal Ballet. She was five years younger than me, so it was strange to bid her farewell when I was carrying on. Everyone has a point when they find they're ready to retire; Darcey had two daughters and had suffered with a hip injury for years. She felt it was her time to go, but it was sad to lose her from the company because she was such a great ambassador for us and for ballet itself. On a personal level, I missed having her around. She was always relaxed and confident in her own skin, generous with everyone. If you needed something she was there; the goodbyes showed how much she was loved.

As for me, I kept motoring on, discovering new territory. I danced Jerome Robbins' *Dances at a Gathering* for the first time, though I've always been heartbroken that I didn't get a chance to perform his *Afternoon of a Faun*, which is one of my favourite ballets ever. I'd also would have liked to have a go at *The Concert*, which is full of sly humour that might have suited me. That autumn I did get an opportunity to dance another great American ballet, George Balanchine's glamorous *Jewels*, with its three abstract acts—*Emeralds, Rubies, Diamonds*—each with a different character, the mood created by music from three separate composers. With Tamara Rojo, Ed, and Ivan Putrov, I was in *Emeralds*, which is the most mysterious section, set to extracts from Gabriel Fauré. I had to master a lingering pas de deux and a filigree solo with feathery phrasing; both are sustained and difficult, but the mood is dreamy. The glamour of the ballet was increased when, to mark the performances, the jeweller Van Cleef & Arpels, in whose showroom George Balanchine and Suzanne Farrell went to pose when the ballet first opened in 1967, commissioned a special book of portraits. They were sponsoring the 2007 Royal Ballet premiere. Marianela and Alina represented Diamonds, Lauren Cuthbertson was Rubies, and I was Emeralds, draped in expensive, heavy jewels which were such a pleasure to wear. The dress they'd brought along for the shoot didn't fit me—nothing ever does—so I found a corset on their rail, wrapped a green band around my waist and put on a little tutu. I loved the resulting photographs.

Jewels apart, I was gradually giving up those tulle and tutu ballets. I felt I could contribute more elsewhere, and when a more senior dancer steps down from a role, it gives the younger ones a chance. I didn't need to dance another *Nutcracker*. I felt it was better that it was given to an aspiring ballerina who would appreciate it and learn from the opportunity to work hard in a big classical role. Monica Mason and I had reached the point where we would discuss what I was going to dance in the coming seasons, and I'd tell her my thoughts. It made a lot of difference. I always remind dancers now that no one can know what's going on in your head. You don't have to keep knocking at the director's door, but I wish I had realised earlier that you need to make it clear what you want, because people can't read your mind. Directors are looking after hundreds of dancers and they won't always know what each individual is thinking, or where they are at in their career plans. If you're passionate about something, then say so. They can only tell you you're not right for the role, or that they don't see you in that. But if you don't speak up, they will never be able to put what you want into the equation. This is also true of life in general. If you want something, you must pluck up courage and go for it.

The one exception to this general policy of letting go of what I came to think of as the tutu classics came in 2010 when Patricia Neary, the Royal Ballet's most regular Balanchine coach, coaxed me into taking on the first movement of *Symphony in C*, which, although abstract, is about as much of a tutu ballet as you can get. I adored Pat, and she'd been watching me in class, and I think she felt I had the quality she wanted for this light, jumpy opening. It was years since I had performed something that required such precision and stamina, all in white tutu and pink tights. It's fantastically exposing if you don't get it right, but I was glad she pushed me to take it on. Sometimes you need someone to persuade you that you are right for something that you have always avoided.

There was one step in it that was difficult for me for some reason—a series of double pirouettes starting and finishing in fifth position, with the feet tightly crossed on the ground. I had a real dread about it that I was determined to conquer, so I asked Loipa Araújo, who was a guest teacher in the company at the time and someone I particularly liked working with, if she could help me. For fifteen minutes after class every day for weeks she took me into a studio, and I did that step over and over again. By the time I made the stage, it was spot on. It's an example of how a dancer works, how you can train to succeed. If I hadn't conquered my fear, I would have missed out, all because of one step. Yet I loved that role, the last big tutu ballerina part I performed.

In this final decade of my career, I had the sensation of having built my own audience at Covent Garden. It was like being an orphan accepted into a new family; I think it took people time to get to know me. As I went on, I had the confidence that you get from knowing there were people who had booked specially to see me, and the warmth of their greeting when I appeared was always a pleasure, like someone opening a door you and saying, 'It's really lovely to see you.' It calms you down, makes you feel appreciated. It's a terrific feeling when you win an audience over. It's up to you to make sure they enjoy themselves and if you can sense they are coming round to you when they've just been dragged along for one reason or another, that's wonderful.

If you've danced badly, no amount of applause will console you, but when you feel you've danced well, the moment when the curtains sweep back to the sound of thunderous clapping is extraordinary. It's as if you're riding on a wave of affection and appreciation. If flowers are thrown, it adds to the theatricality; if they accidentally hit someone, it increases the hilarity. Dancers have their own way with curtain calls too. I wanted to show my own personality, my enthusiasm for the performance, my gratitude for the audience's welcome.

The other moments that are lovely for dancers are the ones behind the curtain. You might hug your partner if it's gone particularly well or pull a face if you feel it hasn't. At the end of some ballets, like *Romeo and Juliet*, the curtains open with just the two leads onstage, often still tear-stained and exhausted. Gradually, as you bow, your involvement in the role begins to dissolve, and by the second or third bow, it's the first time you break character in front of the audience. In other ballets, you begin by taking a full company call, and as the curtains close, coaches, choreographers and friends will start to appear onstage behind them, and there are lots of hugs and cheers and little jumps of excitement. Everyone is energised, elated and happy, though if the show has been flat, it's quite another story.

Afterwards some partners want to discuss everything in depth in the dressing room for hours. Others just want to go home. I tended to want to get out of there after a small debrief with my partner—if it was Ed and there was something we wanted to sort, we'd make a plan on how to get it right for the following show. I was desperate to have a meal as soon as I could. Performance days began as early as any other day, so by eleven in the evening I was what we call in the business knackered, not to mention starving. But I loved the ritual of meeting fans at the stage door afterwards. Tobias, as flower holder in chief, would often find himself waiting for a long time as I met the people who had come round to have their programmes signed. It's the ultimate collective high after a good performance; you are so exhilarated about how you have danced, and the crowd you have danced for are completely satisfied. We all dance out into the street together on those nights. Whether I thought my performance good or bad, I could never sleep. Like a tennis player at the end of a match, I'd be going through every step in my head until the early hours.

CHAPTER 22

FAREWELLS

DANCE IS DEMANDING. WHAT KEPT me going was that I loved the discipline of it, the sweat and exhaustion of daily class. I never missed class, if I could possibly help it, and it gave my career a shape as well as making me capable of constantly pushing myself onwards. That linked to the other thing that kept me going, which was my desire to put all I had learnt at the service of young choreographers.

I spent some of the summer of 2008 in the stimulating and beautiful setting of the Vail Festival. Taking place in a tranquil valley in the heart of the Colorado Rocky Mountains, the event has acted as a springboard for the talents of many choreographers and new companies. I was there with Ed at the invitation of Christopher Wheeldon, who had formed his own company Morphoses, a scratch gathering of some of the best dancers from around the world, who would perform programmes of cutting-edge work. Everything about that summer was new and rather magical, including our rehearsal space, which was a huge, echoing gymnasium.

I loved working with the small group of committed dance specialists that Chris had assembled from companies he knew. Sharing the stage with New York City Ballet dancers such as Maria Kowroski, Wendy Whelan, Tiler Peck, Jason Fowler and Craig Hall was incredible. Their American training was different to mine and it was refreshing that Chris wanted to bring the different styles together in performance. The English schooling is concerned with the placing of the arms, known as 'placement'. Our port de bras are very considered. American dancers seem to move through their arms and feet much faster, which gives them more speed and makes them look more energetic.

In Vail itself, I performed a piece Chris had already created called *There Where She Loves*, plus *The Dream* pas de deux and, later that month in an International Gala evening, the one from *Qualia* with Ed. That's the only time I ever danced through what I thought was a hostile reaction. As we went through our moves, which are quite raunchy, we could hear what sounded like booing. I was worried we were offending somebody's sensibilities, and almost subconsciously started to pull my little top down so that less midriff was showing. As we came off, Ed hissed, 'They hated us.' It was only later that we discovered the commotion had nothing to do with our talent. A woman sitting in the audience was wearing an expensive necklace, and as she sat watching us, someone behind her attempted to pull it off.

Later in the summer, in a small theatre in Beaver Creek, in a Morphoses programme of three new works, I danced a new Adam Houghland ballet with the NYCB dancers, including a beautiful pas de deux with Tyler Angle. We began to get to know those dancers really well, forging links in the little village that is the dance world, developing friendships and sharing knowledge. Tiler Peck, who was about to dance her first Giselle that autumn, asked for my advice and we ended up having an impromptu coaching session in the foyer of one of those big hotels while we were waiting for the bus. Goodness knows what the other guests thought of us as we went through the choreography, marking out the options with the arms, the line of the neck and so on. She is such an amazing dancer, still dazzling audiences.

I spent a lot of time with Morphoses that summer and autumn, too, staying in New York, at the Hudson Hotel in the centre of Times Square. It was an exciting time to be in the United States, as Barack Obama campaigned in his first presidential election, and we rushed home at the end of rehearsals each day to watch the coverage of the huge rallies that greeted him. I'd always wished I had spent some of my career in New York so this stay was a way of having that moment without having to move to a new city. It was also a blissful time creatively. We were a small band and having been in a big company all my life, I relished being a part of that. It was like a family. Chris is a great leader as well as a choreographer and he created a space which felt incredibly positive.

Appropriately enough the ballet Chris was making, *Commedia*, set to Stravinsky's *Pulcinella* score, conjures the sense of a travelling group of performers. Ed and I had a long, warm, pas de deux, which starts as a bit of fun and develops into an expression of sincere affection. Chris also created a witty, jaunty duet for me and the fifteen-year-old Beatriz Stix-Brunell, who was still attending school in between rehearsals. There's a documentary made at the time which shows me heading off shopping in Greenwich Village as she goes back to lessons. Beatriz subsequently joined the Royal Ballet and the bond between us has always been very strong. She had an astonishing technique even in her teens and coped beautifully with all the pressure she must have felt, being the youngest in this professional group.

The duet Chris made for us set my knowledge against her youth. When *Commedia* had its premiere at Sadler's Wells in September, the critic Jann Parry commented that 'Stix-Brunell is pretty and talented, but Benjamin shows just how far the journey can take you. As she works the choreography, inscribing it in space with taut precision, her physical authority is absolute. Stravinsky's music describes the absurdity of the human condition, and Wheeldon, ever ambivalent, offers us innocence and experience too.'[1]

I was back in New York with Morphoses in October for the US premiere at City Center and more of the election, and then went to perform in Amsterdam. In the past I'd loved going abroad, but it was increasingly hard to leave Thomas, to disconnect from home and get on with things wherever I was. Tobias was brilliant and generous, reassuring me that all was well and that I could go off and not worry. Then I'd get home and he would go off somewhere for his work.

In London the same month, I danced in a revival of *L'Invitation au Voyage*, a ballet that Michael Corder had made in 1982. I had seen Alessandra Ferri and Antoinette Sibley perform it then, and I loved dancing it all those years later. Ed was partnering Marianela, while I danced with Federico Bonelli, in a cast Clement Crisp in the *Financial Times* called 'admirably responsive'.[2] It was memorable in retrospect because it was one of the first times I'd been onstage alongside Sergei Polunin, who was already beginning to make a name for himself. 'Power and classical distinction are his,' said Crisp. In a world where everybody is phenomenal, he really stood out. He had so much potential and worked hard in the studio.

My next new creation, which premiered in November 2008, was Wayne McGregor's *Infra*, a dark, dazzling ballet made in collaboration with the artist Julian Opie, who provided a set consisting of an overhead walkway with of LED shapes of people walking by. Featuring twelve dancers, with a score by Max Richter, it's full of huge moments of emotion and despair, including a section where one woman screams silently, unnoticed by the crowd passing her by. I longed to play that woman and do the slow pas de deux. I always ended up dancing at high speed for Wayne. Not that I am complaining. The moment in *Infra* when the six couples are all framed under separated squares of light, dancing simultaneously and incredibly rapidly, is one of my favourites in Wayne's ballets.

In December, I was invited by The Australian Ballet to guest with them in *Manon* at Sydney Opera House, an invitation that brought me back to my family. It was almost too much to take in, a culmination of so many ambitions. Sydney has long been my favourite city. When I'd been a student at the Sydney summer schools, I'd often walked past the Opera House, dreaming of dancing inside it, although like many performers before me, once I got inside, I discovered that the stage is underwhelming; it's like a reverse Tardis, huge on the outside, tiny on the inside. But the walk from Circular Quay station to the Opera House balanced things up, never failing to overwhelm me. Then, emerging from rehearsals in the belly of the building, I'd have another spectacular view walking home at sunset. Working with Australian Ballet, with my partner Robert Curran and with my friend, the then artistic director David McAllister, was also pure pleasure. The performances were wonderfully received.

The icing on the cake was that by that point Mum and Dad had moved to Sydney from Rockhampton, and my brother Tony, and Fiona and David and their three children were also settled there. I had what I had never experienced over my entire career, which had been built so many miles from them: home-cooked meals and time with the family. It was a luxury, a treat.

After I got back to London, I wrote to Mum and Dad: 'No words can express how much I've loved this whole Sydney experience and that all the things that I love—my favourite ballet, dancing at a dream venue, in my favourite city and spending time with my favourite people in the world all came together. Thank you so much. You are such special people and I'm glad that I could show you onstage what you've given up all these years emotionally and financially—with this passion of mine, dancing.' I apologised at the end for not spending Christmas with them but wanted to spend it back in London with 'two very important people': Tobias and Thomas.

The following year began with a satisfying run of revivals, including *DGV* and *The Firebird*. April brought great excitement when I was one of the dancers chosen to host the wives of the leaders of the G20, when the summit was held in London and a tour of the Opera House was one of the attractions. After following the US election so closely the previous year, it felt particularly exciting to meet Michelle Obama. I'd admired her ever since she had first emerged into public view and our in-person encounter as we had photographs taken on stage, confirmed her incredible warmth and the sense she emanates of being so relaxed and secure. Shaking her hand and talking to her made me feel a tiny part of a piece of history.

In July, the entire company made history when we visited Cuba, which no Western company had visited for fifty years. It was an extraordinary and emotional time, especially for Carlos who was performing in his homeland with the company that had become his home. For me, it began with disaster because I had squeezed in a gala in Hamburg at the invitation of the choreographer and director John Neumeier before flying to Havana and had to change planes en route. For the first and only time in my career, my suitcase vanished. It was full of evening wear because we knew we were going to have a lot of galas—and even more disastrously it contained my ten pairs of carefully chosen and prepared pointe shoes. Fortunately, I had remembered the old rules that Peter Wright drilled into us when we were touring with SWRB and stuffed an old pair in my hand luggage as I set off. They were very soft, and not really suitable for performing, but at least they gave me something to dance in. Ballerina Melissa Hamilton kindly lent me a dress and heels for the evenings, so that sorted that out. Otherwise, I just had the trainers, T-shirt and jeans I had travelled in.

By the time I arrived, the company was facing its own problems because a number of dancers had become ill with swine flu and had to be quarantined away from the rest of us. Others were injured. I ended up performing an extract from the second act of *Giselle* in a programme of divertissements with a marvellous dancer from National Ballet of Cuba called Joel Carreño. We'd never met before, and didn't have time to rehearse, but he was an incredible partner. Thanks to lack of practice, I wobble a bit in my unsupported solo—as you can see on YouTube—but the pas de deux all went off smoothly.

Jonathan Cope, who was by this time working as a Royal Ballet coach and hadn't danced for about two years when I hauled him out of retirement to dance *The Firebird* with me in Germany, ended up going on in Ashton's *A Month in the Country*, opposite Zenaida Yanowsky. He had just a day's notice to reconstruct a performance that had once been one of his finest; I stood in the wings and cried, he was so moving.

The heat was sweltering, but the atmosphere was warm and wondrously welcoming, with enthusiastic crowds greeting us wherever we went. There were parties every night. On the second night, at the Gran Teatro, there was a gala in honour of the revered Alicia Alonso, prima ballerina assoluta and director of the National Ballet of Cuba, in which we danced alongside the stars of her company. Monica Mason presented her with a bouquet at the close. Thanks to the efforts of Alonso, ballet is the national art of Cuba and it has a tradition of producing terrific dancers and big productions of the classics. The Royal's programme had been devised to bring works they didn't know. The mixed programme featured *Chroma* and *A Month in the Country* as well as more familiar classical divertissements, and it was followed by *Manon* at the Karl Marx Theatre. Many of the performances were streamed to big screens, and large audiences outside. After the bows in the theatre, we were whisked by little buses, still in costume and pointe shoes, to the huge square where the crowds had gathered to watch and took a second curtain call there. It was an experience unlike any other in my career; with their hero Carlos in our midst, we were treated like a conquering football team, not a touring ballet company.

I'd been to Havana once before with Carlos and Ricardo Cervera, in 2006, when we performed the finale of *Mayerling* as part of a gala in honour of Alonso, so I knew what to expect, but the scale and the excitement of this tour was something else. Our audiences were made up of the most glamorous of Cuban high society, but there were also plenty of people who had queued for days and paid a dollar for a chance to see us. I was completely enthralled by the people, by the beauty of the city and by the vivacity of the culture we discovered all around us. Carlos and our Cuban hosts led us to clubs full of the sound of Cuban music, familiar to me from the recordings of the Buena Vista Social Club that I played at home in London.

With my usual need to get back to Thomas, I left before the end of the stay, and travelled to the airport with the American ballerina Alexandra Ansanelli, who was not only leaving Cuba but her career, having decided to retire at the age of twenty-eight. When we tried to board our plane, we were surprised to be told by armed guards that we needed to pay some additional cash. Neither of us had any money on us, and when we were taken into a small room for questioning, Alexandra burst into tears. We were both terrified.

I had to think laterally and said: 'We've just been performing at the National Theatre.' That didn't seem to work, so I added, 'With Carlos Acosta.'

His name was like a magic charm. Suddenly and abruptly, the guards' attitude and body language changed, and we were ushered onto our flight. Ansanelli vanished into her new life, while I just went home and kept on dancing, throwing myself into the creation of *Limen*, another new work from Wayne McGregor.

One of the qualities Wayne brought into the Opera House, like a breath of fresh air, was a willingness to collaborate with the best contemporary artists. Each of his ballets has a distinctive visual world; each good luck card he sent to his casts as we opened in his new work celebrated the art that was so much a part of his creative process. For *Infra*, the card was a single image of a Julian Opie figure, striding forth. For *Limen*, a ballet about light and darkness, the thresholds between presence and absence, life and death, accompanied by a light installation by Tatsuo Miyajima, it was a sheet of blue Perspex.

I was in the studio creating *Limen*, which opened in November 2009, at the same time that Georgina was in London, working with the cast members who were playing the Empress Elisabeth for an October revival of *Mayerling*. She stayed with us for three weeks in September, spending a lot of time with Thomas. We were so glad she did because it became a very precious memory, the last sustained period we all spent together. When she got back to New York, where she was coaching Natalie Portman and Mila Kunis as they got ready to film *Black Swan*, she began to complain of a sore back. She had had no previous symptoms, and although she had smoked since the age of thirteen, she was incredibly fit, so we didn't have any particular worries when she went in for an examination.

In October, Tobias got a telephone call from his mother: she'd been told that she had lung cancer and it was likely to be terminal. 'They've just told me that I am going to die. But how can I be dying if I feel fine?' she said, with a note of incredulity in her voice.

From that moment, everything unspooled with the unreality of a nightmare. She began chemo, but only with the hope of extending rather than saving her life. By December the cancer had spread and by the time Tobias arrived back in New York, he knew she would die within days. I flew to join him, and we spent hours at her bedside at the New York Presbyterian hospital, where the dancers who had loved her so much were constant visitors, all wanting to say goodbye. Everyone was distraught. On the night of 17 December, Tobias sat with her all night. We decided that I should stay with Roy in the loft. At five in the morning the following day, Tobias slipped into a nearby room to open his laptop and send the payroll for a show he was about to open in London. When he returned, his mother had died. It was shattering. He called me from the hospital to say she was gone, and I told Roy, as gently as I could.

Overwhelmed with grief and with the suddenness of it all, we then faced a dilemma. We really wanted to stay in New York, but we had to get back to London for Thomas's sake. We organised a makeshift funeral the following day at the John Krtil Funeral home. It was bitterly cold, but the room quickly filled up with all the close friends who could make it at such short notice and so close to Christmas. Tobias, Kevin McKenzie, the artistic director of ABT, and John Meehan, a close friend who was running the ABT Studio company, spoke.

Roy was in no condition to do anything but sit and listen, surrounded by us. It was bleak, but full of love. I fixed my attention on a beautiful black and white photograph of Georgina dancing Empress Elisabeth that Roy had taken for the premiere of *Mayerling* in 1978. It's a photograph that we treasure, catching her beauty and grace. Early the following morning, we had to set off for the airport. Snow was coming down and New York was about to close; the terminal was full of people, stranded because their flights had been cancelled. Miraculously, we made it home. We were numb. It seemed impossible that only weeks before Georgina and I were telling stories with a cup of tea around the kitchen table. Tobias had lost his mum, Roy his beloved wife, Thomas his adoring grandmother, and the ballet world one of its treasures.

We'd moved again by this point and were living in Randolph Avenue in Little Venice. We'd first settled there in 2007 in a smallish flat, and then uprooted ourselves again in 2008, to a larger one across the road. It was a fantastic street, and I'd once again revealed an unexpected ability, inherited I am sure from my parents, to make a good property deal and to enjoy doing up a house. Thomas had just started primary school and deciding where to send him put a lot of stress on both of us. Like all parents we wanted the best for our son, but unlike most we were totally at sea in the English education system, having been educated in Australia (me) and New York (Tobias.)

Other stresses were coming to the fore. I was working hard to sustain my position as a world-class ballerina, while, having left the Donmar Warehouse, Tobias was struggling equally intensely to set up his own theatrical production and management company. Like so many couples, we probably didn't allow ourselves enough time to be on our own and relax, and strains began to tell on our relationship. When cracks began to appear, we didn't find time to talk about it; what I know now is that when Tobias has a problem, he doesn't want to burden me with it and feels he must carry it himself. We were both just trying to survive, but little issues became big issues.

Two months after his mother died, we decided to split up—or at least live in different places. He took a flat in Notting Hill and I stayed in Maida Vale with Thomas living between the two. It was horrible. We never stopped liking and loving each other, but we decided we needed time apart. Since we were both committed to Thomas and wanted to make things as normal as possible, we continued to spend time together with him, which kept us closer than we might otherwise have been. When Tobias's dad Roy decided that he couldn't stay in New York any longer without Georgina, he moved into another flat in Randolph Avenue and we all met together as a family. Roy would often come over to my place, and we'd have drinks or dinner, or just long chats. It helped ease the pain of parting and in the long term, it helped bring us back together.

CHAPTER 23

ALWAYS LEAVE THEM WANTING MORE

I THREW MYSELF INTO WORK, pouring all my feelings into my life on the stage. Dancing is a huge escapism, and you can lose yourself in it. I found the daily discipline of class a soothing and necessary part of my routine. I love the music, the way it develops over the ninety minutes, as you move from the barre to the centre of the room, from slow pliés and tendus to your perky glissés and the rounded rond de jambe. The music matches you every step of the way, and it's beautiful. I enjoyed class more some days than others, simply for the way the piano was played.

I was there until the end of every class, surrounded by younger people who acted as a spur. Someone like Ed was a great inspiration because he was so meticulous about work. If you prolong your career as I did, you have to ask yourself whether you would prefer to be the biggest fish in a small pond or stand next to people who challenge you and force you to excel all the time. That was the choice I made by staying in the Royal Ballet so long; I never worried about the young talent coming up behind me. I just wanted to contribute whatever I could—and, if possible, be part of the next most exciting thing.

In January 2010, I was named best female dancer in the Critics' Circle awards, which were awarded on the basis of performances in the previous year. I'd won the same award in 2004 and felt again the quiet satisfaction of knowing that the UK dance critics had noticed my efforts. The early months of the year brought revivals of ballets I really loved, including *Infra* and *The Judas Tree*. Then in May, I stepped into Christopher Wheeldon's *Electric Counterpoint*, which asks its dancers not only to perform, but to be filmed talking about themselves. I can tell you that I never liked the sound of my voice booming around the auditorium, but I did enjoy being partnered by Eric Underwood. The same month saw my performances in *Symphony in C*.

Over the summer, I danced around the world, always enjoying the different atmosphere that each country brought. I had more guesting invitations in my forties than in the whole of the rest of my career and I wanted to make the most of them. That year, for example, I flew to Japan with the company to dance *Mayerling* with Johan Kobborg, and *Romeo and Juliet* with Ed. In the ancient and spectacular setting of the Taormina theatre in Sicily, on a balmy July night, I performed alongside other international stars in a gala of excerpts. In August, Ed and I went to the Chicago Dancing Festival to perform the pas de deux from *Qualia*, and then performed the same piece and a pas de deux from *Romeo and Juliet* in the gala in Perth, held to raise money for a new centre for West Australian Ballet. I took Thomas with me, and Mum and Dad flew the five hours from Rockhampton to meet us at the airport and stay for a few days. It was incredibly hot, I remember, but wonderful to have a bit of time with them before returning to London. Saying goodbye was heart-wrenching.

I also went for the first time on a relaxed, small tour of Danish, Swedish, and Norwegian venues, organised by Johan Kobborg. A band of Royal Ballet dancers, including Alina Cojocaru, Steven McRae, and Sergei Polunin performed a programme of classical excerpts in lovely settings at castles and stately homes. I joined the party in summer 2010, 2011 and 2013, relishing the low-key mixture of holiday and work they provided, though the summer of 2011 was scarred by the cancellation of our performance in Norway after Anders Breivik killed seventy-seven people in the country's worst act of domestic terrorism. It was a terrible, shocking tragedy. In contrast, 2013 threw up another royal encounter in Gavnø Castle Denmark when Steven and I met Mary, Crown Princess of Denmark, who is married to the heir to the Danish throne, but who was born in Hobart, Tasmania. I'd danced the solo Pie Jesu from MacMillan's *Requiem* and she was very moved. She stood up to applaud, making the audience follow her in a standing ovation. The castle was owned by her friends, and we all ended up in the kitchen, having drinks and swapping stories.

Over the first two summers I got to know Sergei a little better, though we were never close friends. As we travelled from place to place by car, he would sit quietly playing computer games. He was always electrifying to watch in performance and was someone I enjoyed being with. You never know what is going on in someone's head, though, and I was taken aback when he walked out of the Royal Ballet in 2012 at twenty-one years old. He's found fame and won multitudes of adoring fans since, but I would have loved to see him tackle more roles at the Royal and have a chance to develop there. At his age, I was still on the road in Scarborough in a big top with the rain coming in. Sergei was in the Royal Opera House with the world at his feet, but something gave inside him, and he went.

The summer of 2010 was quite busy, one way and another, but I also squeezed in a photo shoot for an exhibition of portraits of Royal Ballet principals taken by the designer Paul Smith that were unveiled at his new flagship store in Tokyo, when we were in the city on the Japan leg of our summer tour. As usual, I was too tiny to fit any of the clothes, so I wore my own black top and jeans, and used one of his designer bowler hats as a prop; the result is one of my favourite photographs.

Meanwhile, I was working on *Invitus Invitam*, a new ballet by Kim Brandstrup that premiered in October. I'd worked with Kim twice before, once in making *The Fall of the House of Usher* for the Bregenz Festival, and again in 2008 on his first creation for the Royal Ballet on the main stage. That ballet *Rushes – Fragments of a Lost Story*, took its title from the pieces of film that a director watches at the end of each day, and was a direct reference to Kim's own background in film. That's what makes him so distinctive as a choreographer; all his work is heavily influenced by cinema and he sees dance quite differently than most creators. Because he doesn't dance himself, he works through images that he can see in his mind's eye and then asks you to try to reproduce in the studio. In *Invitus Invitam*, Ed and I were originally cast as alternates to Johan and Alina, but they dropped out early and we ended up creating the ballet and performing every one of its six performances.

The ballet, which was quite short, was inspired by six words in Suetonius about a Roman emperor leaving his lover 'against his will, against her will' and was danced to a gorgeous Thomas Adès score based on the music of François Couperin. Its set was a huge wall that moved and provided the background for video projections and some sumptuous lighting by Lucy Carter. The costumes were lovely too, suggesting the seventeenth century. There were four dancers, but the main meat of the piece was three different encounters between me and Ed, all dissolving shapes and shuddering lifts. In the *Daily Telegraph*, Sarah Crompton wrote, 'It is like a poem, fleeting and lovely.'[1]

Ismene Brown described us as 'one of the most intriguing partnerships of recent years, she tiny but haughty, he broad-shouldered, hunched, riven with tension.'[2] In the *Sunday Times*, David Dougill noted: 'These two dancers are as compelling here as in everything else we have seen them do.'[3] The first night was particularly memorable because Alicia Alonso was sitting in the Royal Box; the bill which ended with Balanchine's *Theme and Variations* in which she had once starred, was in honour of her ninetieth birthday.

I gave an interview to *The Times* in November in which I talked about the way having Thomas had altered my mindset. He was seven by this point, but although he was old enough to come to watch me perform, or to wait for me at the end of a rehearsal, I didn't often take him into the Opera House with me. I wanted him to understand what

I did, but when he was sitting in the audience, I found it difficult to pull myself away from the thought of him. I couldn't disconnect. I wanted to do everything well, both work and home. 'I want to make everything my first priority, that's my problem,' I confessed.[4] Whatever I am going to do, I am going to do well. That's a theme of my life, really. That helped me to stay in my profession for such a long time, because I regarded every day as a challenge. I actually liked the challenge of challenging myself.

As the year unfurled, I got the chance to explore the works I loved. In January, I danced *Giselle* once more with Ed. In March, I returned to *Sensorium*. In April, I opened the company's run of *Manon*, opposite Steven McRae, making what the *Independent* described as his 'stellar debut',[5] when Ed was injured and couldn't perform. After twenty years, I felt I had finally nailed the part and the reviews indicated that other people agreed. In the *Sunday Express*, Jeffrey Taylor commented that I 'broke everyone's heart': 'Not only has Benjamin matured into a fine actress, but, defying all rules of physics, her technique grows more victorious with the passage of time.'[6]

Zoë Anderson[7] talked about the brothel scene, where Manon is passed over the heads of one man to another, extending her legs in languorous arabesques. 'Benjamin's Manon is both passive and working it,' Anderson wrote, noting that throughout I played the character as a woman making choices 'pulled this way or that by the claims of love or money'.

That scene is incredibly difficult to get right. As you are handed from man to man, and brought down over their heads, there's one lift where it is quite easy for the knickers on your costume to get snagged on a button of their coats; it's happened to me on a couple of occasions, but they've always managed to fumble under my skirt and get me free. I had another costume problem in *Manon* because the richly embroidered coat which the character wears at the start of that act was so expensive to make that when I was dancing there were only two sizes—huge and slightly smaller. Neither fitted me, and it is very hard to look a million dollars when your coat doesn't quite fit.

Lots of different things were happening around that time. I was still performing a lot of galas. Over that summer, I'd also been invited by David Bintley to dance at the New National Theatre in Tokyo where he was co-director, in a number of performances of *Romeo and Juliet*, partnered by César Morales. Going to Birmingham to rehearse with him was the first time since I left that I had been back to the company that used to be Sadler's Wells Royal Ballet. The company in Japan had never danced MacMillan's ballet before, so had to be taught step by step. When it came to Act 3 in particular, I suddenly had to reverse the spontaneity I had been striving for over the years and follow the rules so an entire new cast of dancers could respond to me. It made me realise how lucky I had been at the Royal Ballet to work with character principals who were experienced in their roles and allowed me, as Juliet, to make such an impact. But it was also lovely to work with a group of fresh, enthusiastic dancers in Japan, anxious to learn and to stretch themselves. When I coach dancers in this ballet today, I try to remember both experiences, and let them find many alternative ways of telling the same story.

Monica Mason, who had been so important in my career, had decided that the season of 2011–12 would be her last as artistic director. Her swansong season was full of the ballets I loved. From autumn to spring, I danced *Jewels*, *Requiem*, *Limen*, *Gloria*, *Song of the Earth*, *Romeo and Juliet* and *Polyphonia*—a glorious, happy run. For her final production, Monica decided to ask seven choreographers who had been central to the Royal Ballet's creativity during her decade in charge to work together on three ballets inspired by Titian's three paintings based on the myth of Diana and Actaeon, for a programme called *Titian 2012*. Writing in the *New York Times*, Roslyn Sulcas declared the evening to have been 'a resounding success. Not because any one work proves to be a masterpiece but because a real sense of collective creative energy and innovation permeated the exercise'.[8]

I was in the first ballet, *Machina*, choreographed by Wayne and Kim, and dominated by the design by Conrad Shawcross, which took the form of a robot with lights and a gigantic mechanical arm. I danced with Ed, Carlos and Tamara in the spaces around its movements. I really admired the way Monica was thinking outside the box even in terms of her farewell. She had made her mark as a director, taking on the company at a difficult time, opening it up, bringing in new repertory and new creativity. There are dancers who have said they didn't find her style suited them, but she had been pivotal to my career. She worked with me when I was vulnerable and helped me push through difficult times both as a student and under Anthony and Ross. I felt she appreciated hard work and, when she took over, the repertory was very much in my favour, so I could work hard and develop roles. I owed her a lot.

I was fortunate though to have the last year of my career under the directorship of Kevin O'Hare, who took over in July 2012. He is an exceptional director who has opened doors and new directions for the company, making it open and inclusive. I was so excited to see the route of travel that, in a way, I didn't want to leave, but when I saw that his first season was going to end with *Mayerling*, I knew it was time for me to call it a day. I'd come in with *Mayerling*, so leaving with it was a way of completing a circle. It was a hard decision to give up, because arguably at that point my career was going better than it had ever been. Coming back to the stage after having a baby had empowered me. I felt braver than I ever had and was ready to take on the world.

On the other side of the scale, by July 2013, I would be turning forty-nine. It was enough. I wasn't even tempted to try to get to my fiftieth birthday. My motto with curtain calls was 'always leave them wanting more', vanishing into the wings while the applause still filled the auditorium. I wanted to apply the same logic to my life. As far as I was concerned, the years after fifty were going to be about exploring worlds other than ballet. I needed the last year of my forties to reset, retrain and make up my mind in what direction I was going to head. I asked Kevin out for a drink and told him what I'd decided. My only request was that, if possible, I'd go out with a final performance of Mary in *Mayerling*. He didn't try to change my mind about any of it.

Photo: Christian Witkin

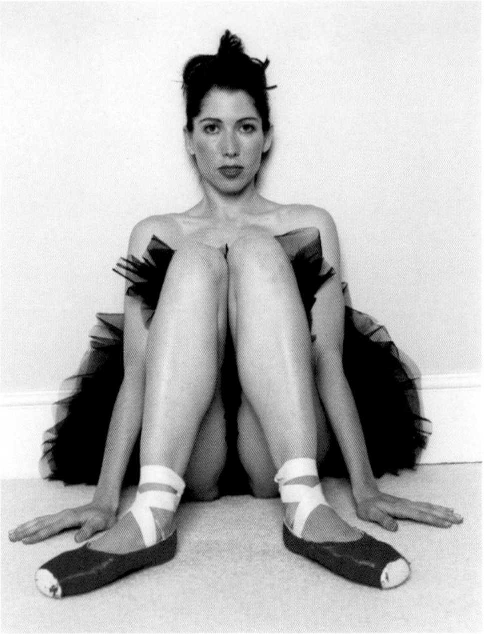

top: Photo shoot for Paul Smith's Tokyo exhibition.
Photo: Paul Smith

bottom left: Photo shoot of *The Judas Tree* for *Dance Magazine* in Roy Round's New York loft studio, 1994.
Photo: Roy Round

bottom right: My photo in 'Polly Borland: Australians'; an exhibition at The National Portrait Gallery, of Australians who have made a significant contribution to British Life.
Photo: Polly Borland

top left: In rehearsal with Edward Watson at the Royal Opera House.
Photo: Johan Persson / ArenaPAL

top right: My first creation post-pregnancy in *Qualia* with Edward Watson, choreographed by Wayne McGregor.
Photo: Bill Cooper / ArenaPAL

bottom left: *The Judas Tree* performance with Edward Watson at the Royal Opera House, 2010, age forty-six.
Photo: Royal Opera House / ArenaPAL

bottom right: Opening night of *Manon* with Steven McRae at the Royal Opera House, 2011.
Photo: Johan Persson / ArenaPAL

top: A moment of fun rehearsing *Mayerling* with Carlos Acosta.
Photo: Roy Round

bottom: Ricardo Cervera helping me with my *Mayerling* hat for a performance at the International Ballet Festival of Havana with him and Carlos Acosta.
Photo: Personal Archive

top: Just Married! Sharing a kiss outside St. Paul's Church in Covent Garden.
Photo: Personal Archive

middle: Even honeymooning in the South of France couldn't stop me from exercising!
Photo: Personal Archive

bottom left: Nine months pregnant outside the Royal Opera House with my darling husband, Tobias.
Photo: Anne McNulty

bottom right: Cuddling with my son, Thomas.
Photo: Personal Archive

top: With Monica Mason after she interviewed me for The London Ballet Circle (LBC), 2019.
Photo: London Ballet Circle

bottom left: Outside Buckingham Palace with Mum after receiving the Order of the British Empire (OBE) in 2005.
Photo: Personal Archive

bottom right: Receiving the Member of the Order of Australia (AM) at Government House in Sydney in 2015.
Photo: Personal Archive

top: With President Bill Clinton at the Kennedy Center in Washington after a performance of *The Sleeping Beauty* with the Royal Ballet Company.
Photo: Personal Archive

middle: Gailene Stock and I chatting to Prince Charles at his London Residence, Clarence House.
Photo: Personal Archive

bottom: Cosying up to my favourite audience member, David Beckham, after a performance at the Royal Opera House.
Photo: Personal Archive

A cartoon that appeared in Rockhampton's *Morning Bulletin* in honour of my retirement, 2013.
Cartoonist: Harry Bruce, The Morning Bulletin, *Rockhampton*

That left me with another difficult decision. For years, I had been dancing with a labral tear and very little cartilage in my left hip. I'd found ways of working around the restrictions and the pain; I'd favour one side of my body, and on occasion slightly change certain steps—with the permission of the choreographer or the stager, obviously. But by the summer of 2012, it had become obvious that if I wanted to go out on a high, as I'd planned, I'd have to take more drastic action. After months of deliberation and consultation, I decided to have invasive hip surgery, and have the troublesome socket resurfaced. The tennis player Andy Murray had a similar operation to try to extend his playing career. I was advised that I'd need six months of rest and rehabilitation before returning to the stage, but I was determined to do it in three because I'd noticed that Christopher Wheeldon's *Fool's Paradise* was scheduled to open the autumn season.

Fool's Paradise is a ballet I'd watched for years and had dreamt of dancing. I saw it for the first time when I was guesting with Morphoses, and I would sit in the wings each night, mesmerised, watching it from beginning to end. I loved everything about it, from the Joby Talbot score to the intensity of the abstract choreography and the simplicity of the stripped-back costumes of flesh leotards and bare legs for the women and flesh tights and bare torsos for the men. It has the most magical moment, too, when paper petals fall from the flies, on the heads of the dancers; I knew it was a ballet I had to perform, especially in my final season. With that at the beginning and *Mayerling* at the close, I thought it was a perfect reflection of everything I had wanted my career to stand for.

I don't know if it was stupidity or sheer determination that made me plan the operation in this way, but I was prepared to take a calculated risk on getting back quickly. I had the rest of my life to take it easy. The procedure was carried out as a day operation at a private hospital in Cambridge, and because we were a little light on childcare, Tobias drove me there with Thomas in tow. It all went well, though I was very woozy after the anaesthetic and still groggy when I got into the car to go home, just four hours after having the surgery. At around seven in the evening, we set off back to London. I get travel sick at the best of times, and by the time we reached the M25, I was feeling so ill that Tobias had to stop the car so I could get out to be sick. However slowly he drove from that point onwards, I felt nauseous. He had to pull over at least four times, and it took us hours to get back to my home.

By the time I was tucked up in bed, I felt entirely better. Then I began the process of trying to get my body back into working order, working methodically like any athlete with a goal to meet, with daily physio, body conditioning, tailored training and massage. By September 2012 I was back in the studio, learning *Fool's Paradise*, which was scheduled to open on 3 November. For the first few weeks I struggled, trying to navigate the new choreography while guarding my hip, anxious not to let anybody down. Although I was on track with my rehabilitation, I was definitely not on top form, and as the weeks passed, the team decided that I wouldn't be ready for opening night. I was bitterly disappointed and pleaded for them to postpone the decision, but I also completely understood. They couldn't take the risk of jeopardising a company premiere just because it suited my plans. I made the second cast performance, four days later. It was bittersweet, but I did make my goal, and I did get to perform a ballet I still utterly love.

That last year began to fly by, with each performance a kind of letting go. But it still contained new excitements, not least making a ballet with Alexei Ratmansky, another of the world's great ballet choreographers, for the first and last time. I liked being in the studio with him. He has the most incredible eye. As I had become older, it was hard for people to give me corrections, because maybe they thought I was too senior and didn't want telling. Now when I work with more mature dancers, I always ask them if they want me to tell them what I think, and generally they do. There's not much point in carrying on otherwise, because you're just churning things out. When Alexei came in to make *24 Préludes*, set to an orchestrated version of

Chopin's piano music, he pushed me, and since I like to be pushed, it was fantastic. He gave me this funny, difficult, wonderfully musical solo. He changed his mind quite a lot as he worked, but I liked that too, because you could see it was for the right reasons—he was still developing what he wanted to see, and he hadn't quite found it. When it opened, Jann Parry described Alina and I as 'quicksilver sprites, darting at speed',[9] quick and flirtatious. It was gorgeous to dance.

In April, the Royal Ballet formally announced my retirement and Kevin issued a statement. 'Leanne has been such a huge part of The Royal Ballet for the last twenty-one years it is hard to imagine the Company without her.' It was equally hard for me to imagine life without the company, it had shaped my days for such a long time. 15 June marked my final performance on the Covent Garden stage. On the same day, the *Telegraph* published the interview I'd given to Laura Thompson, discussing my entire career and explaining that I felt my longevity was partly to do with the long period of rest while I was pregnant. She said that I had 'a grounded quality onstage, a rooted realism that transmits directly to the audience and which became even more palpable after the birth of her son ten years ago'. She also noted my 'wonderfully expansive voluptuous dimension'[10] which was often commented on, and which always struck me as ironic, given my good Catholic upbringing.

I talked about the fact that people went to the theatre to be carried away. 'When I stopped to have my baby, I learnt what was really important—and it wasn't anything that I had thought. What matters is the giving over. If you give one hundred percent of yourself, the audience will know. That's what we're here for.'

Back in Australia, the newspapers also marked the day of my retirement. The front cover of Rockhampton's *Bulletin* was covered with the words 'Swan Song: How a little Rocky girl grew up to become one of the world's greatest ballerinas.'[11]

It was a strange feeling walking into the stage door on that last day and seeing the pile of bouquets that would be presented to me at the end of the night, already beginning to accumulate. I tried to play it straight, following the familiar, non-nutritional pre-performance routine of a trip to the canteen for a hot chocolate and a muffin, settling my stomach, deliberately following my usual pattern. There are always so many people who want to see you before a show, and this night was even worse than usual, with so many heads popping around the dressing room door to say hello. Everyone knew what a huge deal that night was for me; how, having given my life to ballet, I was now preparing to exit Covent Garden as a principal ballerina for the final time.

The audience was full of friends, fans and family. Mum and Dad travelled over from Australia with Fiona and Tony. Madonna was there too, with her family, as was Roy, my father-in-law. That final performance as Mary in *Mayerling*, opposite Carlos Acosta, was everything I wanted it to be. I didn't feel nostalgic. I had a lot of people around me that I loved—and I knew that I had a few more performances scheduled over the summer so this wasn't the final time I would dance. Nevertheless, it was emotional, a blistering performance from all concerned, with Carlos devastating as Rudolf. It ended with me standing onstage, house lights up, flowers raining down from the balconies above. Carlos was unbelievably generous, standing back to let me take all the adulation, always the perfect gentleman with such a gracious presence. While the applause continued, a procession of my partners started to parade across the stage, to kiss me and present me with a bouquet: Gary Avis, Chris Saunders, Ed, Steven, Federico Bonelli, Thiago Soares, Nehemiah Kish. At the end of the line came Thomas, aged ten, carrying his own bouquet.

It was wonderful to experience all this with my entire family in the audience, for the first time in thirty years, and to say goodbye to all those fans who had been so loyal and lovely to me throughout my career. My pigeonhole at the stage door was stuffed with cards and letters, including many from people who had followed me from my earliest days at Sadler's Wells and were saying their own goodbyes. There were enough flowers waiting for me to fill a cathedral. Dancers and teachers who I had worked with over the years had sent cards and flowers. Fans whose knowledge and affection sprang from years of watching from the audience added their thank yous. They were the people I really valued and I tried always to make time for them.

Their letters were warm and generous. One, characteristic of many, ended: 'Thank you for twenty-one years of unforgettable pleasure—too many great roles to mention … I wish you a happy retirement and I hope you can find some way to pass your artistic genius onto future generations—although like all truly great dancers, you are unique, irreplaceable and unforgettable.' Knowing that you have had this effect on people who have paid money for tickets to see you perform, is like gold to a dancer. It makes everything seem worthwhile.

That performance was followed by a period of saying goodbye in different ways. Ten days afterwards, I flew to Monaco to perform *Manon* opposite Carlos for the opening of the Royal Ballet's short residency there, then it was on to Tokyo for a gala of excerpts, in which I danced the *Manon* bedroom scene with Carlos and *Qualia* with Ed. I was so pleased to have an opportunity to say farewell in Japan. I had spent a lot of time there, from my first company to my last, with a lot of guesting in between, and I loved my Japanese fans. On that day, 10 July, Kevin made a heartfelt and generous speech onstage after the performance and presented me with the costume from *Requiem* as a memento, saying that it was the ballet in which he remembered me best.

Johan Kobborg and Alina Cojocaru retired from the Royal the same day, and then we all shot off to Scandinavia for the last of our summer tours. My final, final performances were in August, at the Coliseum in London, where Carlos was presenting *A Classical Selection*, a celebration of his fortieth birthday. There were excerpts from five MacMillan ballets in a programme of thirteen, and I was in three of them. With Carlos I danced the murder-suicide ending to *Mayerling*—'ferociously exciting,' wrote Debra Craine—and then the bedroom duet from *Manon*, opposite Nehemiah Kish. 'She gives lustrous shape to everything she dances,' Craine commented. 'How I will miss her now that she has retired.'[12]

My final appearance onstage was in extracts from *Requiem*, which is set to the spiritually uplifting music of Gabriel Fauré, and which was made by Kenneth as a memorial for his friend and fellow choreographer, John Cranko, after his sudden death in 1973. First we danced in a solemnly beautiful pas de deux, and then Carlos danced a solo, before I returned alone to dance to the soprano solo 'Pie Jesu'. This is one of the loveliest pieces I have ever danced, and I danced it often, finding different accents in it throughout my career.

Kenneth based it on seeing his daughter Charlotte playing, and once I had Thomas, I understood much better how a child's attention span changes so quickly. It's a solo full of delicate arm movements, slow turns, deep bends and little moments of reflection. The music is sublime. To have an entire stage to yourself always made it feel like a very private moment in a very public setting. When she was teaching it to me, Monica Mason emphasised that it shouldn't be mawkish; you shouldn't go with the sentiment of the music. But it is very difficult to dance to such music and not get too intensely carried away. As I danced it down the years, I developed it to be less sentimental—the music sat within me more. It's particularly true of Kenneth's work that you find different things within it as you mature.

On Sunday, 4 August, standing in the makeshift dressing room at the side of the stage, waiting to go on, all the emotion I felt about leaving a lifetime of performing suddenly overwhelmed me. The excitement I'd felt up to now drained away, leaving a powerful emotion—something I had never experienced before. I felt so alone. Suddenly I realised that this really was my last performance ever. It sounds silly, but I don't think I had thought about it until that moment. I was busy, I was happy with my decision, I definitely wanted to stop, and I knew it was the right moment. Ending my career with a piece choreographed by Kenneth was incredibly important to me. I'd watched other people retire in floods of tears, and I thought that would never happen to me. I was very much, yes, I've done it, now drop the mic. But there, on that night, I realised the enormity of my last dance.

It wasn't that I was bereft about the thought of leaving ballet. When people are dying, they supposedly see their whole life flash before their eyes. It was like that for me, in this tiny dressing room with a chair, a table and a mirror, where I was standing fixing my hair. Suddenly everything I had ever danced, from 'Animal Crackers', to my first *Giselle*, to my work in four companies, ran through my mind. All the fun, the laughter, the good times and the bad. I was suddenly emotional in a way that I never imagined I would be.

Worse, Tobias wasn't in the audience. Although we saw each other all the time and although he was instrumental in organising all the celebrations around my departure from the Opera House, we were still separated for this last moment of my career. I wasn't sharing one of the most important moments in my life with the person who had been most important to me. That shook me up a bit, and it made me think about what I really wanted in the future.

All this raced through my mind in seconds; by the time I actually stepped out onto the stage and danced, it was incredibly uplifting. All my senses were clear. At the end, everyone gathered round, and then I went out to dinner with a couple of friends. They were lovely, but I couldn't help thinking that this wasn't where I was supposed to be, and that they weren't who I was supposed to be with. Thomas was with Tobias, so when it was all over, I picked up my bouquets and went home to Randolph Avenue, alone. The house was empty. I closed the front door, had a little sob, and then picked myself up. It was time to get on with the rest of my life.

CHAPTER 24

REBUILDING A LIFE

I HAD MADE A PLAN. I didn't want to wake up the morning after I left the stage and wonder what to do next. I had decided I needed an entirely new life. For the whole of my career, I'd been interested in property and interior design. Between 1987 and the moment I retired, I'd bought and renovated seven different properties, living in six of them, and doing one up just for the fun of it. What I really liked was buying somewhere fairly run-down and making it fantastic; it seemed to me that it was a bit like making a ballet. You start with an idea of something and some ingredients in a raw state, and then put them together to see how good you can make it. The process, the working on things, not just the performance, all appealed to me.

I'd also always been curious to get involved with other things, and I liked to reach out to people beyond the ballet world. Perhaps because I didn't go to a traditional ballet school, but instead wound my ballet training around a fairly normal life in Rockhampton, I could never quite get my head around the idea that being a dancer was the most important thing in the world. I liked life outside the ballet bubble; all my closest friends were not dancers. When I was doing up properties, I loved spending time with builders, plumbers, electricians and architects. I liked the chats and building up teams of people I trusted and could work with.

When I began to think about retirement, it seemed obvious to me that I would need to develop these other interests outside of ballet. I had left school with very few qualifications and I was determined to fulfil a long-held ambition of going to university and getting some kind of degree. Wanting to throw myself into unfamiliar territory, to clear my head of dance, and to explore my passion for property and design, I began to trawl around the internet, investigating various courses. Eventually, I found something that appealed to me, but didn't have quite the right qualifications, so arranged an appointment. I was fortunate that Peter Stickland, who was the head of the architectural design course at the Chelsea College of Art and Design, part of the University of the Arts, happened to have seen me perform and knew who I was. It never occurred to me that someone in the outside world might know me as a dancer. We talked through my lack of qualifications and my enthusiasm, and I persuaded him that I was worth taking a chance on as a mature student wild card on the Diploma for Architectural Design course.

He suggested that I should prepare myself by taking private lessons before I started, to give me some kind of basis for my studies. From May to June in that last hectic year at the Royal Ballet, I ran from rehearsals at the Royal Opera House to my studies with George Rome-Innes, a lecturer in the history of architecture and interior design, and a prolific designer and model-maker. Half of my day was filled with the familiar—*Manon*, *Mayerling*, *Qualia*—and the other half was filled with subjects such as surveying, orthographic drawing, perspective drawing, model making, and elevation. Cushion plumping up it certainly wasn't. After years of filling my mind with the technique of port de bras, adage, and allégro, I had to pick up an entirely new vocabulary, and a totally novel way of thinking, very fast indeed.

By September, I was just about up to speed. I was enrolled on the full-time course at the university, a beautiful old building just next to Tate Britain. One of the great bonuses of the year was getting a student pass that allowed me entry to all the exhibitions, but it was a very unsettling time. I was living with Thomas in Randolph Avenue, fulfilling all my obligations as a mother, and then I'd shoot off to university for a day and sit with my fellow students, studying an unfamiliar subject. On one particularly frenetic day, I dashed from my lectures to the 2013 Critics' Circle awards, where I was given the De Valois Award for Outstanding Achievement. This is the top honour the dance critics can give, and I was surprised, proud and grateful to be awarded it. I gave a speech saying this and then ran straight back to school. The other students were friendly, but they were half my age, and whizz kids in computer skills and technology. We had nothing in common except my determination to conquer the subject.

It wasn't easy. After the discipline, structure, focus and above all the movement of ballet, I found it difficult to get used to sitting down all day. The pace was so different. Instead of moving around studios with a ballet bag stuffed with shoes, I was carrying a large artist's folder full of drawings. I'd put additional pressure on myself because I was trying to do both a foundation year and the one-year course in a single twelve-month period. I went to college each day and had private tuition at night. I was worried about being old, wanting to progress as quickly as I could and get out into the workplace. If I had my time again, I would have taken things at a more leisurely pace, giving myself the chance to digest what I was learning and to enjoy the experience. As it was, I was racing to catch up the whole time, and because I was such a perfectionist, I wanted to excel.

The projects that gave me the greatest pleasure, and those I think I learnt most from, were two design tasks, where I had to work out ways of remodelling a space and then write a little booklet on my plans. For the first, we had to redesign two rooms in the school; they said you should go with something you knew about, so I chose to design a multi-purpose studio for both living and performances, with a great glass wall and a landscaped amphitheatre for the audience in the garden. I based the idea on the rigs used on a stage and invented a way of elevating the furniture, the bed, the table and benches, up to the ceiling when the space was needed for rehearsal or performance. The second task was to find a space and create a business plan. I chose a building in Shoreditch and built a model in which I reimagined it as a launderette that could be adapted for other functions. I'd had to wash so many practice clothes in my time as a dancer that it seemed obvious to design a luxurious and functional launderette called Fluff. I enjoyed the scouting trips, making practical decisions about how to convert the space. I am not really a theorist and I found those aspects of the course difficult. But once I could dig down into the practicalities and make something of a room, that was one of my happiest places. I really love it.

Overall, I honestly think that the entire course was one of the hardest years I have ever lived through. But as usual, I was determined to keep going. The other students, and probably the tutors, laughed at me at first, wondering why I had changed career paths. In the end, I not only got a diploma in architectural design but also won a prize as the most improved pupil in the entire year. My sense of satisfaction was profound, though I was beginning to wonder whether interior design would become my life. It had allowed me to step away from dance with a different interest to absorb me, but I wasn't sure that I was going to enjoy life as a full-time designer. As I investigated the profession more, talking to people about possible routes I might follow, I realised that working for demanding clients might be more stressful than dancing *Swan Lake*. You weren't entirely in control of a project as you were when it was a hobby. I wasn't sure that was what I wanted.

As I celebrated my fiftieth birthday, I allowed myself the greatest indulgence of all: a gap year. I think I needed that time to reassess and re-evaluate everything. Collecting Thomas from the school gates was wonderful, a complete novelty, and it was a pleasure to be able to devote my attention to my son. I also needed time to do all these basic things that had been pushed into the background by my commitment to ballet. I had lunch with friends, and booked holidays without hesitating in case a guesting commitment came in. I went to the theatre and the movies, because I had evenings free without another pair of pointe shoes to sew. I tried sports such as horse riding, skating and skiing, which I was terrible at, but it didn't matter. Finally, I could have a go at such things; before I'd always been worried about falling off or falling down. The list of activities that a dancer can't do is long and surprising. Sometimes you don't want to walk up a hill or climb a long set of stairs because it will pull your muscles in the wrong way before a major performance—although I couldn't say no to walking up the Great Wall of China when on tour with Sadler's Wells. Once I had stopped, I didn't have to worry about the consequences of whether an extra holiday might take too much time away from practice or whether I'd break a bone on the beginners' slopes.

I also started to repair my life with Tobias. We always adored and supported each other, and we had never stopped being a part of each other's lives. Around this time, we made a conscious decision to try to rebuild our relationship. We had to work hard at it, and we went to marriage counselling for a while to help us to begin to talk, properly and deeply. Once we began a conversation, we kept going. We took it slowly, in baby steps, but it helped that I had retired. I didn't any more have to worry about putting the washing out at midnight when I was dancing *Swan Lake* the next day. I was more relaxed, and I could find more time to spoil him. We got better at talking things through. By the time we moved back in together, our relationship was stronger and more secure than when the cracks first began to appear. I doubt that would have been possible without the time apart.

Other pressures were swirling around us. In 2014, Tobias's dad, Roy, was diagnosed with Alzheimer's and by the following year he needed a carer to come into his home to help him get through the day. He hated it and could be quite rude, which was a problem. When he had a bad fall, we had to take the terribly hard decision to try to find him a place to live where he could be looked after properly, and he went to Denville Hall in Middlesex, a care home for members of the entertainment industry which had been recommended to us by Joanna Lumley, whom Roy had photographed on her first job as a model in the sixties. Peter Wright's wife had also been looked after there before her death. It's about as un-institutional as a care home can be, and set in beautiful grounds, but Tobias was still devastated to have to leave Roy there. It was one of the hardest things he ever had to do and from then on, it was just so sad seeing Roy's slow decline. He nearly died in January 2016, and we all said our goodbyes when he was in hospital, but somehow he survived, though he could no longer walk. We would visit him as much as possible, but he was mainly confined to bed, confused and unhappy. In the early days, we could take him out on day trips and visits to places he had loved. By this point, it was impossible.

We spent a lot of time in the car that year because Thomas, out of the blue, said he wanted to go to Charterhouse, an English boarding school in Godalming, Surrey, right out of central casting. Not being a fan of boarding schools after my idyllic upbringing in Rockhampton, I had misgivings about sending him away, but also wanted to do what I could to give him the experience he wanted. I felt I couldn't be selfish and want to see him every day. Things started well, although I will never forget leaving him there on that first day; he looked so small, and I felt he was so young. We called daily, and every weekend we would visit him, or he would come home. While he was doing very well academically and was well liked by his teachers, it became clear that he wasn't enjoying it, and by the end of the year, we knew we would have to find him a change of schools. In the meantime, we used to drive to be with him as much as we could.

In May 2017, at the age of eighty-eight, Roy fell ill once more, with a urinary tract infection. We went to see him, but he was not really awake, and we couldn't stay because it was time to go to collect Thomas forty miles away. As we drew up to the school, Tobias got a call on his mobile to say his father had died. Thomas was distraught that he hadn't managed to see his grandfather. We drove back to London, sad but relieved that his suffering had ended. Dementia was an awful way for the life of such a vital man to end. Roy had always been a huge presence and had lived an amazing life. Looking back, the sense he sometimes gave off of being temperamental, of finding it hard to fit into the modern world, may have been a sign of the onset of Alzheimer's. Once it took hold, it was cruel, slow and took away everything he held precious—independence, dignity, company, memories—one at a time. It is a terrible fate, suffered by far too many.

By this point, Thomas had realised boarding school wasn't for him and got a place at University College School in London. I was over the moon to have him at home and watch him grow into the person he is today. When I look at him, I sometimes see myself: questioning, determined, outspoken. Tobias says it is like living with twins on occasions. I am happy that we are all in the groove of being a family again.

The year of my diploma was a way of separating myself from ballet. Perhaps because I had been through so much in my career, both good and bad, I thought I would walk away from dance when I retired. I had given everything to it, physically and mentally, and I wanted to leave it all behind. I also had very mixed feelings about teachers. Throughout my dancing life, I'd had wonderfully inspiring teachers in the main. But I resisted the idea that former dancers became teachers because it was the easiest and most obvious transition. A lot of dancers think it is the only thing they can do, but it requires an entirely different skill set and you don't know if you are going to be any good at it.

Almost as soon as I stopped performing, however, the phone rang with people asking whether I would take on some private coaching. Curious to see how it worked out, I began to teach a couple of private pupils every weekend and was surprised by how much I enjoyed it.

It became the event that I most looked forward to every week—and has ended up being one of the most rewarding things I have done since I left the stage. It's a way of giving back, which has felt important to me. My criteria for taking a student are that they have to want to work hard and are serious about their training, willing to take lessons that can last hours. I am going to push them to reach their goals. I also have to feel that I can make a difference. I like to teach someone I think has potential, not only someone who is already soaring high, especially if I think there is more to discover.

Dancers thrive in different ways. I knew from the age of fourteen that I would have a career in ballet. Other talents burn more slowly. If you don't have the confidence to stand at the front of class or the ability to pick up the technique as quickly as someone else, you can get slightly left behind or become insecure. One thing about dance that I am not sure is clear to the outside world, is that companies need a great range of dancers. They require corps de ballet, soloists, and character dancers as well as principals. You can have a wonderful career in ballet without being an internationally known star, so if you have talent and the desire to make it your life, the important thing is to discover the best level you can attain. There are a lot of dancers who won't be principals, but who are more than happy to be in the Royal Ballet or another company, and not get leading roles. As a teacher, it's satisfying to work with them one on one to help them reach that ambition.

On the other hand, if you get to the point where dancers are not getting offers to join a company or to work professionally, then there must come a moment when they ask whether they can keep going. You have to weigh up what's right for you, and what's not. That's what my sister did so well. Even after two years in the Royal Ballet she had the courage to recognise that it wasn't going to make her happy. She left and found a career in television, using her creative abilities in making documentary films. She is now Commissioning Editor for documentaries at Channel 4 in London, has two children and has had a much more satisfying and rewarding time than if she had stuck with ballet.

As I've gone on, I've become increasingly interested in mentoring young dancers and trying to help them make the decisions that are right for them. All artists have insecurities, but young dancers are particularly susceptible because they are competing at a young age with their peers. It can be difficult to cope with that. I've worked with students who have been anxious, and I've tried to give them the strength to keep going, keep building, and climb up towards the best they can be. When I was coming up, I had a strong personality and a mindset that would help me to drive through problems, and I still found it hard. If you're not like that, it can be even more difficult.

As a teacher you have to develop a relationship with your students that will help them solve their problems. Without ever thinking you have medical training, or that you know best, you become both teacher and psychologist. You are there to help them master technical issues, but also to make them feel safe about working out any other difficulties they have, because if they tackle their insecurities, it's going to help their body. My aim with the people I work with is to allow them to talk about their concerns in a safe space, so that they gently find their way into the career and life they want.

By late 2014, I had begun my involvement with the Tait Memorial Trust, formed in memory of Frank and Viola Tait, and the Tait brothers, who played such an important part in the establishment of theatre and the performing arts in Australia and New Zealand. The trust supports young artists from Australia and New Zealand by raising money for scholarships at vocational level and enabling them to come to study in the UK. I understand the journey of an Australian in England; leaving the comforts of home to take brave steps forward alone can feel very lonely, so I'm glad to mentor them in any way I can.

It appealed to me to work for an organisation that helps youngsters to develop their talent. I've got more and more involved as the years have passed, have become their patron and there are now dance bursaries awarded in my name. I give talks and masterclasses and organise events in order to fundraise. One of those recitals, at Australia House in London in 2019, was a particularly special occasion for me because it marked the night I was presented with the inaugural Queensland Agent-General award by Paul de Jersey, the Governor of Queensland, who was over in the UK. He made a speech thanking me for the contribution I had made to my chosen art form and to Queensland and thanking Miss Hansen for her contribution to the beginning of my career.

I loved curating the recital and introducing the musicians and singers taking part, including Lachlan Monaghan from Birmingham Royal Ballet and Calvin Richardson from the Royal, who had both been recipients of bursaries from the Tait Memorial Trust. Collaborating with Australia House feels like the sum of who I am, a recognition of the connection between Australia and England.

In December 2014, my ties to my homeland had been recognised in a different way, when I received an honorary doctorate in the performing arts from the Central Queensland University in Rockhampton. Pride doesn't begin to express what I felt, with the additional pleasure of being surrounded by family and friends as I was presented with my degree. I'd flown in directly to the event, which takes more than twenty-four hours and three different aeroplanes, so I was distinctly jet lagged, but as soon as I stepped out into the hot sun, I felt at home. Our old Rockhampton neighbours, Maureen and John Kerr, in whose backyard we had enjoyed endless barbecues and in whose pool we used to swim as children, were also in the audience that day because their son in law was receiving a degree as well. Naturally, my rented red gown (complete with mortar board) was too big for me, but that couldn't take the gloss off a wonderful occasion.

The ultimate honour for an Australian was given to me in April 2016, when I was made an AM (Member of the Order of Australia). It was amazing to go to Government House in Sydney, where I had toured as a ballet student in my summer studies all those years ago, and to have my career celebrated in this way. It was equally lovely to be able to share the event with my parents, without them having to travel thousands of miles to be by my side. The only problem was that I was only allowed three guests. In the end, Fiona was the third and we met my brother Tony and the rest of the family for a celebration later.

Government House sits in its own grounds on the edge of the beautiful Botanical Gardens, overlooking the Harbour, not far from the Opera House. When we arrived, we had an opportunity to explore the high-ceilinged and elegant state rooms, and then the family went off to be seated while the people who were being honoured were taken away to have the formalities explained to them. We lined up on a colonial verandah, looking out across the lush, green vegetation, before being called inside. We were all seated in order of our awards being given and noticed that our family and friends were sitting in another room, just in front of us. As the ceremony began, a dividing wall between us opened into one large room. It was just like a curtain going up on a performance. The ceremony conducted by the Governor General David Hurley was formal, but more relaxed than the one I had experienced when I was given my OBE in the opulent grandeur of Buckingham Palace. Afterwards, there were canapes and drinks in the grounds.

What I was going to achieve next was becoming clearer. The fulfilment I felt in teaching my private pupils and working with the Tait Memorial had clarified my thinking. I was beginning to realise that I could have a positive effect on other dancers, that all I had learnt and experienced could help them flourish.

Then Kevin O'Hare rang me up and asked if I'd be interested in coaching *Mayerling*.

'Next week?' I asked, thinking he hadn't left me much time.

'2017,' he replied.

'I might be dead by then,' I joked. But I said yes.

I knew I had the energy to be a coach, and I knew by that point that I loved ballet. I love it more than I sometimes think I do. People can be sniffy about classical ballet, but I believe it is an art form that can communicate like no other. Because I always viewed myself as an accidental ballerina, it took me a little while to accept that this is a profession that I want to see continue and thrive. In order to do that, it needs to keep current, as well as have a strong sense of its tradition. I suddenly realised that the knowledge I have acquired, my willingness to look both forward and back, meant that I should stay in the industry. I did have a lot to offer and before I knew it, I was walking back into the Royal Opera House.

CHAPTER 25

WHAT I HAVE LEARNT AND WHAT I PASS ON

ALTHOUGH I'D BEEN BACK TO watch performances at Covent Garden since my retirement, I had scrupulously avoided going backstage to the dancers' areas. I didn't want to be hanging around after my moment had passed. When I walked in four years after I had left, it was a disconcerting mixture of the familiar and the strange. I was returning to a place that had been as much a part of my life as my own front room, yet now I was a different person playing a different part.

I'd never, up to that point, sat at the front of the room, directing operations. I'd always been in the middle of the studio, listening to advice. It was a daunting prospect, made all the more so by the fact that on that first day back I was coaching Steven McRae and Sarah Lamb, dancers I had been cast alongside when I was a principal. They had never danced Rudolf and Mary in *Mayerling* before, so they were probably just as nervous as I was. But there was a calming presence greeting us all in the form of Jonathan Cope, whose performance as Rudolf was fabled and whose experience as a coach was already extensive.

He'd been one of my coaches before I retired, and now I would be sitting alongside him, rehearsing.

I had been anxious in advance about what I could bring to the room. I knew I had the first-hand knowledge of having been rehearsed in this role by Kenneth, but I worried about passing on all I knew in ways that would be helpful. I felt curiously vulnerable. I remembered standing alongside these same dancers and rolling our eyes together when we disagreed with something the coach was saying. Were they going to do the same behind my back?

In that first rehearsal, completely out of character, I didn't say much but as I watched I got a sense of things I could develop in both Sarah and Steven that would help them bring the best out in their performances. Over the weeks that followed, I began to feel completely at home in the studio, quickly forgetting any insecurities, as we worked to perfect everything from the choreography itself through to the character, developing possibilities to help them put their personal stamp on the roles. When it was time for their debut, I sat, sweaty-palmed, in the audience on their opening night, dancing every step with them from the safety of my seat. I had never before realised as a dancer how much responsibility a coach feels.

Somewhat to my surprise, I fell instantly in love with coaching and began to realise that I had both the critical eye and the depth of experience to make it a role in which I could contribute. The great tradition whereby a dancer hands on her knowledge to a younger dancer forms the backbone of ballet. It sustains the art form's history, and when it's working at its best, it also looks forward to its future, nurturing a new generation with their own ideas and dreams. I had experienced this time and time again in my career but the most personal was when my mother-in-law, Georgina Parkinson, came to the Royal Ballet to help mount a production of *Les Biches* in 2005 and taught me the part of the enigmatic La Garçonne, the character in white tights and a short blue tunic designed by Marie Laurencin that is one of the most iconic costumes in ballet. Georgina had been taught the role by Nijinska, who choreographed the ballet, and she could tell me what Nijinska had told her when they rehearsed it together.

Nijinska had choreographed the ballet in 1924 for Diaghilev's Ballets Russes, the company that changed the face of modern ballet by making it exciting and contemporary, introducing choreographers such as Balanchine and composers such as Stravinsky. It also inspired the formation of other companies; Ninette de Valois was in the corps de ballet while Nijinska was making *Les Biches*. When Georgina led me through the steps, I was holding hands with ballet's story. But physically, Georgina and I were very different, so I didn't dance it in the same way Georgina had, just as she didn't exactly copy Vera Nemtchinova, who created the role.

I have learnt, both as a dancer and as a coach, that the great balancing act of teaching people ballets from the past lies between the way it has always been danced and the way the individual in front of you is going to dance it today. If ballets are treated like tender greenhouse flowers, they will die when they are brought out into the air. On the other hand, if the choreographer's intentions are not respected, there's not much point in staging the ballet anyway. I try never to say, 'This is how it's always been done' when I am handing on a ballet in which I have danced. I want a new generation to be able to find their own way to interpret the steps to make the ballet relevant for their times and suitable for their bodies, but I am also a real stickler for preserving the integrity of the choreography.

My own relationship with the people who prepared me for roles hasn't always been entirely smooth. No matter how good they are, you don't get on with every coach, and at moments my frustration perhaps showed. But you learn even from your mistakes. One error I made was in my early interactions with Donald McLeary, a fantastic dancer, friend of MacMillan and an amazing teacher. When we first started to work together, I felt he was a little bit old-school, that his methods and his ideas were old-fashioned. He talked a lot about how Margot Fonteyn would approach a role, and the rebellious voice in my head said that I didn't want to be Margot, I wanted to be me. Later, I realised I had misinterpreted what he said. I was worrying too much about the technical execution of the steps, and his intention was to make me think about the meaning and the interpretation. My reaction wasn't a reflection on him or his knowledge, which was huge, or his teaching, which was refined. It was just me and where I was at that moment in my career.

On the other hand, I loved working with Monica because you just got on with the job; she didn't ever stop to tell me about someone else. You did it, she gave you corrections, and you did it again. I felt I achieved a lot in every rehearsal with her. She knew the stamina needed, and what it took to get a ballerina to the point where she could perform a particular ballet. She revved me up and wouldn't let me get away with anything. I'd try to excuse myself from hard work, saying I wasn't feeling so great, and she'd just say, 'All right, darling, let's make a start.' Before I knew it, it was the end of an exhausting rehearsal. It probably helped me that she wasn't a conventional ballerina herself. She had to battle against the odds to achieve all she did. But most importantly, I liked her energy.

From all of my own different experiences with directors and coaches, I appreciate that everybody is different and what you as a coach must do is help the individual standing in front of you. That's why coaching one to one—or one to two if you are working with a couple—is so enriching. You can see people excelling. This happens with a lot of dancers when they reach the level of principal; suddenly they are getting a lot of individual attention and that enables them to improve rapidly.

Coaching is tiring, concentrated work, and that's probably why it suits me. I like applying all my energy for bursts of time. If I come in to work with particular dancers, I can share my knowledge over whatever period we are in the studio together. Surprisingly, I've found it much more exhausting than dancing. When I've been working with different dancers all day, I come home utterly drained. It's like starting a new book when you have twenty piled up to read; you need to immerse yourself fully in the world of each story. A coach has to alter their mindset every time a new dancer walks into the room.

Coaching works best, I think, when a coach sits alongside a notator. Notators have a book of the steps, a bible that will help everyone learn the production; within that rigidity there are likely to be pages of notes about different versions and different interpretations. You have to decide which version you use. The thing I really learnt from Kenneth in the brief time I was lucky enough to work with him is that he had the ability to let each of his leading dancers find their own way. He would sometimes tweak something slightly for each dancer, which is why there are so many nuances to his steps, and so many variations actually written down. Most choreographers are like that. I see my job as helping the dancers find the technicality to execute the steps, to paint the picture—and then let them colour it in with their own individual taste.

I am probably stricter with the younger dancers than with the more experienced ones. I want the young ones, who are taking on parts for the first time, to learn it by the book. They are so confident and smart, and they're used to having a lot of freedom; if they learn ballets properly, they can find the abandon they need later. With more mature performers, I am perhaps more lenient, but I talk to them all in the same way, telling them stories, trying to get them to tell me their thoughts. You're attempting to let the dancer reflect their own personality but also to push the boundaries of what they think they are capable of. For example, a very beautiful dancer might always want to look beautiful, so I am there to say, forget yourself sometimes, elongate the lines, push yourself to be brave, let yourself be spontaneous. The way you communicate is of such importance. It's possible to give a tough note yet explain it in a way that isn't undermining. I'd learnt throughout my career to emphasise that any comment I make won't be personal. It's all about the show.

As a coach, you don't have success every day; it's easy to get it wrong, but I do try. I also want to give the dancers a good time, to make the studio an interesting place to be. In many ways, I try to make it like a performance, to give rehearsals curves, shape, momentum. Some days we will work exceedingly hard physically and other days we will spend a lot of time discussing something. In 2017, after I had helped him get ready for his performance as Lescaut, the brother in *Mayerling*, Ricardo Cervera sent me a thank you card: 'I thought I talked a lot until I rehearsed with you!' We might just explore a small area of the ballet, even something as simple as how they walk or how they make their entrances and exits. Every little detail matters, and the more you accumulate, the better the performance is likely to be.

I can feel my own experiences coming into play all the time I am teaching. 'Your experience and knowledge are hugely inspiring if a little daunting,' wrote Matthew Ball after I coached him and Yasmine Naghdi for their 2018 performances in *Giselle*. I was immersed in the history of that ballet, having been taught by Alicia Markova before the school performance, but as I talked I tried to remember how nervous I felt about the dancers whose performances had become the templates of the classics and not let the weight of history lie too heavily on their shoulders.

Today's dancers face different pressures from the ones we faced. They may have more autonomy and self-determination, and they may be able to build their fanbase via Facebook, Instagram and Twitter, but it's impossible to overestimate the stress that social media puts on them. Not only can they watch just about every great performance of the past on YouTube and put pressure on themselves as they try to live up to them, but also their own performances and lives are always out there for the whole world to see, and to comment on. It takes a lot of mental strength to resist the insecurities that can arise from being bombarded with videos of other dancers doing technical feats with apparent ease. The constant search for perfection isn't made any easier if you are constantly comparing yourself.

The very first piece of coaching I did wasn't for the Royal Ballet and it wasn't for *Mayerling*, though I knew that was around the corner. I began in 2016, coaching Alessandra Ferri in New York for an ABT gala in which she was dancing the solo from *Requiem*. She had stopped dancing in 2007 and then returned to the stage six years later, at the age of fifty, and has continued to dance since then. I had just stopped, even though physically I could have continued. It was great being back at the ABT studios at 890 Broadway where I had spent hours watching Georgina coach, and I hoped that she might be smiling down on me as I sat in her spot in the teachers' dressing room. Alessandra and I had a nice time together, having tea at her house, talking about kids and life in general. Our different experiences reveal just how individual the decision about retirement is for everyone; I am in complete admiration that she has wanted to carry on and her performances since her return, particularly in works created for her by Wayne McGregor, have been absolutely electrifying. For myself, I am so relieved to have stopped, and was much happier once I decided to cede the stage to the young ones. I did, when I retired, keep a skip of new pointe shoes with the half thought that one day I might need them again. They sit and look at me when I am clearing out cupboards, but I have never felt the impulse to put them on.

After that, apart from coaching extensively at the Royal from 2017 in the MacMillan ballets, but also for the classics, in 2019 I took on guest coaching jobs at The Australian Ballet for *Giselle*, and Queensland Ballet for *Romeo and Juliet*. There I discovered, if I didn't know it already, that sometimes the lessons you are passing on are entirely practical. I always advise Juliets to put some tissues backstage because you've only got a moment between the bedroom scene where you are found, supposedly dead, and the crypt scene where you wake up to find Romeo has killed himself. This change happens on the stage behind a black cloth. You will be weepy and emotional by the time you have taken the potion to put you to sleep—so you need to check that the person who is responsible for wiping your brow and doing your hair brings some tissues out to you. My other top tip is about the height of the bed which doubles as the slab of the tomb. At the end, you have to stab yourself and then drag yourself across it. It's much more difficult than it looks to make it seem convincing; the height always took me by surprise. These are the little things you can pass on if you've danced the role and I always hope they help the dancers coming after you to find their way more quickly through its challenges.

After being with the Royal Ballet for twenty-one years, it shines a new light on things to coach abroad, and to see the fresh way other dancers approach roles with which I am so familiar. I was very impressed when I went to Houston Ballet in 2017 to coach *Mayerling* to see how much work they had done to examine the roles before I even arrived. Connor Walsh danced Rudolf and though I've seen a lot of great interpretations, he was for me the closest to David Wall, who originated the role.

The bulk of my work is still with the Royal, and my involvement with the company continues to grow. Since 2016, I've been a governor of the Royal Ballet companies, the board that has oversight of the Royal Ballet, Birmingham Royal Ballet, and the Royal Ballet School and in 2020, I became vice chair. This new position has given me a much broader understanding of how the companies operate and the factors that cover decision-making behind the scenes. As a dancer you only have a partial view; as an administrator, the landscape is much wider.

I know, for example, that as a dancer I worried about being given first nights. It feels important that you open different runs of a ballet, because it is a signifier of how you are seen within the company, and also, if you are the one getting reviewed and noticed, it's a great help in establishing your name to a wider public at home and abroad. Now I recognise that there are a lot of other factors in play: it isn't always the best dancer who is cast. The casting can also be to reward someone, or to try someone out, to see how they react. These are the things I am learning now I am on the other side of things. You think everything is personal when you're a dancer, and it's not.

In 2017, I was invited to return to Switzerland to judge the Prix de Lausanne. It was an emotional moment, and a lot of memories flooded back. They showed me my performances from all those years before aged sixteen and I found myself wiping away the tears as I watched that youthful dancer going through her paces, trying so hard to get everything right in the Sugar Plum fairy variation—and then suddenly looking liberated and happy as I danced the freer piece created for me by Derek Deane, wearing a simple second-hand purple leotard with short skirt attached that they'd found for me in the Royal Ballet costume department. That career-defining performance summed me up as well as anything does; I see my character so clearly delineated, that longing to tell stories and to be free.

It's easier to be yourself these days. The companies I have recently been around have become better at accommodating different types of dancers and giving them space to blossom. As society has changed, ballet has responded. It was a great surprise and pleasure to me when my friend from Sadler's Wells days, Kevin O'Hare, was appointed to run the Royal Ballet. Quietly but firmly, he is making the company in a new image. It is a much more open place than it used to be, and dancers are happier as a result. I see the changes in a lot of ways. Dancers are allowed to make a much more rapid ascension through the ranks; there isn't the old sense of serving your time in the corps de ballet. You're promoted when you're ready, not according to some preordained idea.

At one time, the Royal Ballet was structured around long runs of the classics and if you didn't fit the image of Aurora or Odette, then you were unlikely to be made a principal. That repertory is still there but there are more performances and much more new work, so you can fulfil your potential much more quickly and you may become a principal even if you don't fit the traditional mould. I've always hoped that talent will rise, like cream, yet it hasn't always been true. This wide repertory gives dancers more of an opportunity to show the director what they are capable of, and the result has been the promotion of an extraordinary array of young talent, dancers who will blaze across the stage for the next generation. This is true in the companies I see and work with; the mood is shifting in many places.

Thanks to the efforts of many people, including Deborah Bull, who was at the forefront of trying to improve the way dancers viewed their fitness, the health of dancers is also much better looked after than it was. When I started out, there was a tiny physio room at Barons Court; disciplines such as pilates and yoga were things that you might seek out for yourself, but they were definitely not provided as the norm. Now care of a dancer's body is at the forefront of everyone's mind and that helps today's dancers fulfil their ambition. Towards the end of my career, I'd always fit in a physio session before class, to sort out any little niggles. It helped me extend my longevity as a dancer. With such facilities, you can reduce the risk of injury; when they do happen there is extensive rehabilitation available to help dancers back to the stage. Today's facilities and fitness regimes are much more like those provided for top-class athletes.

It's just one of the changes that makes me excited about the future of ballet. The style of leadership to which I was exposed towards the end of my career as a dancer suited me, and gave me an unexpected period of fulfilment and creativity. Looking around the world of dance, I see that directors have a tough job to do, as they try to satisfy so many groups of people from the dancers to the Board, from the funders to the staff, never mind audiences and critics. No one style of leadership fits all situations. From my point of view, I have been exposed to a positive evolution of leadership which achieves a great deal within ballet while at the same time taking account of the changes taking place in the world today. Evolution is healthy and necessary, in terms of the work being produced and the way organisations are run. When I see new stories being told and watch the development and progression of the use of movement and the artists being given agency to create, I feel sure there is a bright future for ballet.

I've lived my entire career on the cusp of change. I came into dance when the lineaments of the old Royal Ballet culture of unquestioning respect were still in place, and now, as a governor, I watch an entirely different, collaborative, modern company coping with the new challenges our art form faces. I was lucky enough to be a dancer when the repertory was already expanding; to have danced the classics, and dramatically expressive ballets, and the powerful abstract works of my final decade took me on a personal tour of ballet history. The variety fed my art in a way that nothing else could. But it also gave me, in my body and in my bones, an overview of the trajectory of dance from Petipa to Massine, from Balanchine to Ashton, from MacMillan to Wheeldon, from the nineteenth century to the twenty-first.

Going forward, I want to be a mentor for the younger generation, to open doors that eventually lead to success. That's what Kenneth MacMillan did for me and in this he is still my role model. I think because I went through so much, when I retired I thought I would walk away from it all—I had given everything mentally and physically to a long career. But I couldn't leave it behind and I began to realise I could have a positive effect on the future, because of everything I had learned in the past. I've learnt that it is precisely because my career didn't go according to a perfect, pre-ordained plan that I can give so much back. The twists and turns I have taken on the road have made me able to sympathise with others and perhaps to help them avoid some of the pitfalls along the way. I get it wrong sometimes, but I am trying hard not to repeat the negative lessons that sometimes blighted my days. To be positive. To help. To recreate the sense of joy that I felt when I began dancing in Rockhampton all those years before.

I am glad that I had the strength, patience and maturity to ride out the tough times at home and at work and look to the horizon. I was lucky in my timing, in being in the right place at the right time. But I know I was also lucky to have the right body, the support of my parents, excellent training, and the understanding of my friends, teachers, and colleagues. It's important to recognise that pursuing a career like ballet is hard on everyone around you, and there is an entire chorus of people at home and at work who help you and make sacrifices themselves along the way.

I worked hard all the time to get to a better tomorrow, and I discovered how to enjoy every day when it arrived. Nothing was handed to me on a plate. I am much more confident now than I ever was as a dancer. Coaching nourishes me, drawing on everything that I have learnt and turning it into help for others. My aim is to make tomorrow's dancers hold on to the love for their art that I felt from the moment I stepped onto a stage in Rockhampton. Ballet can make people feel better. It can entertain, inspire, provoke, educate and excite. I was built for ballet and how lucky I have been that it is my life.

CONCLUSION

I HAVE BEEN THINKING ABOUT writing this book for years, hoping to write something that would appeal not only to ballet-lovers but to everyone. The insights I've gained in pursuing my artistic career, from a small town in Australia to the biggest stages in the world, seem to me to be relevant to everyone. It's not easy for anyone to succeed. It's particularly not easy for a woman to achieve success young and sustain it alongside a family life. You must believe in yourself and back yourself, even when the going is tough. You need to put metaphorical money in the bank on the good days, to carry you through the bad.

These thoughts were very much in my mind in July 2020 when I was asked to give the graduation speech to the Royal Ballet School. It was the strangest time. The world was in the grip of a pandemic, and the school had only reached the end of its academic year by giving lessons remotely. Everyone had been confined to their home, often away from the people they most loved.

I'd done quite a lot of public speaking by this point; it's something I've developed since I left the stage as a way of finding a voice now my performing days are over. But this speech seemed particularly weighted with significance. I wanted to find a way to inspire the school and its graduates at a time when they were feeling bleak. I spoke via Zoom, live from White Lodge to the graduates, whose faces I couldn't see, watching me from their bedrooms all over the world. An extract seems a good way to finish because it sums up so much of what I believe.

None of you ever imagined that your graduation would look like this! It's been a tough few months, but as we all know—life is full of unexpected situations and this bump in the road on your journey will surely make the class of 2020 more resilient and determined to get to work.

Today is not for worrying about coronavirus. It's about you, your future, and how you take that amazing, fateful, scary but exciting step from student life into professional life. The journey from a classroom to centre stage can be disconcerting because there is a lot of competition and few jobs to go around. But you do it because you have to, you feel compelled to, and as you know, when you achieve your goals, nothing is better.

Having had a long career in the dance world, I'd like to offer up a few things for you to think about …

1. Surround yourself with support.

Throughout my career I was lucky to have support from my work colleagues, family and friends, and I couldn't have done it without them. They were there for me—whether I was riding high from dancing the greatest ballets or suffering the lows of injuries or insecurities.

When things get tough, remember to seek out the support you need, and be there to support others.

2. Compete with yourself, not others.

It is natural to want to compare ourselves to others. Are my fellow dancers stronger than me? Faster? Can they jump higher?

Even the best of us can get caught up in these thoughts and fears. As an impatient dancer, I had to remind myself of a useful saying—'If you look at the peak you might slip on the pebbles.'

Focus on being the best you can be and set realistic goals for yourself that you can achieve day by day.

3. Don't be put off if things don't go your way.

No matter how high up the ladder you go, don't expect things to go your way, all the time, or frankly that often. Even the biggest stars have been rejected far more times than awarded the role they wanted, or given an opening night, or the right partner, or invited on the right tour, or given the right seat on an airplane!

Try not to be defeated over short-term and irrelevant disappointments. Throw yourself into work and continue to learn. You never know when you may be called on to step in, and when that call could change your life.

4. You learn more from criticism than you do from praise.

Let's face it, we all hate criticism but positive correction, particularly in ballet, is necessary. Try not to be discouraged by it, be open minded, stay curious and embrace feedback constructively. And when you get praise—acknowledge it, celebrate and enjoy it.

5. Be consistent and reliable.

This is important going into any job. Be the person who always delivers. If you let people down too many times, no matter how talented you are, they will lose faith in you. Work out what it takes to deliver reliably and without losing your individual spark, be consistent in your training, preparation and performance.

6. Treat people you work with respectfully and expect nothing less in return.

In most professions, and in the arts in particular, there are times when tempers flare or people snap and when that happens, it's almost always a barrier to progress. Treat everyone you work with, from stage door workers to the artistic director, with respect and with compassion.

Be your peers' number one cheerleader, stand up for those that may not be as confident as you, welcome newcomers, and—why not do the English thing … be there with a cup of tea when someone is struggling.

And, finally,

7. Remember your passion.

It's amazing that we get to do what we love, meet exceptional people, travel the world, create new work and unlike most professions, we are lucky to end our evenings with flowers and applause. But with blisters on our feet, the repetition of daily class, and a bad en dedans pirouette, we can lose our inspiration. When this happens, try to remember what made you want to dance in the first place. Hold on to that.

As Martha Graham said: 'Great dancers are not great because of their technique; they are great because of their passion.'

AUTHOR'S NOTE

Sadler's Wells Royal Ballet (now Birmingham Royal Ballet)
The company changed its name just after I stopped dancing with it, moving to Birmingham and taking the city's name in 1990. I have called it Sadler's Wells Royal Ballet throughout the text because that is the name by which it was known all the time I performed there. Historically, like its sister company the Royal Ballet, it grew from Ninette de Valois's original Vic-Wells Ballet, founded in 1931.

London Festival Ballet (now English National Ballet)
This company changed its name while I was dancing there and so I have called it English National Ballet throughout the text. It was founded in 1950 by Alicia Markova and Anton Dolin as London Festival Ballet.

GLOSSARY

Allégro—all steps where the dancer jumps are considered allégro. Petit allégro includes smaller jumping steps. Grand allégro includes large expansive jumps.

Arabesque penché—the dancer's body leans far forward, with the forward arm and head low and the foot of the raised leg behind high in the air.

Chassé—meaning to chase, a basic ballet step of a gliding character.

Épaulement—use of the shoulders, neck and upper back (looking over the shoulder).

Fouetté—a whipped turn, usually performed by ballerinas, where the fouetté or whipping action describes the movement of their raised leg out to the side.

Glissé—a movement in which weight is transferred from one foot, which is slid outward from the body and briefly extended off the ground, to the other, which is then brought to meet it.

Grand défilé—a big parade, when all the dancers present themselves onstage in turn, often from youngest to most senior.

Grand pirouette—to turn on one foot where the raised leg is held in any position; front, back or to the side.

Jeté—a jump from one foot to the other in which the working leg is brushed into the air and appears to have been thrown.

Pas de bourrée—small/tight running steps.

Pirouette—to turn in a spectacular series on one foot.

Pirouette en dedans—a pirouette turning inward towards the standing leg.

Plié—knee bend. It is used in jumps and turns to provide spring, absorb shock, and as an exercise to loosen muscles and to develop balance.

Port de bras—carriage of the arms, a controlled movement of the arms.

Posé—to step (onto a straight leg).

Répétiteur—a tutor or coach.

Rond de jambe—round of the leg where the leg is circled like a protractor on the floor from 0 degrees to either 90 or 180.

Tempo—the speed of the movement in dance; tempi is its plural.

Tendu—means stretched. The working leg is extended along the floor until only the tip of the toe remains touching the floor, with a return closing action.

ENDNOTES

Chapter 1: The Tiniest Competitor

1. *Morning Bulletin*, 25 June 2003.
2. *Morning Bulletin*, 3 October 1968.

Chapter 2: DonnaranLeanne

1. *Morning Bulletin*, n.d. Quoted by Governor of Queensland in his speech in honour of Leanne Benjamin's 2019 Queensland Agent-General award.

Chapter 4: 'Remember the name Leanne Benjamin, we shall undoubtedly hear more of her'

1. *The Stage and Television Today*, 22 January 1981.
2. *Daily Telegraph*, 6 January 1981.

Chapter 5: 'A Giselle like no other'

1. Wright, Peter. *Wrights & Wrongs*. Oberon Books, 2016.
2. Clarke, Mary. *Guardian*, July 1982.
3. Williams, Peter. *Observer*, July 1982.
4. Crisp, Clement. *Financial Times*, July 1982.
5. Archer, Ruth. *Morning Bulletin*, August 1982.

Chapter 6: On the Road

1. *Observer Magazine*, 12 September 1982.
2. Clarke, Mary. *Guardian*, December 1983.
3. Percival, John. *The Times*, December 1983.

4. Parry, Jann. *The Observer*, January 1983.
5. Clarke, Mary. *Guardian*, January 1984.
6. Sorley Walker, Kathrine. *Daily Telegraph*, 12 April 1984.
7. Percival, John. *The Times*, April 1984.
8. Parry, Jann. *The Observer*, April 1984.
9. *Dance and Dancers*, March 1985.
10. *London Evening Standard*, 12 April 1985.

Chapter 7: In the Studio with Sir Fred

1. Wright, Peter with Arrowsmith, Paul. *Wrights & Wrongs: My Life in Dance*, Oberon Books, first edition 2016.
2. Crisp, Clement. *Financial Times*, 17 January 2007.
3. Craine, Debra. *The Times*, 18 January 2007.
4. *Dance and Dancers*, ibid, March 1985.
5. Woodcock, Sarah C. *The Sadler's Wells Royal Ballet*, Sinclair & Stevenson, 1991.
6. Macaulay, Alastair. *Guardian*, 2 May 1985.
7. *Morning Bulletin*, June 1985.

Chapter 8: Pink Tights Syndrome

1. *Wrights & Wrongs*, ibid.

Chapter 9: A Dancer's Life isn't Meant to be Easy

1. Clarke, Mary. *Dancing Times*, November 1985.
2. Clarke, Mary. *Guardian*, 30 September 1985.
3. Crisp, Clement. *Financial Times*, 30 September 1985.
4. Hall, Fernau. *Daily Telegraph*, 30 September 1985.
5. Wright, Peter to Owen, Michael. *London Evening Standard*, 6 January 1986. Quoted in *Sadler's Wells Royal Ballet*, ibid.
6. Croce, Arlene. *New Yorker*, 6 February 1986. Quoted in *Sadler's Wells Royal Ballet*, ibid.
7. Anderson, Jack. *New York Times*, 7 February 1986. Quoted in *Sadler's Wells Royal Ballet*, ibid.
8. Crisp, Clement. *Financial Times*, 30 April 1986.

Chapter 10: 'We Benjamins are always on the lookout for a challenge'

1. Stringer, Robin. *London Evening Standard*, 25 July 1988.
2. Dromgoole, Nicholas. *Sunday Telegraph*, 7 August 1988.

3. Koch, Peta. *Dance Australia*, Feb–March 1990.
4. Sorley Walker, Kathrine. *Daily Telegraph*, 14 June 1989.
5. Jordan, Stephanie. *The Listener*, 29 June 1989.
6. Kisselgoff, Anna. *New York Times*, 29 July 1989.
7. Kisselgoff, Anna. *New York Times*, 29 July 1989; then *New York Times*, 6 August 1989.
8. Brown, Ismene. *Sunday Telegraph*, 21 June 1989.
9. Mackrell, Judith. *The Independent*, 16 July 1993.

Chapter 11: The Smallest Valkyrie

1. Hughes, Chris. *Daily Mail*, 5 May 1990.
2. Stringer, Robin. *London Evening Standard*, May 1990.
3. Lehmann, Wolfgang. *Der Tagesspiegel*, 6 October 1990.
4. Pape, Uli. *Sächsische Zeitung*, 3 February 1991.

Chapter 12: 'Aren't you talking to me then, Benjamin?'

1. Clarke, Mary. *The Guardian*, 27 February 1984.
2. Parry, Jann. *Different Drummer, The Life of Kenneth MacMillan*, Faber & Faber, 2009.
3. *New Statesman*, 2 March 1984. Quoted in *Different Drummer, The Life of Kenneth MacMillan*, ibid.
4. Nitschmann, Jürgen. *Berliner Zeitung*, 30 September 1991.
5. Langer, Roland. *Frankfurter Rundschau*, 4 October 1991.
6. *The Times*, December 1991.
7. Draeger, Volkmar. *Neue Zeit*, 27 December 1991.

Chapter 13: 'Benjamin, you're going to be fine'

1. Crisp, Clement. Interviewed on *South Bank Show Special*, 'Macmillan's Mayerling', 1978.
2. Percival, John. *The Times*, 23 November 1992.
3. Thorpe, Edward. *London Evening Standard*, 23 November 1992.
4. Kisselgoff, Anna. *New York Times*, 18 July 1994.

Chapter 14: Work, Work, Work

1. Lebrecht, Norman. *Covent Garden: The Untold Story, Dispatches from the English Culture War, 1945-2000*, Simon & Schuster, 2000.
2. Anderson, Zoë. *The Royal Ballet: 75 Years*, Faber & Faber, 2006.
3. Percival, John. *The Times*, 5 January 1993.
4. Percival, John. *The Times*, December 1992.

5. Crisp, Clement. *Financial Times*, January 1993.
6. Mackrell, Judith. *Guardian*, April 1993.
7. Thorpe, Edward. *London Evening Standard*, 17 May 1993.
8. Percival, John. *The Times*, December 1993.
9. Sacks, Anne. *London Evening Standard*, January 1995.
10. Craine, Debra. *The Times*, 4 January 1994.
11. Stephen, Andrew. *Telegraph Magazine*, 4 June 1994.
12. Barnes, Clive. *Dance Magazine*, November 1994.
13. Barnes, Clive. Ibid.

Chapter 15: 'You were able to let the choreography speak through you'

1. Stephen, Andrew. Ibid.
2. *Observer*, 4 February 1996.
3. Robertson, Allen. *Time Out*, 31 Jan 1996.
4. Craine, Debra. *The Times*, 9 February 1996.
5. Herd, Julie. *The Weekend Australian*, 15–16 June 1996.

Chapter 16: On the Road, Then Back to the House

1. Kisselgoff, Anna. *New York Times*, 22 January 1997.
2. Lebrecht, Norman. Ibid.
3. Anderson, Zoë. Ibid.
4. Brown, Ismene. *The Spectator*, 17 October 2015.
5. Craine, Debra. *The Times*, 24 July 1998.
6. Allen, Mary. *A House Divided: The Diary of a Chief Executive of the Royal Opera House*, Simon & Schuster, 1998. Quoted in *The Royal Ballet: 75 Years*, ibid.
7. Anderson, Zoë. Ibid.
8. Brown, Ismene. *Daily Telegraph*, 22 April 1999.

Chapter 17: Love and Marriage

1. Craine, Debra. *The Times*, May 2000.
2. Parry, Jann. *The Observer*, 4 June 2001.

Chapter 18: New Arrivals

1. Christofis, Lee. *The Australian*, 19 September 2001.
2. Anderson, Zoë. Ibid.
3. *The Catholic Leader*, 2 June 2002.
4. Anderson, Zoë. Ibid.
5. Ibid.

Chapter 19: A Career Reborn

1. Craine, Debra. *The Times*, 18 November 2003.
2. Frater, Sarah. *London Evening Standard*, 17 November 2003.
3. Craine, Debra. *The Times*, 26 November 2003.

4. Mackrell, Judith. *Guardian*, 4 December 2003.
5. Bishop, Clifford. *The Sunday Times*, 7 December 2003.
6. Jennings, Luke. *Observer*, 24 April 2004.
7. Craine, Debra. *The Times*, 16 November 2004.
8. Johnstone, Helen. *Daily Telegraph*, 19 March 2005.

Chapter 20: 'Don't f* it up'**

1. Winship, Lyndsey. *The Guardian*, 7 October 2020.
2. Craine, Debra. *The Times*, 19 April 2006.
3. Frater, Sarah. *London Evening Standard*, 4 February 2008.
4. Craine, Debra. *The Times*, 5 February 2008.
5. Winship, Lindsey. Ibid.

Chapter 21: Spreading My Wings

1. Christiansen, Rupert. *Telegraph Magazine*, 29 April 2006.
2. Mackrell, Judith. *Guardian*, 7 October 2006.
3. *Morning Bulletin*, 16 November 2006.
4. Ibid.
5. Symons, Kate. *The Weekend Australian*, 16–17 December 2006.
6. Brown, Ismene. *Daily Telegraph*, 27 March 2006.
7. Frater, Sarah. *London Evening Standard*, 5 May 2009.
8. Craine, Debra. *The Times*, 11 April 2007.

Chapter 22: Farewells

1. Parry, Jann. *Observer*, 28 September 2008.
2. Crisp, Clement. *Financial Times*, 30 October 2008.

Chapter 23: Always Leave Them Wanting More

1. Crompton, Sarah. *Daily Telegraph*, 18 October 2010.
2. Brown, Ismene. *The Arts Desk*, 15 October 2010.
3. Dougill, David. *Sunday Times*, 24 October 2010.
4. Wilson, Fiona. *The Times*, 8 November 2010.
5. Anderson, Zoë. *Independent*, 25 April 2011.
6. Taylor, Jeffrey. *Sunday Express*, 24 April 2011.
7. Anderson, Zoë. *Independent*, 25 April 2011.
8. Sulcas, Roslyn. *New York Times*, 16 July 2012.
9. Parry, Jann. *Dance Tabs*, 25 February 2013
10. Thompson, Laura. *Saturday Telegraph*, 15 June 2013.
11. *Weekend Bulletin*, 15–16 June 2013.
12. Craine, Debra. *The Times*, 1 August 2013.

INDEX

C

D

T

KODAK PXP 605
48
AK PXP 6057

KODAK PXP 6057
49
6057

KODAK PXP 6057
50

KODAK PXP 6057
51